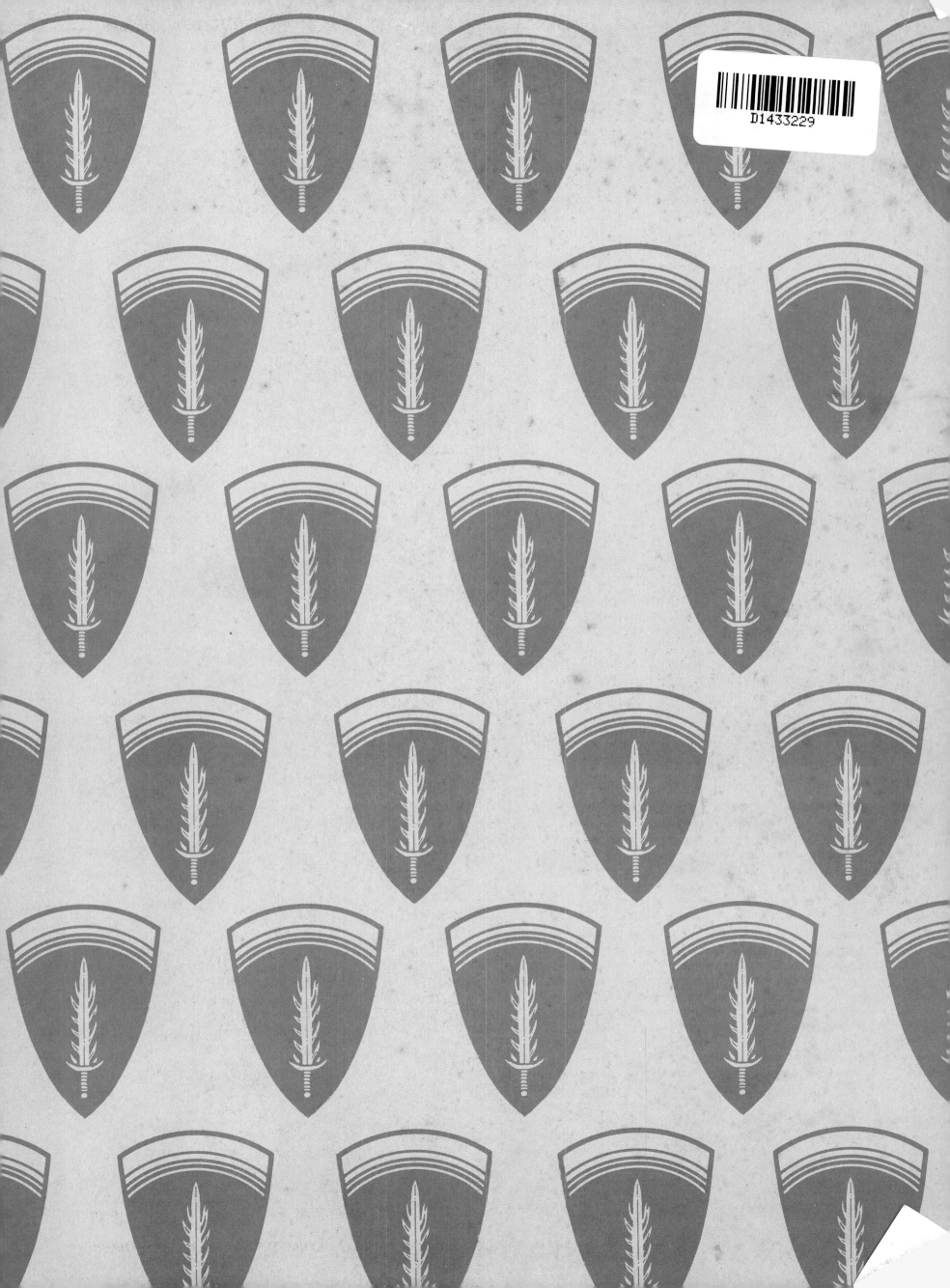

DEDICATION
To Charles Percival (1904-1991)
who, as Squadron Leader Czeslaw Tadeusz Perzenowski RAF,
fought for both his countries in the Battle of Normandy

TEXT Dr. Stephen Badsey

ADDITIONAL TEXTS Michael C. Tagg (Air Power),
Colin McIntyre (Sea Power), Andrew Preston, Richard O'Neill

DESIGNER Philip Clucas MSIAD

LOCATION PHOTOGRAPHY Neil Sutherland, Tria Giovan

PHOTO RESEARCH Leora Kahn, Miriam Sharland,
Andrew Preston, Brereton Greenhous

DIRECTORS OF PHOTOGRAPHY Leora Kahn (USA), Andrew Preston (Europe)

CAPTIONS Richard O'Neill

EDITORS David Gibbon, Andrew Preston, Brereton Greenhous

COMMISSIONING EDITOR Andrew Preston

DIRECTOR OF PRODUCTION Gerald Hughes

2637
This edition published 1994 by
Tiger Books International PLC, London
© 1993 Coombe Books
All rights reserved
Printed and bound in Italy
ISBN 1-85501-390-8

D-DAY

FROM THE NORMANDY BEACHES TO THE LIBERATION OF FRANCE

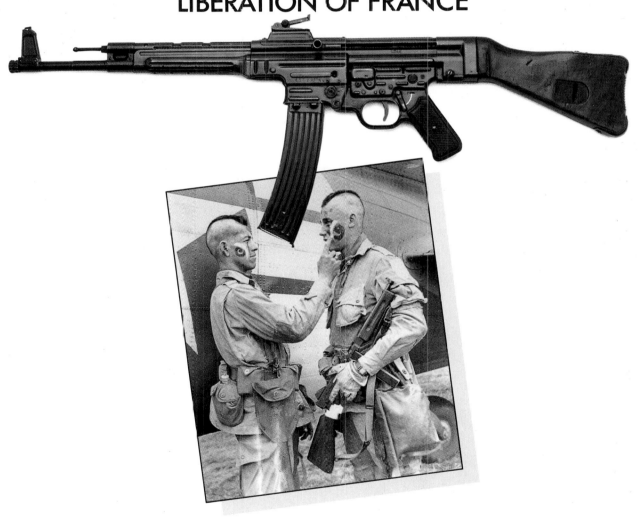

...RED URGENT URGENT – JUNE, 6,1944 ... WAR JDJD...
COMMUNIQUE NUMBER ONE SUPREME HEADQUARTERS
ALLIED EXPEDITIONARY FORCE UNDER THE COMMAND OF
GENERAL EISENHOWER, ALLIED NAVAL FORCES, SUPPORTED
BY STRONG AIR FORCES, BEGAN LANDING ALLIED ARMIES
THIS MORNING ON THE COAST OF NORTHERN FRANCE.

D-DAY

FROM THE NORMANDY BEACHES TO THE LIBERATION OF FRANCE

STEPHEN BADSEY

TIGER BOOKS INTERNATIONAL
LONDON

SUPREME HEADQUARTERS
ALLIED EXPEDITIONARY FORCE

Soldiers, Sailors and Airmen of the Allied Expeditionary Force!

You are about to embark upon the Great Crusade, toward which we have striven these many months. The eyes of the world are upon you. The hopes and prayers of liberty-loving people everywhere march with you. In company with our brave Allies and brothers-in-arms on other Fronts, you will bring about the destruction of the German war machine, the elimination of Nazi tyranny over the oppressed peoples of Europe, and security for ourselves in a free world.

Your task will not be an easy one. Your enemy is well trained, well equipped and battle-hardened. He will fight savagely.

But this is the year 1944! Much has happened since the Nazi triumphs of 1940-41. The United Nations have inflicted upon the Germans great defeats, in open battle, man-to-man. Our air offensive has seriously reduced their strength in the air and their capacity to wage war on the ground. Our Home Fronts have given us an overwhelming superiority in weapons and munitions of war, and placed at our disposal great reserves of trained fighting men. The tide has turned! The free men of the world are marching together to Victory!

I have full confidence in your courage, devotion to duty and skill in battle. We will accept nothing less than full Victory!

Good Luck! And let us all beseech the blessing of Almighty God upon this great and noble undertaking.

Dwight D Eisenhower

CONTENTS

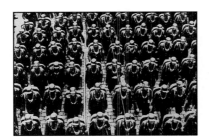

FOREWORD BY

VISCOUNT MONTGOMERY of ALAMEIN CBE

If the Battle of Alamein was, as Winston Churchill said, the end of the beginning, then surely D-Day was the beginning of the end. The assault on the fortress of Europe began on D-Day, but the preparations had been in hand for many months and required a massive effort in planning, coordination, leadership and dedication to duty. The invasion of Normandy in June 1944 was the initiation of the last phase of war, leading to the liberation of France and the Benelux countries. It was the largest military operation in the history of warfare.

Under the supreme command of General Eisenhower, the ground forces of the Allies comprising American, British, Canadian and others combined under my father. This was a good choice, as he had proved himself a master of the set piece battle. During early 1944 in a period of tireless activity, he addressed every officer and man who would take part in the battle. No one was in any doubt as to what he had to do, and what would be the outcome. Good training and high morale were to be the keystones of this great endeavour. On 5 June, on the eve of D-Day, when the final decisions had been taken for the operation to proceed, my father issued an historic message which included a verse from Montrose, the soldier poet of the 17th century:

> "He either fears his fate much,
> or his deserts are small,
> who dares not put it to the touch,
> to win or lose it all."

We must be ever grateful for the courage and sacrifice of those who gave their lives for us to enjoy the fruits of peace, and to the leadership that made victory possible. The study of these historic events does not glorify war, but reminds us of the horror, and of the vital need for continual vigilance to ensure a just and lasting peace.

Montgomery of Alamein

Montgomery considers his great task as commander of ground forces on D-Day.
(US National Archives)

The Detroit Free Press

On Guard for Over a Century

Vol. 114—No. 35

EXTRA

Five Cents

WEATHER

TUESDAY, JUNE 6, 1944

INVASION!

SUPREME HEADQUARTERS, Allied Expeditionary Force—(AP)—Gen. Dwight D. Eisenhower's headquarters announced Tuesday that Allied troops began landing on the northern coast of France Tuesday morning strongly supported by naval and air forces

Under the command of Gen. Eisenhower Allied naval forces supported by strong air forces began landing Allied armies this morning on the northern coast of France.

The Germans said the landings extended between Le Havre and Cherbourg along the south side of the bay of the Seine and along the Northern Normandy coast.

Parachute troops descended in Normandy, Berlin said.

Berlin first announced the landings in a series of flashes that began about 6:30 a. m. (12:30 a. m. Eastern War Time).

The Allied communique was read over a trans-Atlantic hookup direct from General Eisenhower's headquarters at 3:32 E. W. T., designated "Communique No. 1."

A second announcement by Shaef said that "it is announced that Gen. B. L. Montgomery is in command of the army group carrying out the assault. This army group includes British, Canadian and U. S. forces.

Berlin Says Landing Is at Seine River

Murphy Says He Will Return Bribe Money

Allies Cross Tiber; Chase Routed Foe

Rome Hails Liberators in Wild Joy

F.D.R. Hails Fall of Rome

All Warned to Quit Belt 20-Mi. Deep

Victor Quits as Ruler; Umberto to Control Italy

Report from Dover

HELL ON WHEELS

D-Day and the Battle of Normandy is far too large an event to be described completely in just one book. Instead, in telling the story of the battle I have tried to show it from different levels and perspectives, from the high command to the front lines, in the hope that something of the nature of this very hard fought battle will emerge. It need hardly be added that responsibility for success or failure in this, and for any errors of fact and interpretation, rest with me alone. Even my bibliography, which seems alarmingly long, includes only those works which I found most useful in writing this particular book. It represents only a small fraction of what has been written on Normandy and the Second World War, and a rather larger fraction of the material on the battle which I have studied over the years.

While the opinions expressed in this book are also entirely my own, I have benefited greatly from the exchange of ideas with my colleagues in the Department of War Studies at the Royal Military Academy Sandhurst. I would particularly like to thank Major (rtd) R d'A Ryan, who first pointed me in the direction of the Battle of Normandy, Dr Andrew Lambert who did his considerable best to help me understand sea power, and G.D. Sheffield for his tolerance. The major battle sites of Normandy have been extremely well preserved, and I have been lucky enough to visit them in the company of experts, notably Nigel and Martine de Lee of Sandhurst Staff Rides, and Lieutenant-Colonel (rtd) Michael Chilcott of the Airborne Assault Normandy Trust, who between them provided kindness, knowledge, and hospitality. Thanks are due also to Professor Brian Bond and the members of a battlefield tour held under the auspices of the British Commission for Military History, which turned into a walking seminar on the battle. In England, Andrew Orgill, the Librarian at Sandhurst Central Library, and his staff were as efficient and courteous as always, while Andrew Preston, who first suggested this book to me, has seen it through to completion with remarkable smoothness.

My family, an unfailing source of support over the years, are also my sharpest and most honest critics, and I hope that my latest work has come up to their standards. My wife Phylomena managed to turn the curse of being married to a historian into a blessing by taking the opportunity of my obsession with Normandy to master its cooking. My thanks are due to her, and to Sean and Susan McKnight for coming to sample the results, and for introducing me to some good wines.

Stephen Badsey
Hampton
June 6, 1992

CHAPTER ONE
EUROPE AT WAR

In the bleak hours before first light on June 6, 1944, the first American, British and Canadian assault troops climbed down the scrambling nets from the ships that had taken them to the Normandy coast into their pitching landing craft, and set off on the long and uncertain trip to the shore. Even as they approached the Normandy beaches the battle was already under way. Since midnight, glider and paratroop forces had been fighting for a perilous foothold inland, while French Resistance fighters blew up bridges, derailed trains and sabotaged telephone lines to hamstring the Germans. Out at sea, the guns of the big warships threw out plumes of smoke against the gray water with each massive salvo, while overhead Allied fighter and bomber aircraft left contrails in the brightening sky as they sought out their enemy. D-Day, the Allied liberation of France, had come at last.

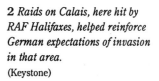

2 Raids on Calais, here hit by RAF Halifaxes, helped reinforce German expectations of invasion in that area.
(Keystone)

3 Badly damaged in the Japanese attack on Pearl Harbor in 1941, the veteran battleship USS Nevada *was rebuilt to become the USN's D-Day flagship and add the weight of her 14-inch guns to the Normandy bombardment.*
(US National Archives)

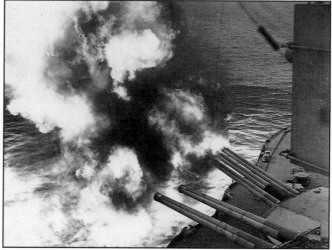

1 On guard on the Atlantic Wall, the German coastal defense line extending from Norway's North Cape to the Pyrenees. It was strongest in northern France, in the Pas de Calais, where Hitler most anticipated invasion. But although Hitler cited it in support of his claim to be "the greatest fortress builder of all time," Field Marshal Rommel, who suspected invasion would come in Normandy, pointed out the Wall's weaknesses.
(Bundesarchiv)

Most of the 70,000 Allied soldiers who landed in the next few hours, soaked through, seasick or sick with apprehension and fear, were heartily glad to exchange the perils of their journey even for those of a bullet-swept beach. Altogether 156,000 came ashore or dropped from the sky that day, and although each man knew that this was the biggest amphibious invasion in history, the climax of the Second World War, few had much time to reflect on the fact. That was for the generals and admirals watching anxiously from the big ships lying offshore, or following the maps at their headquarters back in England. For most of the men on the Normandy beaches it was enough, at the end of the day, to be ashore and still alive.

In the history of warfare, nothing quite like this invasion had ever been attempted. Certainly, the Allied landing at Salerno in Italy nine months earlier had been almost as big, and in some respects bigger, but D-Day at Normandy was different. For the first time a major coastal fortress – the Germans' boasted Atlantic Wall – would be attacked directly from the sea instead of from the landward side. In the next two months the Allies planned to land in Normandy over two million men, 500,000 vehicles and three million tons of stores, the biggest seaborne invasion force in history. It was the force with which they would drive the Germans out of occupied Western Europe within a year. Already Germany's war effort was massively overstretched and visibly crumbling, but Normandy was to be the death blow. At stake on the beaches was nothing less than the survival of Hitler's Third Reich.

4 In all wars, combat is a young man's business.
(US National Archives)

5 "Hit the deck!" – one soldier's instant, life-saving reaction to a shellburst on the beach.
(Keystone)

HITLER'S WAR

D-Day came in the fifth year of the war, and the fourth of the German occupation of France and most of the Continent of Europe. At first, the German blitzkrieg, using air power and mobile forces to fight short, aggressive campaigns, had proved almost unbelievably successful. The German invasion and over-running of Poland in September, 1939, had brought declarations of war from Britain and France, but neither could save Poland from the Germans. The first winter of the war had been the "phoney war," in which most of Europe had remained neutral and even the belligerents had done little fighting. Peace had been broken only by border fighting between Finland and the Soviet Union, by the start of the German U-Boat campaign against Britain, and by a few largely ineffective air raids. In April, 1940, the British and French were humiliated and suffered heavy losses when their attempted intervention against Germany's invasion of neutral Denmark and Norway was checked by the Luftwaffe. In the face of this defeat the British government collapsed, to be replaced on May 10 by a new coalition government under Winston Churchill, dedicated to a more effective prosecution of the war. Just as Churchill took office, the phoney war ended with the long-awaited German attack on the West. To astonishment and horror, the Germans overran and occupied neutral Belgium and Holland and defeated France within days. While much of the British Army escaped through Dunkirk, France surrendered and signed an armistice with Germany on June 22.

6 Signaling the triumph of German arms in France, May 1940, such headlines gave Americans food for thought about a conflict in which they were not yet involved.

DAILY MIRROR
2¢　　　2¢
NAZIS CUT DEEP INTO FRANCE
In Control, Says Paris; British Hold Louvain
F. D. R. ASKS BILLION AND 50,000 PLANES
6

9

9 Mussolini, Italy's fascist leader, fully committed his country to Hitler's cause when he entered the war on June 10, 1940.
(Keystone)

10, 11 Britain's "finest hour" began in summer 1940, when Hitler's threats, here headlined in New York, were defied, as a London newspaper proclaims, by a new war leader, Winston Churchill.

7

7 Where World War II began: German infantrymen thrust aside a border barrier bearing the Polish eagle on the morning of September 1, 1939. Massive air attacks immediately preceded the ground forces' assault and the German blitzkrieg – lightning advances by armored units and motorized infantry, with close air support – overwhelmed Poland inside three weeks.
(Keystone)

11

DAILY NEWS FINAL
YIELD OR DIE, HITLER ROARS AT BRITAIN
"One More Appeal to Reason."

10

Daily Mirror
WE NEVER SURRENDER
DUNKIRK —LAST MEN GO
The Noble Story of Calais

IRONSIDES FOR HOME DEFENCE

RUMOUR-MONGER TO BE CHARGED

400,000 Local Defence Volunteers

LIVESTOCK LEAVES COAST

FRY'S retain pre-war prices

8

8 A civic dignitary solemnly proclaims Britain to be at war; September 3, 1939.
(Fox)

Churchill's description of the next months as Britain's "finest hour" is hard to contradict. The German defeat in the Battle of Britain meant that German plans for an invasion of Britain had to be abandoned, but Britain remained in a desperate position. Benito Mussolini's Italy declared war as France collapsed, and except for a handful of neutral countries the whole of Europe, including the puppet state of Vichy France, came under Hitler's domination. No help could be expected from Josef Stalin, General Secretary and effective dictator of the Soviet Union, who sent Hitler a message of congratulation on his victory. In spring,

HITLER

Born on April 20, 1889 in Brannau-am-Inn, Adolf Hitler was the second surviving son of a minor Austrian customs official. Drifting to Vienna in 1907, he made a precarious living as a painter and illustrator. In 1913 he moved to Munich in Germany, volunteered for the German Army at the start of the First World War, and served on the Western Front, being promoted to corporal, badly gassed twice, and winning the Iron Cross.

After Germany's defeat Hitler became a member of the extreme right-wing NSDAP or Nazi Party in 1919, and its leader a year later. In November, 1923, backed by the former First World War commander General Eric Ludendorff, Hitler and the Nazis tried unsuccessfully to overthrow the government in Munich, for which he was briefly imprisoned. On his release he changed his tactics, mixing street violence with political deals. In 1932 Hitler ran for President and, although unsuccessful, won enough support to make the Nazis the largest single party in elections later that year. In January 1933, President Paul von Hindenburg appointed Hitler to the Chancellorship of Germany, and on Hindenburg's death in 1934 he made himself Führer, or dictator. In 1935 he moved

1 A formal portrait of Adolf Hitler gives very little indication of the demonic power that enabled the former non-com (dismissed as the "Bohemian Corporal" by some aristocratic generals) to hurl Germany into history's most terrible conflict.
(Keystone)

troops into the Rhineland, demilitarized since the First World War, and in 1936 forged an alliance with Mussolini's Italy while building up his own armed forces. In March, 1938, Hitler bluffed and bullied his way to the unopposed occupation of Austria, creating the beginnings of the Third Reich, or new German Empire, adding northern Czechoslovakia in September, 1938, and the rest of the country in March, 1939. His attack on Poland in September, 1939, led to declarations of war by Britain and France and the start of the Second World War.

Spectacular early German successes led Hitler to believe in his own military genius, and in December, 1941, he fired the army commander-in-chief and began to direct battles personally from his headquarters at the Wolf's Lair in eastern Germany, which he hardly left for the rest of the war. As the tide turned against him he became an increasingly isolated figure, at odds with most of his generals, refusing to believe that the war was lost. On April 30, 1945, with Soviet forces closing on his underground bunker in Berlin, he married Eva Braun, who had been his mistress since 1936, and both of them committed suicide. Churchill characterized him as "a bloodthirsty guttersnipe."

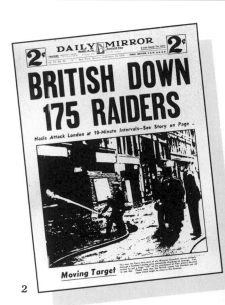

2 In the "Battle of Britain," July-September 1940, German air raids sought to crush Britain's resistance to invasion. London suffered heavy bomb damage (inspected here by Churchill), but although the Luftwaffe's daily losses were never so great as this contemporary headline claims, German invasion plans were canceled.

1941, Britain lost the last of its possible supporters in Europe as the Germans overran Yugoslavia and Greece, including the island of Crete, while in North Africa the Italian and German forces threatened to take the Suez Canal and cut Britain off from the raw materials and manpower of its Empire, its only certain source of supply and support.

3 Hitler's bold plans for lightning conquests in Scandinavia, Holland, Belgium, and France included the use of airborne units (paratroopers and glider troops) to assault strongpoints ahead of the main invasion forces. Here he poses with paratroopers (Fallschirmjäger) whom he has just decorated with Iron Crosses for their part in the operations of summer 1940.
(Keystone)

4 Some say Hitler was fonder of his German Shepherd dogs, notably his favorite Blondi, than of any other living creatures.
(Keystone)

Without military allies, and facing an enemy in overwhelming strength, Churchill based his strategy on keeping Britain from defeat or starvation while looking for aid from the United States, where President Franklin D. Roosevelt was deeply sympathetic to Britain's position. Despite his country's neutrality, Roosevelt came to Britain's assistance with ships and arms supplied under the Lend-Lease Agreement, creating what he called the "arsenal of democracy" by moving United States industry onto full war production after the collapse of France. But an understandable desire to keep out of the war ran deep within the United States, and Roosevelt was not in a position to declare war on Germany. Britain remained without direct military assistance, and with no prospect of victory.

In two years Hitler had conquered most of Europe. But a brutal occupation policy, including the use of torture, slave labor and concentration camps, guaranteed that the Germans would face resistance in all the occupied countries, tying down troops and resources. The German failure to conquer Britain also gave Hitler's enemies a base just off continental Europe from which to attack him. At the apparent height of his military achievements Hitler over-reached himself. In July, 1941, he launched a surprise attack on the Soviet Union, expecting it to collapse like France. Instead, the German blitzkrieg was held just short of Leningrad in the north and Moscow in the center before the onset of the Russian winter. Thereafter, the sheer scale of the Eastern Front made demands on the German war machine which could not be met. Not content with this, Hitler fulfilled Churchill's greatest hope. In December, 1941, responding to the Japanese attack on Pearl Harbor, he kept his earlier promise to them by declaring war on the United States.

5 Japan's surprise attack on Pearl Harbor on December 7, 1941, brought the USA into World War II. Germany and Italy declared war on the USA on December 11.

6 Nazi Germany's vilest war aim was to enslave or exterminate the "sub-human" peoples of Eastern Europe, like this Jewish woman and child menaced in Poland's Warsaw Ghetto in 1943. (Keystone)

7 Germany's sudden attack on the Soviet Union in July 1941 was at first successful but ultimately made such huge demands on military resources as to prove Hitler's greatest mistake. Anti-communist Soviet peoples, notably in the Ukraine, were initially disposed to welcome the Germans as liberators, but Nazi brutality alienated many potential supporters. Many of those who resisted occupation ended as in this photograph – a "souvenir" of anti-partisan activities taken from the body of a German soldier killed in action on the Russian front in 1943. (Keystone)

8 In April 1943, c.60,000 survivors of some 450,000 Jews orginally penned in the Warsaw Ghetto rose in arms. About 14,000 died in 28 days' fighting. Survivors were summarily executed in the Ghetto's ruins, as seen here, or shipped to death camps. (Keystone)

THE TIDE TURNS

Although there would be some German gains in 1942, it was clear by the end of that year that Hitler had placed Germany in a virtually hopeless position. Against Britain and its Empire alone, Germany and the other Axis powers might have won the war in Europe. But against the United States and the Soviet Union as well, Hitler stood only the slightest of chances. Unlike the Allies, Germany had no spare industrial capacity to develop long-range bombers or naval forces. Major German surface ships like the *Graf Spee* or the *Bismarck* did not last long on the open sea, while the U-Boats were defeated in the crucial battle of the Atlantic in 1941. In January, 1943, at Casablanca the Allies agreed on a policy of unconditional surrender for Germany.

By the middle years of the war Germany had about ten million men in uniform, compared to twelve million each from the United States and the Soviet Union and five million more from Britain. In the course of the war Germany and Britain both produced about 23,000 tanks and over 80,000 combat aircraft. But the United States alone produced a further 88,500 tanks and 96,000 aircraft. By D-Day, American factories were producing aircraft around the clock, at least one new plane every five minutes. In the same year the three main Allies produced $69 billion-worth of combat munitions ($42 billion-worth from the United States alone), compared to $17 billion-worth from Germany. In the course of the war, Germany was outproduced by four to one.

1250 PLANES RAID COLOGNE; CITY IN RUINS

1 In long-term preparation for invasion, Allied air forces waged a strategic bombing offensive against Germany. In the first "Thousand Bomber Raid" (The Daily News's headline is a slight exaggeration: 1,046 bombers took part), then by far the largest bombing operation ever launched, the RAF devastated 600 acres of Cologne on the night of May 30-31, 1941.

3 British battleships in line ahead. In 1939 the Royal Navy was well prepared for fleet actions, but German strategy favored commerce raiding by single, powerful units.

2 A British plane's bomb narrowly misses a German warship during the "Channel Dash" of February 11-13, 1942.

Threatened by RAF bombing at the French port of Brest, the German battle cruiser Scharnhorst and two other heavy

units made a successful (although two were damaged), high speed run through the English Channel to Wilhelmshaven in Germany. (Keystone)

Translating this massive superiority into military success was not as easy as it might appear. In defense Hitler had the advantages of his early victories, giving him a strong central position dominating the continent of Europe, with short overland supply lines and the ability to switch forces from one front to another. The German Army and the apparatus of the Nazi state also effectively held the population of Europe as hostages against Allied attack. American first priorities were given to seapower and airpower. To cope with supply lines which literally ran halfway round the world, from San Francisco to Suez, the Americans produced over 2,500 "Liberty" ships – 7,000 ton merchant vessels made to a standard pattern – at an average rate of one every fifteen days, and over 46,000 landing ships and craft, including the Landing Ship, Tank (LST) of 4,000 tons which could carry twenty tanks. This great transport fleet made a build-up of forces almost anywhere in the world possible, but only at the cost of massive effort and planning periods stretching into years. The question was not whether the Allies could invade Hitler's Europe, but how it might best be done, or even if it needed to be done at all.

4 With bayonet fixed, one of Hitler's "Aryan supermen" is prepared to enforce the Nazi doctrine in Europe.

5 Inside the "arsenal of democracy:" US factory hands at work on a B-17 bomber. (US National Archives)

ALLIED STRATEGY

At their first planning conference of the war, in Washington, within a month of Pearl Harbor, Churchill and Roosevelt agreed upon their basic strategy of giving priority to Europe and the defeat of Germany before Japan. It would take about a year for American industry to produce enough ships, planes, tanks and guns

CHURCHILL

Winston Leonard Spencer Churchill was born on November 30, 1874 at Blenheim Palace, England, home of his grandfather, the Seventh Duke of Marlborough. His father, Lord Randolph Churchill, was a prominent Conservative politician, and his mother, Jennie, was the daughter of a wealthy New York businessman. After education at Harrow School he passed through Sandhurst and joined the British Army in 1895, seeing action as a cavalry officer and part-time war correspondent in Malakand, the Sudan and South Africa between 1897 and 1900. That year he followed his father as a Conservative member of parliament, but in 1906 switched his allegiance to the Liberal party. In 1908 he married Clementine, granddaughter of the Earl of Airlie. He held three cabinet posts in the Liberal government before the First World War, becoming First Lord of the Admiralty in 1911.

In 1915 Churchill was blamed for the failed Dardanelles expedition and dismissed from the cabinet, spending three months in 1916 as an infantry battalion commander on the Western Front. In July, 1917, he returned to the cabinet as Minister of Munitions, a

6 *Popularized by Winston Churchill, the "V for Victory" sign, made with the fingers or chalked on walls, became a symbol of resistance throughout occupied Europe.*
(Keystone)

post he held for the rest of the war. In 1919 he was made Secretary of War in a peacetime coalition, losing his own seat in parliament when the government collapsed in 1922. Changing allegiance once more, he served as Chancellor of the Exchequer for the Conservative government between 1924 and 1929, before again being ejected from office in a lost election. He spent the next ten years as a back-bencher, his political career apparently over.

Churchill was recalled to the Conservative government in September 1939 at the start of the Second World War, once more as First Lord of the Admiralty. In May, 1940, the government collapsed, to be replaced by a coalition with Churchill as Prime Minister. Thereafter he directed the British war effort with great skill and personal energy. With the defeat of Germany Churchill dissolved his coalition government, and his Conservatives lost the subsequent election in July, 1945. He continued as leader of his party, becoming Prime Minister again between 1951 and 1955, before retiring through ill-health. Although knighted in 1953, he refused any higher honors. He died of a stroke on January 24, 1965.

7

to make a major assault on Hitler's empire practical. (Italy was seen as an offshoot of Germany rather than as a separate threat). In the interval, the Germans would be defeated in the Atlantic and their homeland attacked by bombing. Despite this decision, several of Roosevelt's advisers, particularly his naval chief Admiral Ernest King, believed that the country's main effort should be made against the Japanese who had attacked them first, rather than against Germany, and tried to get the American emphasis changed back to the Pacific.

7 *Facing a superior British force off Norway's North Cape, Scharnhorst went down fighting; December 26, 1943.*

8

9

8 *The end of HMS* Glowworm; *April 8, 1940. The destroyer engaged the heavy cruiser* Admiral Hipper: *ablaze, she rammed and damaged the enemy before sinking.*
(Central Press)

9 *Anglo-American Combined Chiefs of Staff look on as Roosevelt and Churchill confer at Casablanca; January 1943. The two leaders had earlier decided Germany's defeat should take precedence over that of Japan – although some American commanders, notably Admiral Ernest King (left in lineup), disagreed.*
(Keystone)

10

From the very start of their involvement in the war the Americans, with their straightforward business approach, thought and planned in terms of a direct assault on Fortress Europe in 1942. The British also recognized that to defeat Germany a landing in France was needed, and had begun planning for one even before Pearl Harbor. But, as Churchill and Roosevelt well understood, the decision was not driven by military logic alone. Other issues at stake included the conflicting ambitions of the various Allies who, despite calling themselves the "United Nations," did not necessarily agree on the shape of Europe and the world after the war. Another very human problem was the number of casualties

10 *In the Far East, despite the optimistic headline of this newspaper, the Japanese made huge gains in 1941-42.*

ROOSEVELT

Franklin Delano Roosevelt was born on January 29, 1882, at Hyde Park, near Poughkeepsie, New York, the son of a wealthy land-owner and a distant cousin of past president, Theodore Roosevelt. Educated at Harvard and Columbia, he married Theodore Roosevelt's niece Eleanor, in 1905. A lawyer by profession, he entered politics as a Democrat, becoming a New York State senator in 1910 and Assistant Secretary for the Navy in the Wilson administration in 1913, serving throughout the First World War. In 1920, he won the Democratic nomination for the Presidency, but lost the election to Warren Harding. A year later polio left him crippled, but with his wife's help he gradually resumed his political life, becoming Governor of New York State in 1928.

In 1932 Roosevelt was elected as 32nd president on a platform of recovery from the economic depression. His success led to his election for a second term in 1936, and again for a third term in 1940, the only

1 *The grit he had shown in fighting off the effects of polio in earlier life was again evident in President Roosevelt's war leadership.*
(Keystone)

American president to be elected three times. Roosevelt found himself drawn into increasing opposition to the Axis powers, and with the collapse of France in 1940 he embarked on a massive rearmament program. In December, 1941, with Japan's attack on Pearl Harbor and the Philippines, followed by the German and Italian declarations of war against the United States, Roosevelt devoted himself entirely to the war, creating the massive "arsenal of democracy" provided by the United States for all the Allies. In 1944, although increasingly infirm, he was elected once more for a fourth term of office. He died of a cerebral hemorrhage at Warm Springs, Georgia, on April 12, 1945, just three weeks before Hitler's death.

4 *Hitler's need to capture "Stalin's city" approached obsession. As the headline states, he committed huge forces to the* investment of Stalingrad in late 1942, notably General Paulus's 6th Army of some 230,000 men.

Marines Crush Jap Attack
16 Pages of Comics + 16 Page Color Magazine
WALL ST. SPECIAL
Journal American
5¢
800,000 NAZIS MASSED AT STALINGRAD!
Jimmy Roosevelt In Thick of Fight At Solomon Base
Smash Attack By Japs on Solomons | Own Story —Typical Life Of Criminal | ALP to Name Third Party Ticket Today | **Soviets Crush Enemy Force At Don River**

2 *Joseph Stalin held supreme power in the Soviet Union from the 1920s until his death in 1953. In World War II he was popularly seen as the benevolent ally "Uncle Joe." Most modern historians portray him as a savage tyrant in the Hitler mold.*
(Europan)

3 *In the Soviet Union and elsewhere in Eastern Europe the winter months often saw Germany's blitzkrieg slowed to a crawl by ice and snow.*
(Keystone)

5 *"General Winter" was said to be Russia's major ally. Germans rushed to the East Front without proper winter clothing suffered severely.*
(Keystone)

the Allies might suffer, and how much of Europe itself might be devastated. Also affecting the issue were the immense practical problems of mounting and sustaining a major invasion from the sea, something of which the British and Americans had virtually no experience. A failure or defeat would greatly strengthen the argument that America should give priority to Japan, something which Churchill regarded as potentially disastrous for Britain.

A large part of the American desire for an early invasion was the fear that the Soviet Union might collapse in the face of German attacks, and make a separate peace. Stalin, in turn, called repeatedly for a "Second Front" in Europe against Hitler, conveniently ignoring his own policy of cooperation with Germany between 1939 and 1941, and the fact that his country continued to remain at peace with Japan. But the British, having fought one long, bloody, stalemated campaign in France in the First World War, preferred a strategy of striking at the outer ramparts of Hitler's fortress until they were more certain of success. This view was reinforced by the disastrous Dieppe raid in August, 1942, a test of British amphibious landing capabilities which resulted in the loss of 3,500 out of 6,000 assault troops, most of them Canadian soldiers sent by their government to fight alongside the British.

A further problem for the British was that a large part of their forces were already threatened with defeat in North Africa by the Germans and Italians under Field Marshal Erwin Rommel. Badly needing a victory, Churchill convinced Roosevelt that the Allies stood to gain more in the short term from an invasion

6

6 Stalin and Churchill at the Yalta Conference, February 4-11, 1945, where, with Roosevelt, they attempted to settle the shape of post-war Europe. Wartime relations between the "Big Three" leaders had been strained when the USA and Britain refused to heed Stalin's demands for an early "Second Front" (i.e., an invasion from the west) in Europe.
(Keystone)

7

8

7 Landing craft alongside a British destroyer off Dieppe; August 19, 1942. The raid on the Channel port was described by Churchill as "a reconnaissance in force" for a full-scale invasion: to test the strength of German coastal defenses and to try out new weapons and methods of amphibious assault.
8 Although it is claimed that lessons learned at Dieppe contributed to the success of the D-Day operations, the raid itself was a disaster, as this German post-battle photograph dramatically shows. Well prepared for such an attempt, the Germans raked the beach with small arms and *artillery fire. Of 27 tanks landed, 12 were knocked out at the water's edge; few of the 6,000 troops committed got beyond the sea wall – and about 3,500 were lost.*
(Bundesarchiv)
9 The newspaper headline is pure propaganda: the Germans had only about 600 casualties and shot down 106 Allied aircraft for the loss of 48 of their own.

of French and Italian North Africa than from a landing in France. By the terms of the French surrender to Germany in 1940, only the northern part of France had been occupied. The French government at Vichy kept control of southern France and the French colonies as reluctant allies of the Germans. An invasion of Tunisia, Algeria and Morocco from the sea would cut Rommel's supply lines and win at least part of the Vichy forces over to the Allies. Codenamed Operation Torch, the Anglo-American landing took place in November, 1942, just after the defeat of Rommel's forces in Egypt at the Battle of El Alamein by the new British commander, Lieutenant-General Sir Bernard Montgomery. On hearing that his work had been for nothing, the American staff officer who drafted the plan for the invasion of France in 1942, Brigadier-General Dwight D. (Ike) Eisenhower, lamented that the missed opportunity might be "the blackest day in history" for America.

10

11

10 A German observer keeps a lookout on the East Front.
11 Visiting the East Front, Albert Speer, Minister of Armaments and Munitions, wears the armband of the Todt Organization which, under his direction, made extensive use of slave labor to construct fortifications, roads, and similar military facilities.
(Keystone)

The Torch landings produced a massive military victory for the Allies, with the crushing of German and Italian forces in North Africa. But, even with all the Allied advantages in numbers and equipment, to attack against German troops fighting for their lives was as hard as the British had feared, and harder than the inexperienced Americans had expected. It took until May, 1943, for the last German strongholds in Tunisia to fall. Although, as hoped, most of the Vichy forces in North Africa defected to the Allies after the landings, the Germans responded by occupying the whole of France, ruling out any chance of help from Vichy itself.

Together with the disaster at Dieppe, the long planning times needed to assemble ships and landing craft, and the growing evidence that Italy might abandon the Axis, placed the idea of a cross-Channel attack, even in 1943, in jeopardy. At the Casablanca Conference in January the Americans agreed, with some reluctance, to a British proposal to continue the Mediterranean

6 *A British tank surrenders to Rommel's armored forces, who won notable victories in North Africa, often against odds, until their defeat at El Alamein late in 1942.*
(Keystone)

U.S. INVADES FRENCH NO. AFRICA

F.D.R. CALLS ATTACK OUR SECOND FRONT

EXTRA

ALGERIA AND MOROCCO SURRENDER

d of Campaign Frees Yanks or Drive on Axis in Tunisia

ZI OCCUPATION OF ANCE COMPLETED

Stories on Page 3

4 *The vital supply port of Tobruk, Libya, was the scene of fierce fighting until late 1942. An aerial photograph shows A.A.A. emplacements; part of a 30-mile defensive perimeter built at Tobruk by Axis forces in 1940-41.*
(Keystone)

1 *US Army combat engineers and an officer of the British 8th Army study the Tunisian terrain in 1943.*
(Keystone)
2, 3 *Headlines proclaim the Allies' swift conquest of Algeria and Morocco in November 1942. Tunisia proved a tougher nut to crack.*

strategy. The invasion of Sicily in July, 1943, was followed by an invasion of mainland Italy at Salerno two months later. The shock of Allied troops on Italian soil led to the overthrow of Mussolini's government, with the new Italian government declaring war against Germany in October. By the end of the year Italian soldiers were fighting alongside the other "United Nations." The German forces in Italy, however, simply turned themselves into an army of occupation for their former partner, and brought the Allied advance to a halt in the mountains south of Rome for the winter.

By 1943, as American military power reached its peak, far outstripping that of Britain, Churchill found it increasingly difficult to impose his views of grand strategy upon Roosevelt and his advisers. In turn, many on the American side had grown increasingly wary of Churchill and his military staffs, whom they suspected of having little enthusiasm for a campaign in France. Stalin was also deeply suspicious that his Second Front might never materialize, and insisted at the Tehran Conference in November, 1943, on a firm date and commitment to

5 *A British 6-pounder anti-tank gun in action near Tripoli, early in 1943.*
(Keystone)

the invasion from the British and Americans. Despite his own preference for a continued Mediterranean strategy and an invasion at the head of the Adriatic, which he misleadingly described as "the soft underbelly of Europe," Churchill accepted the realities of the situation and agreed. An invasion of France would take place in May or early June 1944.

8 Allied forces in the Far East sometimes complained they were "forgotten" as plans concentrated on Europe. Here, a B-25 bomber of US 5th Air Force makes a run on a Japanese escort warship. (Keystone)

January 1943 that the campaign in Europe should take priority over that against Japan, but huge resources still had to be committed to the Pacific. (Central Press)

9 Japan's great initial successes in the Pacific in 1941-42 included what Winston Churchill termed "the greatest disaster in the history of the British Empire." This was the capture of the naval base of Singapore by General Tomoyuki Yamashita, seen here (seated, left) accepting the surrender of British commanders on February 15, 1942. (Keystone)

7 Fire fighters on the flight deck of a US aircraft carrier struggle to contain the blaze begun by a Japanese bomb during the reconquest of the Philippines, 1944-45. It was agreed at the Casablanca Conference of

11 Eisenhower and a British aide in Italy, where the Allies landed September 1943. (Keystone)

10 Skirting a Sherman tank knocked out by a mine, US Marines advance on a Japanese strongpoint on Bougainville Island, Solomons, in late 1943. The Pacific "island hopping" campaign saw some of the war's most savage combat. (Keystone)

Serious planning for the invasion had been in progress for almost a year. The Casablanca Conference had led to the establishment in London of an Anglo-American planning staff under the British Lieutenant-General Frederick Morgan, designated as Chief of Staff to the Supreme Allied Commander, or COSSAC. Despite considerable problems, Morgan and his COSSAC staff worked out the basics of what would become the invasion plan by July, 1943. Although the invasion would be mounted from Britain, the bulk of the forces were to be provided by the United States, and it was inevitable that the Supreme Allied Commander would be an American. General George C. Marshall, the US Army Chief of Staff, was himself considered for the post, but recommended instead one of his own protégés, who had come a long way already since his first plans for the invasion. In December 1943, Roosevelt appointed Eisenhower, now a full general, as Supreme Allied Commander, with orders to "enter the Continent of Europe, and in conjunction with the other United Nations, undertake operations aimed at the heart of Germany and the destruction of her armed forces." Eisenhower's original codename for the invasion, Operation Roundup, was changed to Operation Overlord.

CHAPTER TWO
COUNTDOWN TO OVERLORD

Britain in the early months of 1944 was an armed camp of over 3.5 million soldiers, sailors and airmen. About 1.7 million of these were themselves British, some of whom had been training for more than four years. As Eisenhower and his staff arrived, they brought the numbers of American forces up to more than 1.5 million, together with a further 220,000 troops from every continent of the world. Canadian troops had been in Britain for some time, with Australians and New Zealanders also playing an important part in the British air and sea effort. Throughout Britain, men who had escaped from countries occupied by the Germans were preparing, armed and equipped by the Allies, to fight in Normandy, including French, Poles, Belgians, Dutch, Norwegians and Czechs. Altogether more than a dozen nationalities were getting ready for the invasion.

Every one of these men (and women) needed accommodation, food, clothing, equipment, supplies and training. The British provided most of the barracks and camps, but they depended on the Americans for a quarter of their weapons and vehicles, including the famous Sherman tank. American troops and equipment were shipped across the Atlantic to Britain in a build-up of forces which stretched back over two years, under the codename Operation Bolero. By June, 1944, the US Army in Britain alone needed 2.5 million tons of equipment from overseas, 124,000 hospital beds, and 54,000 cooks to feed itself. For the invasion an air armada of 13,000 aircraft and 3,500 gliders was assembled. Over 1,200 fighting ships, 4,000 assault ships and craft, and 1,600 merchant vessels lay in harbors and anchorages around the coast of Britain. Eisenhower, in one of his rare jokes, observed that "only the great number of barrage balloons floating constantly in British skies kept the islands from sinking under the seas."

Not only did these forces have to be housed and made ready for the invasion, they needed transport from their training areas down to the south coast ports and across to France, the equivalent of moving the populations of Boston and Cleveland combined. The ports themselves, from London around to Bristol and Cardiff, were taking merchant ships and supplies until the last possible dates in February and March before their docks were cleared and filled again with the invasion fleet. Beginning with the COSSAC plan, special organizations of staff officers used

Previous page: pre-invasion blessing on an English quayside for US Army men.
(UPI/Bettmann Newsphotos)
1 Stockpiled for bombardment: 1,000lb aerial bombs stored in a disused British mine.
2 The "Springbok" badge worn by a South African unit.

5 Heavy bombers building for the RAF. Britain's war industries produced about 130,000 military aircraft in 1939-45.
(Fox Photos)

3 A Canadian paratrooper's camouflage is approved by Britain's queen.
(National Archives of Canada)
4 Women workers in a British shipyard look on proudly as a tank landing craft they helped build is launched.

In 1944 Southern England was a huge military storehouse.
6 *Serried ranks of Bofors 40mm light A.A.A.*
7 *Tons of small arms and*

ammunition crated at an ordnance depot.
8 *An American non-com checks out aerial ordnance.*
(US National Archives)

rooms full of filing cards and diagrams to keep track of every single military unit in the country in order to plan the movement and embarkation.

In January, 1944, in an attempt to disrupt the massive preparations, the Germans began the Little Blitz, their first regular nightly air raids since 1941 against London and the ports, killing or seriously injuring over 115,000 civilians. Generally, the British people were determined but resigned after four winters of war in which privation and separation had become a way of life. Few doubted that the war was worthwhile, or that they were winning. But they had yet to see the proof, and they could not yet see the end.

9 *B-17 Fortresses await deployment in Britain.*
10 *Women made an invaluable contribution to America's war industries. This "Rosie the Riveter" worked at Brooklyn's Bendix plant.*
(US National Archives)
11 *Units formed by men from Nazi-occupied countries joined the Allies. This badge was worn by Czechs fighting with the Canadian Army.*

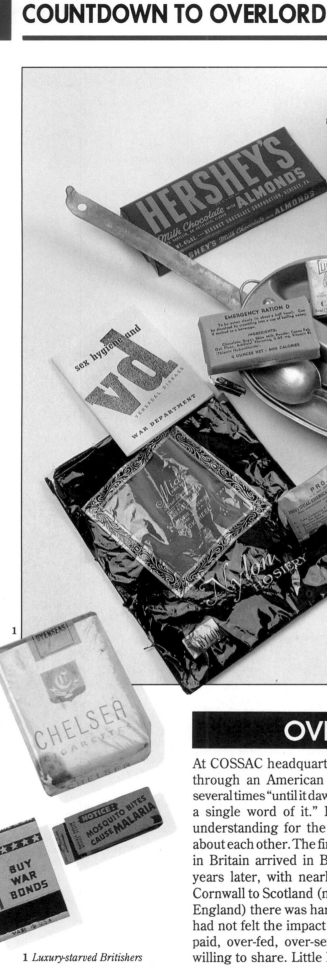

1 *Luxury-starved Britishers marveled at the GIs' supply of cigarettes and chewing gum. Most Americans were generous with their handouts.*
2 *Few soldiers' pocketbooks were without a photograph of a film star or the girl back home.*

OVER THERE

At COSSAC headquarters, Morgan admitted to reading through an American planning paper on the invasion several times "until it dawned on me that I did not understand a single word of it." It took time, patience and great understanding for the British and Americans to learn about each other. The first American troops to be stationed in Britain arrived in Belfast on January 26, 1942. Two years later, with nearly one million GIs billeted from Cornwall to Scotland (not counting the airmen in eastern England) there was hardly a village in the country which had not felt the impact of these friendly invaders, "over-paid, over-fed, over-sexed and over here," but mostly willing to share. Little luxuries like cigarettes and razor blades which had been scarce for years suddenly became readily available. Children waving at passing jeeps in the country lanes were showered with chewing gum and chocolate bars. Their elder sisters, more interested in nylon stockings, dyed their hair peroxide blonde and became accomplished jive dancers. Altogether 70,000 GIs took British war brides back home with them.

With young men in a strange country in wartime, there were always going to be problems. American wealth, directness and different social customs could easily offend British sensibilities, while British reserve was easily

confused with open dislike. "I've come from Bragg," one American greeted his British colleague, only to be told "Yes, I can believe that." With wicked humor, some black GIs even convinced their hosts that they were night-fighting troops given a special chemical to darken their skin for the duration of the war.

Remarkably, in a country of warm beer and cold houses, of people who drove on the wrong side of the road and claimed to enjoy cricket, the Americans made themselves at home. The last American troops arrived in Britain in May to an unexpected and welcome spell of warm weather. Few knew it, but the planning date for the invasion, the date by which everything had to be ready, had been set as June 1.

SHAEF

On his arrival as Supreme Commander, Eisenhower replaced Morgan and his COSSAC staff with his new Supreme Headquarters Allied Expeditionary Forces, or SHAEF, headed by the American and British officers who had served under him in the Mediterranean. Based at Bushy Park near Hampton Court, west of London, it was

3 *"London can take it!" was a frequently quoted slogan at the time of the "Blitz" bombing of 1940-41, and here newly arrived Americans see just how hard London took it. Almost untouched, St. Paul's Cathedral rises in the background.*
(Keystone)

4 *Before they were sent "over there," US servicemen underwent tough training at home. These US Marine Corps paratroopers, making their graduation jump in California, are destined for the Pacific Theater.*
(Keystone)

5 *Jump to it! Men of US Army Air Service Command begin their day with a brisk session of calisthenics.*
(US National Archives)

6 *This US Navy pilot, Lieutenant Robert Callard of VCS-7, originally flew seaplanes. For the Normandy invasion his outfit was re-equipped with speedy British Spitfire fighters, in which they flew missions helping to direct naval gunfire.*
(US National Archives)

On D-Day plus one (June 7, 1944) the German high command ordered the veteran 1st SS Panzer Division, recently rushed back from the East Front, to move up from Bruges towards Caen. The Waffen-SS, more than 900,000 strong (some 40 divisions) in 1944-45, was Himmler's "private army," subject to regular Army command only in tactical matters. It was largely a volunteer force, and its fanatical loyalty to Himmler and Hitler was reflected in its role in the Normandy campaign, where its armored units' heavy tanks provided the Allies with their most savage opposition. The names of the six Waffen-SS divisions thrown into Normandy reflect their elite status in the Nazi war machine: 1st SS Panzer ("Leibstandarte Adolf Hitler;" the "Bodyguard Regiment"); 2nd SS Panzer ("Das Reich"); 9th SS Panzer ("Hohenstaufen"); 10th SS Panzer ("Frundsberg"); 12th SS Panzer ("Hitlerjugend"); and 17th SS Panzer-grenadier ("Götz von Berlichingen").

2 Even in uniform – note Totenkopf ("Death's head") hat badge – Reichsführer-SS Heinrich Himmler does not cut a military figure. The chevron on his sleeve was a mark of honor worn by SS men who joined the organization before January 30, 1933.
(Keystone)

2

1

1 A recruiting poster shows an idealized specimen of Aryan manhood. Requirements for "Nordic blood" were lowered in divisions formed by ethnic Germans from foreign countries and non-German volunteers – at times about half the Waffen-SS's fighting strength.

3 SS troops present arms for the Führer and Himmler (left) at Nuremberg in 1938.
(Keystone)

3

4 *SS Armband.*
5 *Jacket worn by an Unterscharführer (Lance-Sergeant) of 1st SS Panzer Division ("Leibstandarte Adolf Hitler"). Shoulder straps with pink piping (Waffenfarbe) denote an armored unit and incorporate the cypher "LAH." The SS rune is on the right lapel; badge of rank on the left.*

6 *Himmler founded the SS (Schutzstaffel: "Protection Squad") in the early 1920s as Hitler's personal bodyguard.* (UPI/Bettmann)
7 *Radioman of 12th SS Panzer Division ("Hitlerjugend") wears a non-standard black leather jacket "liberated" from Italian naval stores.* (Bundesarchiv)
8 *The Waffen-SS took a good share of around 7,000 Iron Crosses awarded in World War II.*

1 *Lieutenant-General Omar N. Bradley commanded US First Army in 21st Army Group.* (US National Archives)

2 *Lieutenant-General Carl Spaatz (center), commander of US Strategic Air Forces in Europe, cranes to get a look in as Major-General Brereton and Eisenhower discuss invasion plans. Note SHAEF insignia (shown larger to right of facing page) on Eisenhower's sleeve.* (Keystone)

a well-practiced team, with his American Chief of Staff, Major-General Walter Bedell Smith (known as "Beetle" Smith), overseeing a headquarters of 750 officers and 6,000 men.

In theory, Eisenhower had control of the Allied forces within his designated area of command, the European Theater of Operations, or ETO, regardless of their nationality. But as Eisenhower well understood, in coalition war things are seldom so simple. The chain of command for the Allied Liberation Forces (not "invasion" out of respect for French sensibilities) brought together some of the most powerful and explosive personalities on the Allied side, and threatened to expose the national differences which exist in any wartime alliance. Eisenhower knew that many of the British in particular thought him a desk soldier rather than a winner of battles. Churchill's chief military adviser, the Chief of the Imperial General Staff, General Sir Alan Brooke, noted in his diary after one meeting that "Ike knows nothing about strategy."

"Teamwork," as Eisenhower liked to stress in pep-talks to his troops, "wins wars." While the German defenders of Normandy were beset by several conflicting command authorities, with the Navy, the Luftwaffe and the Waffen-SS (the Nazi Party's own army) often refusing to take orders from Army generals, the whole basis of SHAEF was one of cooperation. Eisenhower's Deputy Supreme Commander was a British airman, Air Chief Marshal Sir Arthur Tedder, who had championed air support for ground forces in the early years of the war. Obviously, while British naval and air facilities were crucial, Eisenhower could not command the British Home Fleet or the Air Defence of Great Britain, whose support was needed for the invasion. The solution was to appoint two British

3 *The "Second Front" must have been discussed at this meeting of the Combined Chiefs of Staff (the British Chief of Staffs Committee and the US Joint Chiefs of Staff) at Washington, D.C.; 1943.*
4 *Lieutenant-General Sir Miles Dempsey would command British Second Army in 21st Army Group.* (US National Archives)

EISENHOWER

Dwight David Eisenhower was born in Denison, Texas, on October 14, 1890 of humble German immigrant stock, and grew up in Abilene, Kansas. Entering West Point in 1911, he was commissioned in the infantry. He served in the United States throughout the First World War, organizing and training soldiers for the Tank Corps and rising to temporary lieutenant-colonel, a rank he did not reach again until 1936. Slowly acquiring a reputation as a staff officer after the war, he served under General Douglas MacArthur from 1933 to 1939, first for MacArthur's term as Army Chief of Staff until 1935 and then as his Military Assistant in the Philippines. In 1940 he returned to the United States, rising rapidly in staff appointments through the expanding Army, and in February 1942 was appointed Chief of the Army War Plans Division by General Marshall.

Although Eisenhower showed great skill in staff work and organizing armed forces, he had only commanded a battalion for a brief period in peacetime, and had never led troops in battle. Nevertheless, with Marshall's support Eisenhower became Allied Commander in Chief for the Torch landings in North Africa, being promoted to full general, made Supreme Allied Commander Mediterranean in February, 1943, and finally Supreme Allied Commander Europe in December, 1943.

Eisenhower owed his rapid promotion and eventual high rank to a formidable grasp of the complexities and politics of coalition warfare. In December, 1944, he was promoted to the new rank of General of the Army (five stars), equivalent to a British field marshal. From 1945 to 1948 he served as Army Chief of Staff, and from 1950 to 1952 as the first Supreme Allied Commander Europe for the newly-created NATO alliance. In 1952 he ran as a Republican and was elected as 34th President, serving two terms and retiring at the end of 1960. He died at his home in Abilene on March 28, 1969.

officers as the Allied Air and Naval Commanders in Chief, Air Chief Marshal Sir Trafford Leigh-Mallory and Admiral Sir Bertram Ramsay.

Eisenhower had no direct control over the Allied strategic air forces, the fleets of four-engined bombers of RAF Bomber Command and USAAF 8th Air Force, which he saw as crucial for Normandy. The British and American bomber barons, Air Chief Marshal Sir Arthur Harris and General Carl (Tooey) Spaatz, put up considerable resistance to being placed even temporarily under Eisenhower's control, and it was not until April that their aircraft were switched away from their usual target of German cities and industrial plants. Between then and D-Day, 76,200 tons of Allied bombs rendered the French railways ninety percent ineffective, making it extremely difficult for the Germans to move reserves or supplies and almost cutting off Normandy from the rest of France.

SHAEF's ground forces were designated as 21st Army Group, a number made up by joining together its two components, British Second Army under Lieutenant-General Sir Miles Dempsey and US First Army under Lieutenant-General Omar N. Bradley. Only a fraction of 21st Army Group could land on D-Day, however, and there was no question of Eisenhower commanding the landings. Instead, a separate land forces commander for 21st Army Group would also plan and fight the battle for Eisenhower until sufficient troops had arrived in Normandy for a second Army Group to be formed. With an American as Supreme Commander, Churchill could insist on a British officer for this post, and General Brooke argued successfully for his own protégé, General Sir Bernard Montgomery, described by Eisenhower as "a good man to

5 *Air commanders included (top left) Major-General Lewis Brereton of US 9th Air Force, vital tactical force.* (UPI/Bettmann)

6 *Eisenhower: Supreme Allied Commander from December 1943.* (Keystone)

5

1, 2 For the invasion to succeed, intimate knowledge of the Normandy coastline was essential and, as once "Top Secret" documents show, was meticulously gathered. Detail planning for a cross-Channel invasion began in March 1943 under British General Sir Frederick Morgan (COSSAC: Chief of Staff to the Supreme Allied Commander), who in July 1943 advised that the landing should be in Normandy rather than the easier – and therefore more obvious – Pas de Calais. Early in 1944 Eisenhower changed COSSAC to SHAEF (Supreme Headquarters, Allied Expeditionary Force), with US Lieutenant-General Walter Bedell Smith as its head and Morgan as deputy.

serve under; a difficult man to serve with; and an impossible man to serve over." Montgomery's reputation was far higher among the British than among the Americans, while his belief in his own military genius, and his habit of regarding superiors as an interference, made Eisenhower's job all the harder.

THE CHOICE OF NORMANDY

Since 1942 British Intelligence had been collecting photographs, tide and current tables, soil samples and other information on the French, Belgian and Dutch coastline, looking for a suitable spot for the liberation to begin. The landing beaches had to be within range of fighter air cover from southern England, and both firm and shelving enough to make a landing possible. Analysis ruled out all but two areas: the Pas de Calais and Normandy.

The direct route across the Straits of Dover to the Pas de Calais would give the Allies very short supply lines, and place them in a better position as they advanced inland. Many argued that the Pas de Calais was the better

choice. The Germans also came to this conclusion, giving priority to the Atlantic Wall defenses in the Pas de Calais and strengthening the defending Fifteenth Army at the expense of Seventh Army covering Normandy.

Because a landing at the Pas de Calais was so obvious, Morgan and COSSAC instead advised in July, 1943, on a landing in Normandy within the Bay of the Seine, close to the regional capital of Caen. This promised the advantage of surprise and better landing beaches. Since October, 1943, under conditions of considerable secrecy, nearly 37,000 skilled workers had been laboring in closed-off coastal areas of Britain on the reinforced concrete caissons, shelters and pierheads for the prefabricated harbors, codenamed "Mulberry," which would keep the invasion force supplied until a French port could be captured intact. The Mulberry harbors and specialist landing craft reduced the need to capture a port in the first days of the invasion. Afterwards, the main Norman port of Cherbourg was considered close enough to the landing area for the Allies to capture it within a week or two of landing.

On establishing SHAEF, Eisenhower and Montgomery accepted the choice of Normandy, but insisted on the landing force being stronger than Morgan had planned. The landing would be made on five separate beaches

3

4

5

6

3, 4, 5, 6 A "Phoenix" caisson, major component of "Mulberry" prefabricated harbor, in building and on tow across the Channel (note A.A.A.). Some 150 caissons were built, ranging from 10 of 1,672 tons (the smallest) to 60 of 6,044 tons, to allow construction of a large "Mulberry" off both American and British beaches. (US National Archives)

AIR POWER

For some some months before D-Day, Allied air power was committed to Operation Pointblank.

This was the code-name for an airborne offensive by which the enemy's capability to make war would be progressively reduced to a point at which the invasion would be a viable possibility.

The plan had many aims. It had to ensure that the Allies would have air supremacy over the invasion beaches; it had to make it impossible for the enemy to predict the area in which the attack would be made; it

to be put out of commission, from D-Day until at least D+4, within a radius of 150 miles from the beachhead. The bombing went ahead, and by D-Day a severe paralysis had spread over the Region Nord railway network. Fortunately, French civilian casualties were less heavy than had been feared. Allied aircraft flew almost 22,000 sorties against the railways, and poured over 66,000 tons of bombs onto eighty chosen targets. The disruption of the railways was then complemented by a concerted program of attacks against road bridges within a wide radius of Normandy.

1 *The Short Stirling was the first of the RAF's four-engined heavy bombers to become operational, in February 1941.* (Fox Photos)
2 *Railroad yards in France were a major target for Allied heavy bombers in the buildup to invasion.*

1

had to supress his ability to detect and to resist the invasion once it was launched, and inhibit his ability to reinforce the defenses once it had landed; and it had to provide the reconnaissance which would give the Allies the intelligence they needed of the enemy's activity in the proposed landing area.

Supremacy of the air was achieved, not over northern France, but in the skies above Germany itself. The German policy had been to retain the bulk of its fighter forces for the defense of the Fatherland against the Allied bombing offensive, and the impact of this had been felt most strongly by the massed daylight formations of the USAAF 8th Air Force. To combat this the 8th Air Force had launched an offensive against Germany's centers of aircraft production and repair. Initially this operation seemed almost ineffective, but when the American long-range Mustang fighter became available to escort the bombers all the way to their targets, the effect of the combined bomber/ fighter offensive became dramatically clear. German losses rose to over 2,000 aircraft per month, as the fighters coming up to safeguard the production of their own reinforcements fell prey to the superior Mustangs. The decimation of these aircraft and more significantly the high losses of experienced aircrew, meant that on D-Day the Luftwaffe was almost totally absent from the Normandy skies.

It was predicted that the enemy's most precious asset in the task of reinforcing the defenses of the beachheads would be the French railways. Initially the threat to French civilian lives inhibited the listing of railway targets in what was known as the "Transport" plan, but Montgomery insisted that the railways had

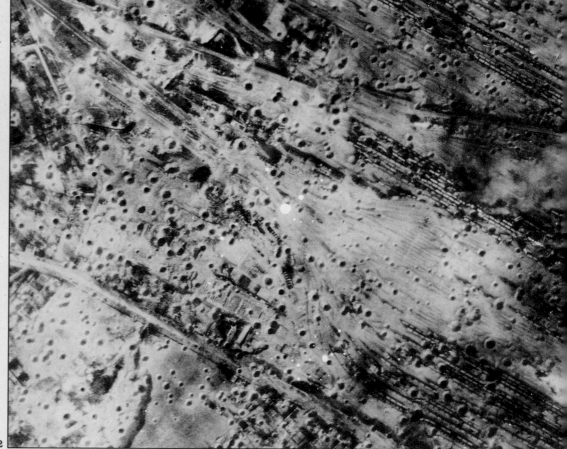

2

During the ten weeks preceeding D-Day Allied aircraft flew 2,500 sorties against German coastal batteries in the assault area. At the same time, fighter-bombers were attacking radar stations which could be used to report shipping movements or control gun batteries.

Each of the Allied services had extremely varied requirements for reconnaissance photography, and in the early planning stages, a vast amount of information about the area to be invaded was collated and verified. As D-Day approached there were more requests for photography of the designated beaches and their exits, airfields and sites for possible airfields, dropping and landing zones, German motor transport parking lots, gun batteries, emplacements, strong points, and every other type of military installation. The detailed information required demanded that a large proportion of sorties had to be flown at low level over heavily defended areas, and between April 1 and June 5,

3

3 *Cap badge of the British Air Training Corps, whose graduates were perhaps responsible for the wreckage at Caen railroad yard, raided by Allied bombers, July 1944.* (IWM: B 7953)

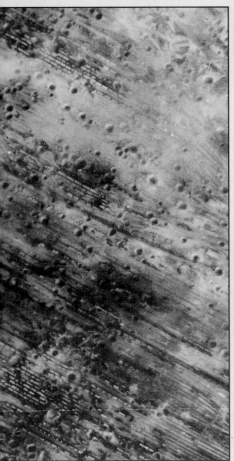

4 *The cap badge of the Royal Air Force – proudly worn by some 1,200,000 men and women in 1939–1945.*

5 *Aircrew of an RAF night fighter squadron stand beneath the Rolls-Royce Merlin engine of a Mosquito. The twin-engined Mosquito was for much of the war the RAF's fastest plane (420 mph) and certainly its most versatile, with major reconnaissance,*

fighter, and bomber roles. It made strikes of pin-point accuracy on buildings, ships, and railroad installations.

(Keystone)

nearly 5,000 Overlord reconnaissance sorties were flown.

It was vital that the enemy should be given no hint of where the attack would be, and to this end, an overall deception plan was created. This was code-named Bodyguard, after the Winston Churchill quote: "In wartime truth is so precious that she should always be attended by a bodyguard of lies." The deception kept the enemy uncertain as to where the invasion might be launched; in the Pas de Calais, Norway or even the Balkans. For instance, every time a reconnaissance mission was flown over Normandy two were flown over the Pas de Calais, and for every ton of bombs dropped on coastal batteries west of Le Havre, two tons were dropped to the north.

The total effort amounted to almost 200,000 sorties, and over 195,000 tons of bombs were dropped. In just nine weeks 1,953 Allied aircraft were lost, at a cost of more than 12,000 airmen.

6 *Cap badge of the Royal New Zealand Air Force. Some 41,000 Dominion air crew were serving with the RAF by 1945.*

MONTGOMERY

Bernard Law Montgomery was born the son of a London clergyman on November 17, 1887 and grew up in Tasmania, where his father became bishop in 1889. Educated at St Paul's School, London, he entered Sandhurst in 1907 and was commissioned in the infantry. He served on the Western Front throughout the First World War, being severely wounded in 1914 and ending the war as a major and chief staff officer of a division. Between the wars he served in Ireland, as an instructor at the Army Staff College, and in Palestine and India.

Montgomery started the Second World War as a major-general, taking his division to France under Lieutenant-General Sir Alan Brooke as his corps commander. He made a good impression in the 1940 campaign, being evacuated with his men at Dunkirk. With Brooke's support Montgomery was promoted to lieutenant-general and given command of the Eighth Army in Egypt in August, 1942. Leading it through the desert and Tunisian campaigns, and through the landings in Sicily and Italy, he was promoted to general.

In December, 1943, Montgomery was appointed to command 21st Army Group for D-Day and the campaign in Northwest Europe, and in September, 1944 was promoted to field marshal. Cautious and thorough in command, he inspired either fierce devotion

or equally fierce dislike, while his offensive vanity and lack of political skills often causing embarrassment and difficulties. In 1946 he was ennobled as Viscount Montgomery of Alamein and appointed Chief of the Imperial General Staff in succession to Brooke. In 1951 he became Eisenhower's Deputy Supreme Commander Europe at NATO, and served until his retirement in 1958. He died on March 24, 1976.

1 *Field Marshal Montgomery.*
(IWM: B 5339)
3 *An RAF Mitchell bomber hits a European target, June 1944. Air activity ranged widely, to keep the Germans guessing over the true invasion area.*
(IWM: CL 217)
4 *On the alert: the rear gunner in a British bomber.*

across a front of more than forty miles, with five divisions in the first wave and four more divisions coming ashore in the first 24 hours, requiring nearly 4,500 landing ships and craft. This demand for more of everything was typical of Montgomery, who believed firmly in playing safe to keep his own casualties low rather than in taking risks to defeat the enemy. Given that most of the American troops were stationed in the west of Britain, it made sense to land them on the western beaches, codenamed Utah and Omaha, which lay on either side of the River Vire estuary. The British and Canadian beaches, codenamed Gold, Juno and Sword, stretched eastward as far as the River Orne estuary near Caen itself. Montgomery also demanded an

assault landing by airborne divisions, one British and one American, to secure both flanks of the seaborne landing. Responding in typical style, the Americans gave him not one but two airborne divisions for his western flank.

PLANNING THE INVASION

Just as it had taken years of organization and training to make Overlord possible, so at SHAEF and 21st Army Group nearly five months were spent finalizing the plan. On the German side, the man placed in charge of defeating the invasion, Montgomery's old adversary, Rommel, worked

5

tanks and engineers to the usual infantry in order to clear the beach defenses and get inland quickly. Previous Allied amphibious landings had been made at night in order to conceal and protect the ships and landing craft from enemy attack, but Montgomery wanted daylight for the landings and advance inland, particularly for the fire support from aircraft and ships. As a compromise, and to allow for the tides, the Allied fleets would cross the Channel after dark and the landings would be made within an hour of dawn after a preliminary bombardment. This in turn meant that the airborne landings, the biggest ever planned, would have to be made at night. In order to improve their chances, the airmen and airborne commanders wanted a full moon. The right combination of moon, tide, winds and weather would last for three days starting on June 5, Eisenhower's choice for D-Day.

Montgomery's plan was for British Second Army to capture Caen on D-Day itself and push armor forward as rapidly as possible onto the open areas to the south. Meanwhile, US First Army would expand westward across the Cotentin peninsula and north to capture Cherbourg. This would provide the space in which to land and deploy troops, armor and fighter aircraft for close support. By the end of the month, if all went well, Montgomery expected to be in possession of the whole of Normandy. At this point or shortly after, enough Allied troops would be ashore for Montgomery to hand over to Eisenhower a firm base in France for the rest of the campaign. For planning purposes, 21st Army Group judged that the Germans would be driven across the River Seine about three months after the first landings.

The first problem would be securing the beachheads on D-Day itself. Once the Allies were safely ashore and the advance inland had begun, Montgomery's greatest concern was that Rommel might assemble enough troops in Normandy to create an armored reserve for a slashing counterattack, as he had done so often in the North African desert. The biggest fear of all was that the Germans might discover when and where the invasion was coming, and meet it on the beaches with overwhelming force.

FORTITUDE

Whatever their skills or bravery on the battlefield, in the hidden war of intelligence and espionage the Germans had little success in penetrating the veil of secrecy which lay over the Allied invasion preparations. From April the entire British coastline was closed to civilians, and all foreign diplomats (except the Americans) were prevented from entering and leaving the country. Allied high command introduced a separate codename of Operation Neptune for all documents which mentioned the date or place of the landing (mainly concerning naval operations), and a new security classification of Bigot, ranking higher even than Top Secret, to cover the Overlord secrets.

Even so, there were some alarming security scares, with secret papers on the invasion turning up in a Chicago post office and an Exeter train compartment, and being blown out of the windows of Whitehall offices. The most gruesome Bigot story was the loss of ten officers, who knew the secret, with 700 others off Slapton Sands in May, when German E-Boats broke into an American landing rehearsal exercise to sink two landing ships. Not until all the bodies were recovered was it clear that none of the officers had been captured by the Germans. The most

2 A German fatigue party on the "Atlantic Wall" prepares to lay Tellermine type mines on the landward side of a barbed wire barrier. From the size, these appear to be the Tellermine 42, the major German anti-tank mine, with a diameter of about 12.5 inches and packing 12 pounds of Amatol or TNT explosive. Some 240-400 pounds pressure was required to set it off. (Bundesarchiv)

5 An Allied reconnaissance plane got this pre-D-Day shot of beach obstacles below the tide line at Cherbourg, intended to rip the bottoms from landing craft (Library of Congress)

6

7

6, 7 American posters stress the necessity for everyone to observe the requirements of wartime secrecy. As a British slogan warned: "Careless talk costs lives!"

with great energy to build improvized defenses and obstacles on beaches throughout the possible invasion areas, and to strengthen the Atlantic Wall. Rommel shared the majority German view that the Pas de Calais was the most likely invasion site, but believed firmly that wherever the invasion came his best chance of defeating it was on the beaches in the first 24 hours. "For both sides," he insisted, "it will be the longest day."

In April Montgomery decided that the landings would be made with the tide high enough for the landing craft to get close to the shore, but low enough to avoid the main shoreline obstacle belt. The first landings would be made by specially-organized assault brigades, adding amphibious

1, 2, 4, 8 *Coastal areas where invasion troops rehearsed were "no go" areas where secrecy ruled and civilian movement was limited. Even so, on April 28, 1944, two flotillas of German torpedo boats attacked US infantry landing craft off Slapton Sands, Devon. More than 600 GIs were killed and others wounded.*
(US National Archives)

3 Did someone's idle gossip tip off an enemy agent about the exercises off Slapton, enabling German "E-boats" to spring an ambush?

Allies convinced the Germans that their forces in Britain were roughly double their real size. The non-existent British Fourth Army was created in northern England for Fortitude North, a threatened invasion of Norway which kept twenty-seven German divisions tied down in Scandinavia. For Fortitude South, a landing where the Germans expected it at the Pas de Calais, an entire Army Group, FUSAG or First US Army Group, was created from a mixture of dummy units and real divisions intended for the later stages of the Normandy battle. The Allies let the

bizarre story concerns the crossword puzzle in a British newspaper, which for the last week in May had several D-Day codewords as answers to clues, much to the astonishment of its totally innocent compiler.

It was obvious to the Germans that an invasion was being planned, and by January Admiral Wilhelm Canaris, head of German military Intelligence, knew both the codeword "Overlord" and the signals which would alert the French Resistance. What the Germans needed was information on the strength of the Allied forces and their likely landing area. German agents in Britain were told to report troop locations and movements. In fact, although the Germans did not realize it, every one of their agents in Britain had been caught and turned by the British in the years before 1944. They were being controlled through the British Intelligence Twenty Committee (20 in Roman numerals being a double cross), and their reports were being dictated by Allied officers.

The work of the Twenty Committee was part of a much larger Allied deception plan, Operation Fortitude, to convince the Germans that Normandy was not the chosen invasion site. Using the double agents together with planted stories in newspapers, faked radio traffic, dummy encampments and other deception methods, the

In poster: **BITS OF CARELESS TALK ARE PIECED TOGETHER BY THE ENEMY** / England / Convoy sails for tonight

Germans believe that the man in charge of FUSAG was the commander they most feared, Lieutenant-General George S. Patton Jr. Always a controversial figure, and on persistently bad terms with Montgomery, Patton was admired for his aggression and battlefield skills, and the Germans did not believe that the Allies would leave him out of their D-Day plans. Indeed, for weeks after the D-Day landings they convinced themselves that FUSAG under Patton was still waiting to carry out the main invasion against Fifteenth Army in the Pas de Calais.

6 Germany used Enigma to produce coded information. It was basically an electric typewriter: the operator manipulated three rotors over the keyboard to achieve a supposedly unbreakable code – but the Allies cracked it.
(IWM: MH 27174)

THE ULTRA SECRET

A large part of intelligence work on both sides during the war was the interception and decoding of enemy radio signals, which often carried crucial information. Before the war the Germans had adopted for their armed forces, diplomatic service and even the police and railways, a mechanical system of encoding messages based on a device resembling a small portable typewriter, called an Enigma machine. In theory, Enigma cyphers were unbreakable, and the Germans relied on them throughout the war. The first work on breaking the Enigma was done by the Poles, then the French and the British, from their Government Code and Cypher School (GCCS) at Bletchley Park, north of London, where a primitive electronic calculating machine was used to help break the codes. The British gave the material produced from Bletchley the codename Ultra, and throughout the war – and for some time afterward – it was their most closely guarded secret, known only to the very highest Allied commanders.

Ultra was a tremendous advantage, but it was not by itself a war winner. The messages which it provided often needed careful interpretation, and it was most useful in providing routine information on the size, strength and locations of German forces. To plan the Normandy landings this was exactly the kind of information the Allies needed. For the build-up to D-Day and the Battle of Normandy itself, the British were breaking the Enigma key used by the Luftwaffe on a regular basis, and the presence of Luftwaffe liaison officers with German Army divisions often provided valuable information.

5 Camouflage netting shields GIs from possible aerial surveillance as they enjoy a final hot meal before facing cold "C" and "K" rations aboard invasion transports.
(UPI/Bettmann)
7 British tankers make sure their Sherman is similarly shrouded against snoopers.
(US National Archives)

1 *Loading up for invasion: US Army artillerymen see that a field piece is safely stowed aboard a US Navy LST (tank landing ship). With a maximum speed of only about 11 knots, these vulnerable, 1,625-ton vessels were aptly nicknamed "Large, Slow Targets."* (US National Archives)

1

4 *A view from the bridge: the five-pointed stars on the vehicles' tarpaulins will identify them to Allied gound attack aircraft.* (US National Archives)

THE CRUCIAL ISSUES

Putting the information from Ultra together with less glamorous radio interception work, aerial reconnaissance photographs and the work of agents and observers in France, including the Resistance, the Allies identified nearly all the German divisions defending Normandy, and the strength of the Atlantic Wall. Most of the German forces were static formations, made up of second-class troops and without transport, intended only to hold their positions. But the identification of even one German armored division, 21st Panzer Division, near Caen caused deep concern. Getting ashore and inland in the face of the Atlantic Wall defenses – "Operation Bloodbath," one British officer called it – was going to depend on the weight of fire with which the Allies could support their landing forces. Eisenhower also needed to be certain that troops and supplies could get across the Channel unhampered by interference from German U-Boats and E-Boats, which had proved so effective at Slapton Sands. This placed a massive responsibility on Ramsay and his two naval task forces, Eastern Task Force to support the British beaches and Western Task Force for the Americans. Almost twelve hours before the landings, minesweepers had to start clearing channels off the Normandy coast up to the beach approaches, while some of the supporting warships had to steam from Scapa Flow in the Orkney Islands, past the northern tip of Scotland, to the invasion beaches without being spotted by the Germans.

4

2

2, 3 *British Admiral Sir Bertram Ramsay was the Allied Naval Commander in Chief for what his Special Order of the Day characterized as "the greatest amphibious operation in history."*

Nearly eighty percent of the warships involved were British. In January 1945 Ramsay was killed in an air crash. (IWM: A 23443)

3

Ramsay's warships, nearly eighty percent of which were British, also depended heavily on air power for their concealment and protection from attack. Whichever way the problem was viewed, air power was seen as the key to the Battle of Normandy. From April onward, by attacking the French transportation system the Allied airmen forced the Luftwaffe to come up and fight to defend it. By D-Day there were fewer than 300 Luftwaffe fighters left to confront Leigh-Mallory's air armada. Thereafter, as long as they controlled the skies over France, the Allied aircraft could prevent or slow the movement of German reinforcements to Normandy while protecting their own ships across the Channel, allowing the Allies to win the build-up battle. But aircraft needed space, particularly airfields in Normandy for the fighters and fighter-bombers of RAF 2nd Tactical Air Force and USAAF 9th Air Force, which would also be needed as flying artillery to support the Allied advance. Tedder and his airmen, worked to support Montgomery's land battle rather than control it, but nevertheless felt the weight of their own responsibility very heavily. They were to become Montgomery's severest critics over his handling of the Normandy battle.

5 *A few of the 4,000 landing craft assembled for D-Day.*
(IWM: A 23730)

6 *A nerve center: US Navy's recording/processing room at SHAEF HQ, London.*

7 *US newsman Ed Murrow makes a broadcast on the invasion. But alongside a censor from the British Ministry of Information has his finger on a switch that will bleep out Murrow if he strays into classified information.*
(US National Archives)

8 *Part of the assembled armada. Note the large liner, possibly a hospital ship.*

9 *In the Nelson spirit: a message from one of the naval force commanders.*

TO ALL IN FORCE "S"

The great day for which we have all been training is at hand. The task allotted to us is a formidable one, and calls for all that is best in every one of us.

The 3rd British Infantry Division has been entrusted to our care. They are old friends of ours; we have grown up together; we have come to look on them as our own. Let every officer and man in the Force feel a personal responsibility for the comfort, safety and maintenance of his "opposite number" in the 3rd Division.

And, above all FIGHT;
FIGHT to help the Army;
FIGHT to help yourselves;
FIGHT to save your ship;
FIGHT to the very end.

A. G. TALBOT,
Rear Admiral.

SEA POWER

Operation Neptune – the naval side of Overlord – was the largest operation of its kind ever undertaken. No opposed amphibious invasion on this scale had even been attempted before. Immediately involved in the Normandy landings were seven battleships, two monitors, twenty-three cruisers, three gunboats, 105 destroyers and over 1,000 smaller naval vessels. There were over 4,000 landing ships and landing craft and 864 merchant ships to take in troops and supplies.

Overlord as a whole was made possible by Allied naval superiority in European waters and the Atlantic generally. This dominance had been won over years of hard struggle against German battleships and other surface-raiders, U-boats, and the Luftwaffe.

By June, 1944, the Battle of the Atlantic had effectively been won. The main units of the German Navy had either been sunk, or were holed up in Norwegian ports, no longer trusted by Hitler as an effective weapon.

the tactical minefields laid by E-boats in the Channel, as the invasion began.

Against the massive Allied forces in the Channel, the Germans only had five destroyers, some thirty torpedo boats, their own minesweepers and around 100 assorted patrol boats and gun-carriers, with another five destroyers, more minesweepers and sixty patrol boats along the Atlantic Coast between Brest and Bayonne.

Operation Neptune was above all an overwhelming victory by the planners. They got it right, and all the efforts by local German naval forces were thwarted. Naval and air cooperation insured that only the relatively small number of U-boats equipped with *schnorkel* breathing apparatus were effective. The German destroyers were kept at bay, and despite a few determined forays, most of the Allied naval losses during the month of June were caused by air attacks or mines. Many ships had narrow escapes, but it was on the whole the Allied navies which called the tune.

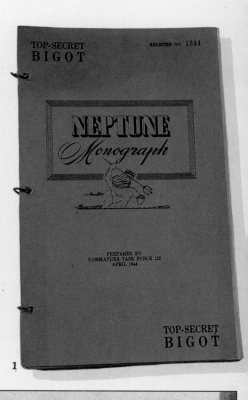

1

2,3 *In mid-1944 most of Germany's remaining U-boats formed anti-invasion groups, in bombproof pens on the Norwegian and French coasts. As the poster suggests, they still were thought a threat.*
(Keystone)

2

The arrival of vital supplies (and troops) from the United States was made possible thanks to the tremendous American Liberty Ship program, with some 2,700 being built by the end of the war. Most of them were now getting through safely as a result of the use of strong naval escorts including escort carriers, better tactics developed against attacking U-boat groups, and a more aggressive use of RAF Coastal Command aircraft.

Victory in the Atlantic was signalled when Admiral Doenitz withdrew most of his submarines to form two anti-invasion U-boat groups: "Landwirt" based in France and "Mitte" based in Norway. Almost to the last, Hitler believed that the main invasion force would land in the Pas de Calais area or alternatively, Norway, as was suggested by Allied deception tactics.

The Allied navies and supply ships off Normandy still faced German destroyers, E-boats and mines. Over 100 Allied minesweepers were used against the defensive minefields along Hitler's Atlantic Wall and

3

A careless word...

...A NEEDLESS SINKING

4

1 *Monograph on Operation Neptune bears the codeword "BIGOT," denoting highest security classification.*
4 *Close on 150 major warships, from battleships to destroyers, guarded the invasion armada. Among them was the 9,050-ton heavy cruiser USS Augusta (CA.31), with nine 8-inch guns.* (US National Archives)

5 *British sailors man conning positions on a Royal Navy assault landing craft (LCA) carrying GIs to a transport on the eve of D-Day.* (US Army)
6 *Assault landing craft head for an invasion beach at maximum speed. Such small craft were carried across the Channel by larger ships specially developed for amphibious operations, such as the US Navy's LSD (landing ship, dock).*

7 *A tank landing ship – LST.289; US-built but transferred to the Royal Navy pre-D-Day – lies alongside a supply vessel in a British harbor.* (US National Archives)

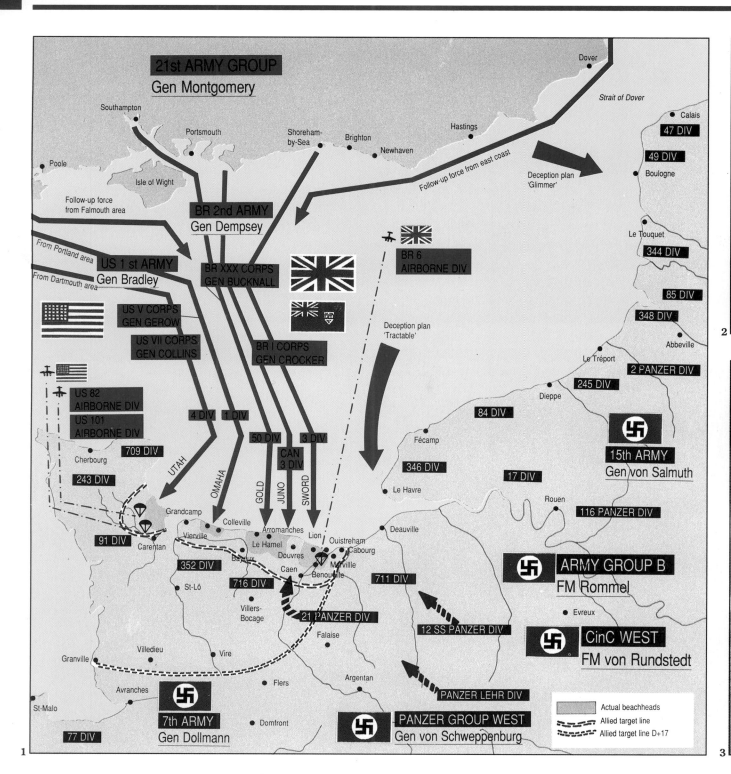

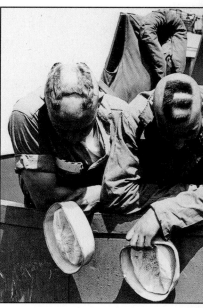

1 *Map shows routes of the armada carrying US First Army to Utah and Omaha beaches and British and Canadians to Gold, Juno, and Sword. Note deception plans "Glimmer" and "Tractable": a few ships, along with aircraft dropping "chaff" to clutter German radars, suggested that forces were also heading for Boulogne and Le Havre. The dispositions of German units at June 6 are also shown.*
2 *Some US sailors chose a novel way to make a pessimistic forecast about the reception the Allies might receive!*
(US National Archives)

THE LAST HOURS

For D-Day itself Eisenhower moved his forward SHAEF headquarters to Southwick House outside Portsmouth, where the senior Allied commanders gathered for the final decisions on the invasion. On May 25, while the last of their stores and equipment were loaded into barges and landing craft, the troops which would make the first landings moved to their embarkation camps, which were then sealed. Inside the camps the final briefings were given, and the men learned of their destinations and the date of the attack for the first time. A few days later, the first embarkations onto landing ships, craft and barges in the harbors began. Eisenhower's biggest concern was now the weather, as the fine spell came to an end on June 1. A sustained period of good weather was essential for Operation Overlord to succeed. Indeed, many in German Intelligence predicted that without four or five days of clear skies Eisenhower would not risk launching his invasion.

On June 3, with the invasion date still set for June 5, the first naval units began their deployment, only for the SHAEF meteorologists to tell Eisenhower early next day that a gale, the worst in twenty years, was on its way into the English Channel. Eisenhower had no choice but to order a postponement of the invasion for 24 hours. As the COSSAC staff had determined long before, this was just possible, but the finely-tuned plans could not be left in suspension for much longer. A second day's delay would mean a postponement until mid-June or even July. On the ships and in the camps the men waiting to go wrote letters, played cards or dice, read or talked or stared into space. Some unfortunates had been on board their ships for nearly a week, sick with the stench and the swell as they rocked in the gale. Some of the ships and craft destined for Utah beach had actually set out according to schedule before Eisenhower's decision to postpone, and faced the disappointment of returning.

At 9:30 PM on June 4, Eisenhower met his commanders, Tedder, Ramsay, Leigh-Mallory and Montgomery with Bedell Smith in attendance, to hear the meteorological

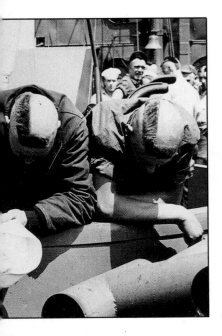

3 *British Horsa gliders that carried some of the airborne troops dropped early on June 6 are lined up with Halifax bombers that will tow them.*
(IWM: CL 26)
4 *Calling the roll: final check-out for GIs and their gear. Note the equipment cart towed by men in foreground: most airborne forces used such light, handy devices.*
5 *Aboard an invasion ship: weather scares forced some men to endure such crowded, nerve-wracking conditions for several days.*
(US National Archives)

assessment once more. The weather was starting to clear, and would remain clear over Normandy for the night of June 5, and through into the morning of June 6, before closing up again. Eisenhower asked for opinions: Tedder and Leigh-Mallory disliked taking chances with the uncertain weather, Ramsay and Montgomery both wanted to go ahead. Eisenhower considered. "I am quite positive we must give the order," he said slowly, "I don't like it, but there it is. I don't see how we can do anything else." As the hours and the storm dragged by the weather predictions remained good, and Tuesday June 6, was set as D-Day.

Once the decision had been made at Tehran over eighteen months before, Winston Churchill had worked for Operation Overlord with all his formidable energy, and had even tried to get himself onto a British warship for the invasion. But as darkness fell on June 5, all his old anxieties welled up once more. "Do you realize," he told his wife, "that by the time you wake up in the morning 20,000 men may have been killed?"

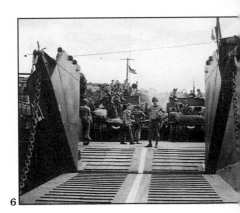

6 *An American LCT (landing craft, tank) is all set to "up ramp" and begin the hazardous journey to the beaches of Normandy.*
(US National Archives)

CHAPTER THREE
OUT OF THE NIGHT

The role of the three Allied airborne divisions on D-Day was to prevent German reinforcements interfering with the seaborne landing by capturing villages, bridges, road junctions and strongpoints inland and on either flank of the invasion beaches. The American 101st Airborne Division (Screaming Eagles) was made up of three regiments (each of three battalions) of parachute infantry. The 82nd Airborne Division (All American) also had three parachute regiments, plus a regiment of air-landing infantry in gliders. The British 6th Airborne Division was made up of two brigades – equivalent to American regiments – of the Parachute Regiment (formed in 1940 and already famous as the Red Devils from its distinctive berets) including a Canadian battalion, and an air-landing brigade of British line infantry battalions given special glider training. Each paratrooper carried up to 100 pounds of weapons and equipment strapped so tightly that most could hardly sit down, and jumping into battle always carried with it the risk of personal injury. The glider troops faced instead a deliberate, controlled crash landing in which most would be dazed or knocked unconscious. If spotted by the enemy, only the fittest men could recover from a parachute jump or glider landing fast enough to fight back.

For the night landing, 1,087 aircraft, mostly American C-47 Dakotas with some British Stirlings and Albermarles, were used to deliver the men to their target. Even with the vast Allied resources, there were not enough aircraft to carry three complete divisions at once, and each division led mostly with its paratroopers. Reinforcements and heavier weapons followed in gliders later, or the next day. To make the drop the pilots had to fly at no more than 120 mph, only a few hundred feet above the ground, through German anti-aircraft fire. Coming by night made them more difficult targets, but also made it much harder to be sure of the drop zones. A pessimistic Leigh-Mallory told Eisenhower that his two American divisions might suffer up to 80 percent losses on the night.

Previous page: *Invaders' dawn: British gliders and their tugs head for Normandy.*
(UPI/Bettmann)
1 *Hitler consults with Generaloberst Alfred Jodl, Chief of Wehrmacht Operations Staff. Both were initially slow to realize Normandy was the "real" invasion.*
(Keystone)

2

2 *This cloth patch was worn on the overseas cap of US airborne forces.*
4 *On the alert for aircraft or paratroopers, searchlights create a cone of brightness.*
(US National Archives)

The aircraft carrying the sticks of between 15 and 18 paratroopers each, or towing the first gliders, took off for France shortly before dusk on June 5. At 101st Airborne headquarters, Eisenhower exchanged a few words with some of the troops an hour before watching them fly into the darkness. A little after midnight the divisional path-finder teams, assigned to mark the drop zones and clear away German obstacles for the main formations, arrived over their target and the men jumped on command. Seconds later, their feet touched French soil. The credit for being the first Allied paratrooper to land in France probably goes to Captain Frank Lillyman, commanding the 101st Airborne's pathfinders.

3 *Following their D-Day operations, US 82nd and 101st Airborne Divisions and British 6th Airborne, with other Allied airborne units, were unified for planning purposes into First Allied Airborne Army, reviewed here by General Eisenhower.*
(UPI/Bettmann)

4

6 *Douglas C-47 Skytrains (known to the British as Dakotas) overfly invasion shipping. The standard US troop carrier, the C-47 could carry 28 paratroopers.* (US National Archives)

5 *Ready to jump: a trooper of US 82nd Airborne Division. The divisional patch is on his left sleeve; the American Flag patch on the right was worn by US paratroopers in Normandy for mutual recognition in enemy-held areas. A breast pack holds his reserve parachute; above it are a flashlight and M1 hand grenades on a ring clip. Other visible arms are a scabbarded carbine (but not the folding stock model of the M1A1 made for airborne troops) and a fighting knife strapped to his right calf.*

7 *US paratrooper's qualification wings: a cloth patch worn on the left breast of the field jacket.*

THE FRENCH RESISTANCE

Members of the Resistance, or Armée Secrete, in Normandy had been preparing and hoping for the liberation for more than four years, during which many had been captured or killed by the Germans. The Resistance was not a single organization but a loose grouping of different loyalties. In May, a headquarters for the *Forces Françaises de l'Interieur,* or FFI, was set up in Britain under General Joseph Pierre Koenig to command the Resistance in France for the invasion. Its work was coordinated with the British Special Operations Executive (SOE) and Special Air Service (SAS), and the American Office of Strategic Services (OSS).

Before D-Day, Resistance members in Normandy, working in great danger under the noses of the Germans, provided the vital detailed information which allowed the Allies to plan their attack. When the Germans made a minor change to the defenses of Pegasus Bridge, knocking down two buildings to improve the field of fire, it was communicated by the Resistance and appeared on the British briefing model next day. Other Resistance messages failed to get through in time, including the arrival near Carentan on June 5 of a new German anti-aircraft battery which cost the American airborne divisions several aircraft that night.

Resistance groups were warned of the invasion mostly by coded radio messages sent out by the BBC on the night of June 4/5. The most famous of these, two lines from the poet Verlaine, *les sanglots longs des violons d'automne blessent mon coeur d'une langueur montone,* was known to German Intelligence serving Fifteenth Army in the Pas de Calais, which went on alert, but not to Seventh Army in Normandy. Because of the uncertainties involved, few Resistance groups were meant to link up with the Allied paratroopers on

the night of the invasion, but many had specific tasks to aid the invasion. One team cut the telephone cable linking Cherbourg with Paris and the outside world. At Caen railway station, the stationmaster and his staff smashed water pumps and sabotaged the engines, while another team blew up railway lines all over Normandy. Paratroopers who landed miles from their targets fought for weeks or sometimes months with the local Resistance before rejoining their units, while during the night of the invasion many locals armed themselves and joined in with the airborne forces.

1 "Patrol wagon" of a French Resistance group is marked with the Cross of Lorraine.
(IWM: B 9420)

2 Risking severe penalties from the occupation power, a French family tunes in a homemade radio set. Coded messages transmitted by the BBC alerted Resistance groups to the imminent invasion.
(IWM: B 8704)

3 This pro-Nazi French poster attempted to show that the "heroes" of the Resistance were in fact criminal types of non-French origin, given to savage atrocities.

4 *The other side of the propaganda war prevailed after D-Day. "Up with the Resistance – and carry on!" is the inspiring* message *on a poster that shows French civilians greeting one of the Allied liberators.*
(US National Archives)

THE SCREAMING EAGLES

101st Airborne Division's drop zones were next to Utah beach, where less than a mile inland the sand dunes gave way to a belt of marsh. The task of the 101st Airborne was to land west of this marsh and secure four designated exit causeway roads from the beaches, together with the bridges and crossing points over the River Vire and its tributary the Douve, close to the town of Carentan, to prevent the Germans from cutting Utah beach off from Omaha on the far side of the Vire estuary. But almost from the start the American airborne assault started to go wrong. The weather which had caused Tedder and Leigh-Mallory such anxiety played its part, as low cloud and fog broke up aircraft formations and pilots drifted off target. Several Dakota pilots, weaving to avoid German flak, came in too fast and too low to identify their drop zones. Only thirty-eight of the 120 pathfinders were put down on target.

This failure was to be repeated throughout the night, leaving the American paratroopers bitterly critical of their pilots and of the whole idea of night assaults, as both divisions were scattered throughout Normandy. Some men of the 101st Airborne landed over 20 miles from their objectives, and in extreme cases claimed to have been dropped closer to Paris than to the beaches. A few sticks were given the jump signal while still over the sea and drowned helplessly, or were dropped so low that their parachutes had no time to open properly. Other men reached the ground only to find themselves in the marsh, deliberately flooded by the Germans as part of their defenses, or in defended hamlets and villages. By the end of the day, of 6,600 men of the division who had set out from England, 3,500 were listed as missing.

5 *A Flying Fortress air drops supplies to men of the* Maquis *(literally "bush country"), the generic name given to French Resistance fighters.*
6 *Identification brassard worn after D-Day by members of the Forces Françaises de l'Intérieur (FFI), which attempted to unify the forces of the Resistance.*

7 *An American paratrooper boards a Normandy-bound troop carrier. He appears heavily loaded, but some of the bulk is accounted for by the rear and front packs holding his main and reserve parachutes. (Equipment weight totaling above 30 pounds made paratroopers much more liable to injury on landing.) He carries a Thompson M1 sub-machine gun and has a fighting knife in a sheath strapped to his leg.*
(US National Archives)

8 *Dummies like this, about half the size of a man, made of sackcloth filled with sand, and with an integral parachute, were dropped before the airborne landings to create confusion among the defenders. Some included small, timed explosive charges to simulate gunfire.*

1 *101st Airborne's "Screaming Eagle" patch commemorated "Old Abe," eagle mascot of the Union Army's "Iron Brigade" in the Civil War.*
5 *"Ike jackets" of a corporal, 101st Airborne, and sergeant, 82nd Airborne, flank a jump jacket. Note jump boots, overseas cap, and other airborne memorabilia.*

The first wave of the 101st Airborne's main body, its three regiments of paratroopers, arrived over the drop zones at about 1:30 AM. But not one single aircraft carrying the men of 502nd Parachute Infantry put them down on their intended drop zone, next to two northern exits from Utah. Instead, almost half the regiment parachuted onto the next drop zone, two miles to the south. To compound the problem, the regimental commander, Colonel George Moseley, broke his leg on landing. One of the regiment's three battalions was so badly scattered that, together with the division's artillery, it took virtually no part in the day's fighting. Fortunately, the remaining paratroopers under Lieutenant-Colonel John Michaelis were able to collect themselves and secure the two northern exits from Utah without meeting serious opposition, except from isolated German units. There were numerous sharp firefights and

2 *Troops inspect the wreckage of a Waco CG-4 glider.*
3 *British GA Hamilcar gliders swoop in to land. This big glider could carry a 7-ton light tank or other vehicles or troops up to a maximum load of 17,500 pounds.*
(IWM: B 5198)

acts of individual bravery as the paratroopers established their positions, including the virtually single-handed clearance of a German barracks at the village of Mesières by Staff-Sergeant Harrison Summers. By the evening of D-Day, the 502nd had made contact with the landing force on Utah, but not with 82nd Airborne to their north and west, whose fate was unknown.

The German defenders of 709th Static Division and 91st Airlanding Division went on full alert soon after one AM, as Allied bombing raids intensified and reports of the landings reached them. The Allied plan included diversions by aircraft flying deep inland to mislead the Germans, and dummy parachutists were dropped all over northern France.

4 *British Horsa gliders lie higgledy-piggledy, but apparently mostly intact, in a landing zone. Note "skid tracks" made on landing.*
6 *Gliders were necessarily flimsy craft, and landing crackups were not uncommon. Here, casualties lie beside a smashed Waco "box car," once capable of carrying 15 fully equipped soldiers.*
(US National Archives)

Resistance fighters also spread confusion to aid the airborne assault. Neither side could form a clear picture of where the enemy was, as isolated German garrisons fought with equally isolated bands of Americans. The training and determination of the paratroopers showed as men from different battalions or even divisions collected themselves together and set off through a long and confused night, knowing that their safety and that of the approaching invasion force depended on their reaching their objectives. 7

In the division's center, close to the two southern causeway exits, only nine aircraft of 506th Parachute Infantry put their men down on target. Once more an entire battalion was dropped on the wrong zone and did not reach its objectives until early afternoon. At least two sticks of men were dropped onto Ste Mère-Eglise itself and slaughtered by the Germans. The divisional commander, Major-General Maxwell Taylor, found himself safe on the ground with the division and regimental staff and just 85 men to secure the southern exits. "Never," he observed grimly, "have so few been led by so many!" In fact, on the initiative of Taylor and two of his junior commanders, three separate groups were rounded up and sent independently to secure the village covering the exit roads.

Over the southernmost of the division's drop zones, the Dakota pilots, by accident or design, put virtually all their troops down in the right place. But the Germans had

7 Airborne troops were not the only ones to reach Normandy ahead of the main invasion force. British "X-craft," midget submarines some 45 feet long and carrying a crew of four, engaged in hazardous but most successful reconnaissance off the beaches. As landing ships approached, they surfaced and flashed colored lights as navigational beacons. (IWM: A 22903 B)

OUT OF THE NIGHT

1 *Because resupply on the ground might be delayed, paratroopers dropped with as much personal equipment as they could safely carry. The model wears a steel helmet with camouflage netting – to which a first-aid pack is taped to be available for instant use. A musette bag is slung, and from the web belt hang pouches for carbine magazines, a larger GP ammunition bag, and a holster for a .45 inch pistol. A compass is strapped to the left wrist. Note the capacious "leg bags" in the combat trousers.*

1

2

4

spotted this as a probable landing site and prepared a trap, illuminating the area by setting fire to buildings soaked in oil for the purpose, while anti-aircraft guns, machine guns and mortars caused heavy American casualties. The two battalions assigned to secure the crossings over the Vire and its tributaries both lost their commanding officers killed and every company commander missing. However, a third battalion landed reasonably intact and the survivors, mainly from the 501st Parachute Infantry, secured the drop zone and their principal objective, the lock at La Barquette over the River Douve.

While the paratroopers fought, the first of the gliders started to arrive at about four AM. Of the first wave of 52 gliders, only six came down on their intended landing zone, and the division's assistant commander, Brigadier-General Don Pratt, was killed, his neck broken when his glider crashed heavily. But throughout the day more stragglers arrived, and the division strengthened its position, with all four exits from the causeway roads to Utah firmly under control. At nine PM, shortly before nightfall, a second fly-in by 32 gliders landed for the loss of 44 killed and injured out of 157 men. The division's known losses for D-Day were 182 killed and 537 wounded. But 1,240 men remained missing, and most were never found.

THE ALL AMERICAN

The original plan for the invasion called for 82nd Airborne to land in the middle of the Cotentin peninsula. But with ten days to go, Allied Intelligence reported that the enemy 91st Airlanding Division had moved into the area and the plan was changed. The 82nd Airborne would now drop just to the west of the 101st Airborne, on either side of the River Meredet near Ste Mère-Eglise, securing the town and both banks of the river before moving westward. What the Americans did not know, and what aerial photographs could not tell them, was that the meadows on either side of their drop zones had been turned into flooded marshland by the Germans. The slightest error in putting the troops down would drop them into a swamp.

The pathfinders of the 82nd Airborne, arriving over their target a little before 1:30 AM, had no better luck than those of the 101st Airborne. Those pathfinders destined for the drop zone to the east of the Meredet near Ste Mère-Eglise, target for 505th Parachute Infantry and the divisional headquarters, were put down accurately. But the remaining pathfinders either never reached their drop zones, or could not light them due to nearby Germans, before the main body of 82nd Airborne began to arrive at just after two AM.

Thanks to its pathfinders and a good jumpmaster, Lieutenant-Colonel Ben Vandervoort of 2/505th in the leading aircraft, 505th Parachute Infantry landed virtually on target, with over two-thirds of the men put down on the drop zone or within two miles of it. The divisional commander, Major-General Matthew Ridgway, parachuted in with the regiment. About 30 men came down in the center of Ste Mère-Eglise, and Private John Steele of 3/505th had an incredible escape when his parachute snagged on the church steeple. In the middle of a firefight, Steele hung by his harness feigning death for two hours until he was cut down and captured by the Germans.

The other two regiments had no more luck, as the rest of the 82nd Airborne's drop turned into a shambles.

2 *Men of 82nd Airborne are helped by their buddies to adjust their heavy loads.*
3 *In Normandy, a German infantryman awaits the enemy.* (Bundesarchiv)
4 *US paratroopers in Normandy. Compare with (3): it is obvious that, especially in poor light, the German camouflage combat suit might appear not unlike Allied gear. In the confusion that often followed an airborne landing, incidents of friendly units shooting each other up occurred.* (US National Archives)

5

6

5 *Patch of the US 82nd Airborne Division. In World War I it was an infantry division raised from all states of the Union: thus "All American." Reactivated as an airborne unit in World War II, it retained its original name and insignia.*
6 *Sliding into base: a US Waco glider makes a good landing. Some 9,000 Wacos saw service in World War II, most in Europe.* (US National Archives)

Fewer than half the men of 508th Parachute Infantry came within two miles of their drop zone, and it took over four days for the regiment to reform. Nearly a third of the paratroopers ended up in 101st Airborne territory, with over 100 men actually landing on one of its causeway objectives. Some fell on Ste Mère-Eglise and the waiting Germans. An even worse fate awaited 507th Parachute Infantry, the last of the regiments to arrive. The drop went reasonably well, but only forty-eight men hit their drop zone. Instead, over half the regiment fell a mile to the east, into the swamp of the Meredet. Weighed down and hampered by parachutes and equipment, men drowned in only a few feet of water. Those who survived had little idea of where they were, and many believed that they had fallen into the Douve, about three miles to the south. The rest of the regiment came down anything up to twenty-five miles from the target. As the Dakotas turned overhead for England, two-thirds of the men of 82nd Airborne were already out of the fight.

From this position, the most that Ridgway could achieve was to secure Ste Mère-Eglise, his most important

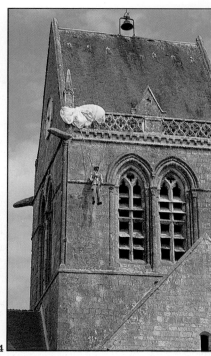

1 *With .30 caliber M1 carbine across his knee, a staff sergeant takes time out as paratroopers advance.*
2 *Landing might be hazardous, but an advantage of glider delivery was that a sizable squad – up to 25 men in a big machine like this British Horsa – could be set down at the same spot. Dropped by parachute, they might land widely dispersed.*
(US National Archives)
3 *Men of 3/505th Parachute Infantry flush out snipers at Ste Mère-Eglise, secured on D-Day after fierce fighting.*
(Keystone)
4 *Some men of 82nd Airborne fell into the center of the strong German garrison at Ste Mère-Eglise. One viewed the subsequent battle (which he survived) while suspended from the church tower.*

5 *As soon as it became apparent that the landings on June 6 were no feint, German reinforcements, like this self-propelled anti-tank gun, began to move into the invasion area. Rommel had earlier advocated that more armor should be committed to the Atlantic Wall, to oppose the Allies from the moment of landing, but Hitler and other commanders believed large armored forces should be held back in reserve.*
(Keystone)
6 *Time out for regrouping: many of the airborne units dropped on D-Day had become widely dispersed.*
(US National Archives)

objective. The 3/505th under Lieutenant-Colonel Edward Krause, consisting at the time of 108 men and a drunken French guide, had captured the town by five AM. Vandervoort, who had broken his foot on landing, commandeered a hand cart to carry him, and recruited two men of the 101st to pull it. He joined in the defense with his battalion by mid-morning. The two weak battalions, virtually surrounded by Germans, fought off attacks for the next thirty-six hours. Directing the defense from his headquarters west of the village, Ridgway had no contact with the outside world or knowledge of how the invasion had fared. In the confusion of the night Ridgway's adversary, Major-General Wilhelm Falley commanding 91st Airlanding Division, was ambushed and killed on the road by paratroopers of the 508th. "Well," Ridgway remarked on being told, "In our present situation killing divisional commanders does not strike me as being particularly hilarious."

Meanwhile, the bridges and causeways across the Meredet west of Ste Mère-Eglise, at La Fiere and Chef-du-Pont, acted as magnets for stragglers and small groups of soldiers from both sides. There were several fierce 5

Above: *The cloth insignia of a Canadian Parachute Battalion: note the "maple leaf" emblem.*
1 *Model shows staff sergeant of British Airborne at dual controls of a Hamilcar glider.*
2 *The cloth shoulder insignia of British airborne troops.*

engagements as the Americans began to coalesce into a defensive line along the east bank of the Meredet, led by the 82nd Airborne's assistant commander, Brigadier-General James ("Jumping Jim") Gavin. A few small parties of the division held on west of the river for another two days before retreating or being forced to surrender. The heroic defense of Hill 30, on the far side of the Meredet from Chef-du-Pont, by 300 men under Lieutenant-Colonel Thomas Shanley of 2/508th, maintained a small but vital bridgehead.

The 82nd Airborne's first reinforcements and anti-tank guns arrived successfully by glider at four AM. A second glider fly-in south of Ste Mère-Eglise landed at

beach; to seize the two bridges across the Orne and the canal, at Benouville, about halfway between Caen and the sea. Its mission also included destroying five bridges over the River Dives, five miles east of the Orne, to seal off the eastern edge of the battlefield.

To take the bridges at Benouville intact, the divisional commander, Major-General Richard Gale, sent in a special assault party in six gliders to land silently between them. Coming down at 12:15 AM, five minutes before the division's pathfinders, all but one of the gliders landed on target. After a brief firefight the bridges – known to the British as Pegasus Bridge – were secured and pronounced clear of demolition charges. As this was happening, the division's

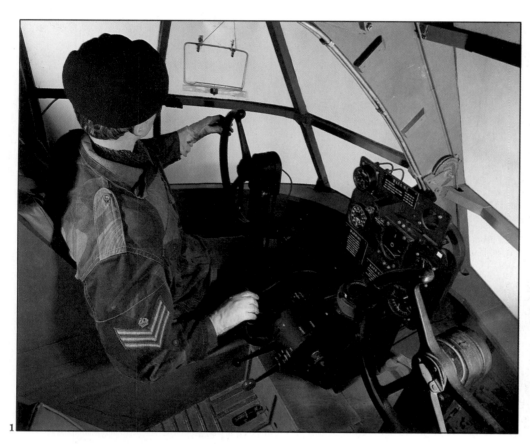

3 *One of the two pilots of a Hamilcar glider steers towards a D-Day landing. The big Hamilcar was designed to carry one light tank, or two Bren gun carriers, or two scout cars, or a field gun and tractor. A few were built with two 965 hp engines, mainly intended to aid takeoff and help maintain stability in flight.*
(IWM: B 5197)
4 *Having landed safely by glider, British airborne troops dig defensive positions in Normandy.*
(UPI/Bettmann)

nine PM. on a zone still under heavy German fire, but surprisingly most of the men survived the landing. A final fly-in by 100 gliders carrying part of the divisional artillery landed successfully at eleven PM, and early the following morning, 325th Airlanding Regiment flew in to reinforce the division. At the end of D-Day, 82nd Airborne placed its losses at about 4,000 out of 6,209 men who had taken part in the drop. Most of these later straggled back to the division, and the final figure was 347 wounded, 156 known dead and 756 missing presumed dead. Although the drop had gone badly, by securing Ste Mère-Eglise and the line of the Meredet, the division had removed any possibility of German reinforcements reaching Utah beach.

THE BRITISH AIRBORNE

The eastern flank of Sword Beach, the most easterly of the British landing beaches, lay on the estuary of the River Orne and the Canal de Caen, which flow roughly parallel to each other, separated by a few hundred yards, from Caen to the sea at the little port and resort town of Ouistreham. British 6th Airborne's task was to destroy the German coastal battery at Merville, across the estuary from Ouistreham, which it was feared could shell Sword

5 *A Halifax bomber acts as tug for a Hamilcar glider.*
7 *Insignia of the British Army's Glider Pilot Regiment.*
8 *"Wings" worn by a qualified British paratrooper.*

6 *The model wears the famed "red beret," with winged parachute badge, of The Parachute Regiment. On the sleeve of the battledress jacket, worn beneath a sleeveless jump smock, is the insignia of 6th Airborne Division: "Pegasus," the winged horse of Greek myth.*

63

1 *Major-General Richard Gale, seen here at his D-Day headquarters (with "Pegasus" pennant), commanded British 6th Airborne Division, tasked on D-Day with the destruction of coastal gun emplacements that might threaten the invasion beaches and with blowing or seizing bridges of vital tactical importance.*
(IWM: B 5352)
2 *The return journey is slower, but maybe safer, as US glider pilots, their job well done, are taken off the Normandy beaches.*
(US National Archives)

1

2

3

PARACHUTE REGIMENT

4

3 *A squad of British airborne troops rides away from a Horsa glider. The Horsa could carry up to 20 men along with a jeep and cargo trailer.*
(IWM: B 5205)
4 *The cloth shoulder insignia of The Parachute Regiment.*

pathfinders arrived. Despite bad weather, anti-aircraft fire and German flooding, the British suffered fewer problems than the Americans in landing, although two pathfinders were unfortunate enough to land on the lawn next to German 711th Static Division headquarters. "Awfully sorry, old man," one of them told the astonished German commander, "but we simply landed here by accident."

The main body of the 6th Airborne, 4,225 paratroopers, arrived over their drop zones at 12:50 AM. Roughly half of them dropped in the right place, and the remainder mostly within five miles. The 5th Parachute Brigade, under Brigadier Nigel Poett, dropping around Pegasus Bridge, arrived with half its men and joined in a confused but persistent firefight with the nearby Germans. By 3:30 AM. the perimeter around Pegasus Bridge and the drop zones, although under constant attack, was secure enough for a glider landing, bringing anti-tank guns and the divisional commander. As a way of moving quickly Gale (known as "Windy" to his men) found himself a horse to ride, and set up his divisional headquarters in a nearby chateau.

The 3rd Parachute Brigade, with two separate drop zones close to Merville and the line of the Dives, was more badly scattered on landing than 5th Parachute Brigade. Its commander, Brigadier James Hill, dropped on the wrong side of the Dives and was out of touch for several hours. He was slightly wounded, and several of his men were killed by a stray RAF bomb. One pathfinder team, intended for the drop zone close to the Dives, was put down instead next to Pegasus Bridge and attracted 230 men of its battalion down with it. Like the Americans, the British paratroopers in small parties collected themselves together and went into action against the Germans. By morning all five of the Dives bridges had been destroyed.

The brigade's main task, given to 9th Battalion, The Parachute Regiment, under Lieutenant-Colonel Terence Otway, was to clear the Merville battery, a position later described by a commando who saw it as "a stinker." The four guns were in concrete emplacements reinforced with earthworks and protected by barbed wire, mines and machine-guns. The scattering and uncertainties of the night drop reduced Otway's elaborate plan, involving special equipment, extra gliders and supporting heavy bombers and naval gunfire, to chaos. Instead, shortly before dawn, having collected 150 men together, Otway

led them in a direct assault on the battery, capturing it in 15 minutes for the loss of nearly half his men. The guns turned out to be 100mm Czech pieces, fully capable of shelling Sword beach, but not the heavier calibres that the British had expected. In the darkness, the smoke and confusion of the fighting, Otway and his men retired without actually having destroyed the guns, and the Germans reoccupied the battery.

For the rest of the day 6th Airborne held off German attacks of increasing strength and determination, including tanks of 21st Panzer Division. At one PM reinforcements, 1st Special Service Brigade of commandos who had landed at Sword beach, arrived at Pegasus Bridge, and starting at nine PM, two battalions of 6th Airlanding Brigade were flown in to complete the defense. By nightfall, of 6,256 men who landed in Normandy, 6th Airborne had suffered about 650 casualties.

5, 9 Apparently bearing the scars of a rough landing, a captured sergeant of the British Army's Glider Pilot Regiment (note insignia on breast; seen in color below) undergoes interrogation by a German officer.
(Bundesarchiv)

7

8

7, 8 At the Merville battery, seen here post-war, massive, well-defended concrete emplacements sheltered heavy guns capable of shelling Sword invasion beach. It was stormed and taken by 150 men of 9th Battalion, The Parachute Regiment.

5

6

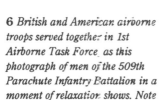

9

6 British and American airborne troops served together in 1st Airborne Task Force, as this photograph of men of the 509th Parachute Infantry Battalion in a moment of relaxation shows. Note the recognition patches: Union flags on British sleeves, and "Old Glory" for the Americans.
(US National Archives)

PEGASUS BRIDGE

The British airborne troops who captured Pegasus Bridge (named for the airborne forces' shoulder patch) at 12:16 AM were the first Allied soldiers to land in France. For the mission Major-General Gale selected and specially trained a force of 181 men of D Company, 2nd Battalion, Oxfordshire and Buckinghamshire Light Infantry under Major John Howard, augmented by two platoons of B Company, some thirty Royal Engineers, and six members of the Glider Pilot Regiment, one for each Horsa glider. Three gliders were to land next to each of the two bridges, which were garrisoned by about fifty Germans. Casting off from their tug aircraft at 5,000 feet so that the engines would not be heard, the lead glider for the canal bridge party smashed through the barbed wire defenses around the bridge as planned, knocking everyone on board unconscious. The second glider landed fifteen yards away and the third twenty-five yards away in a marshy pond, where one man drowned before he could recover. Leigh-Mallory later described this fly-in, done with maps and stop-watches, as the finest piece of airmanship of the war.

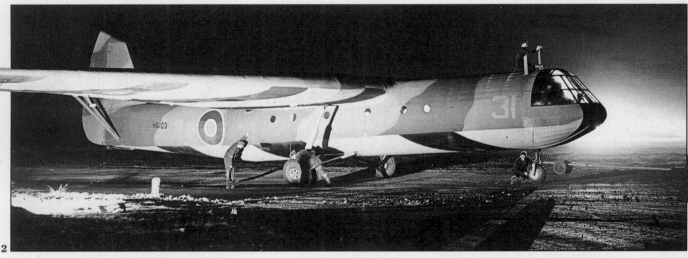

Regaining consciousness in seconds, Howard's men burst from their gliders and charged the bridge before the German sentries could react. From start to finish the whole action lasted only five minutes. Lieutenant Danny Brotheridge, who led the attack, became the first Allied soldier killed in action in Normandy, and five men were wounded. Of the three gliders intended for the Orne bridge, one missed the site and landed close to a bridge over the River Dives. The others landed 300 and 700 yards from their target bridge, and reached it to find that its defenders had already fled. Although both bridges had been prepared for demolition, the charges were not in place.

Brigadier Poett reached the bridge with one other man shortly before one AM. There then followed an anxious wait, and two further skirmishes with the Germans, including one with tanks, before the arrival of more paratroopers at three AM allowed Howard to put his men into reserve. More hard fighting was to follow, and by the end of D-Day, Howard's force numbered only 76 unwounded men.

1 *"Pathfinder" officers, who will be first to drop at Pegasus Bridge, synchronize their watches.* (IWM: H 39070)

OXF, & BUCKS.

2 *Horsa glider pilots in training for night flying.*
3 *Training paid off: they made pin-point landings.* (IWM: B 5233)
4 *British Airborne insignia.*
5 *British paratrooper, with camouflage smock over khaki battledress, carries a 9mm Mark 5 Sten sub-machine gun.*
6 *Red Cross jeep evacuates casualties at Pegasus Bridge.* (IWM: B 5286)
7 *Men of the Oxfordshire and Buckinghamshire Light Infantry wore this flash.*
8 *British troops cross the bridge on a Bren gun carrier.* (IWM: B 5234)
9 *Scars of the brief, brutal action at Pegasus Bridge.*

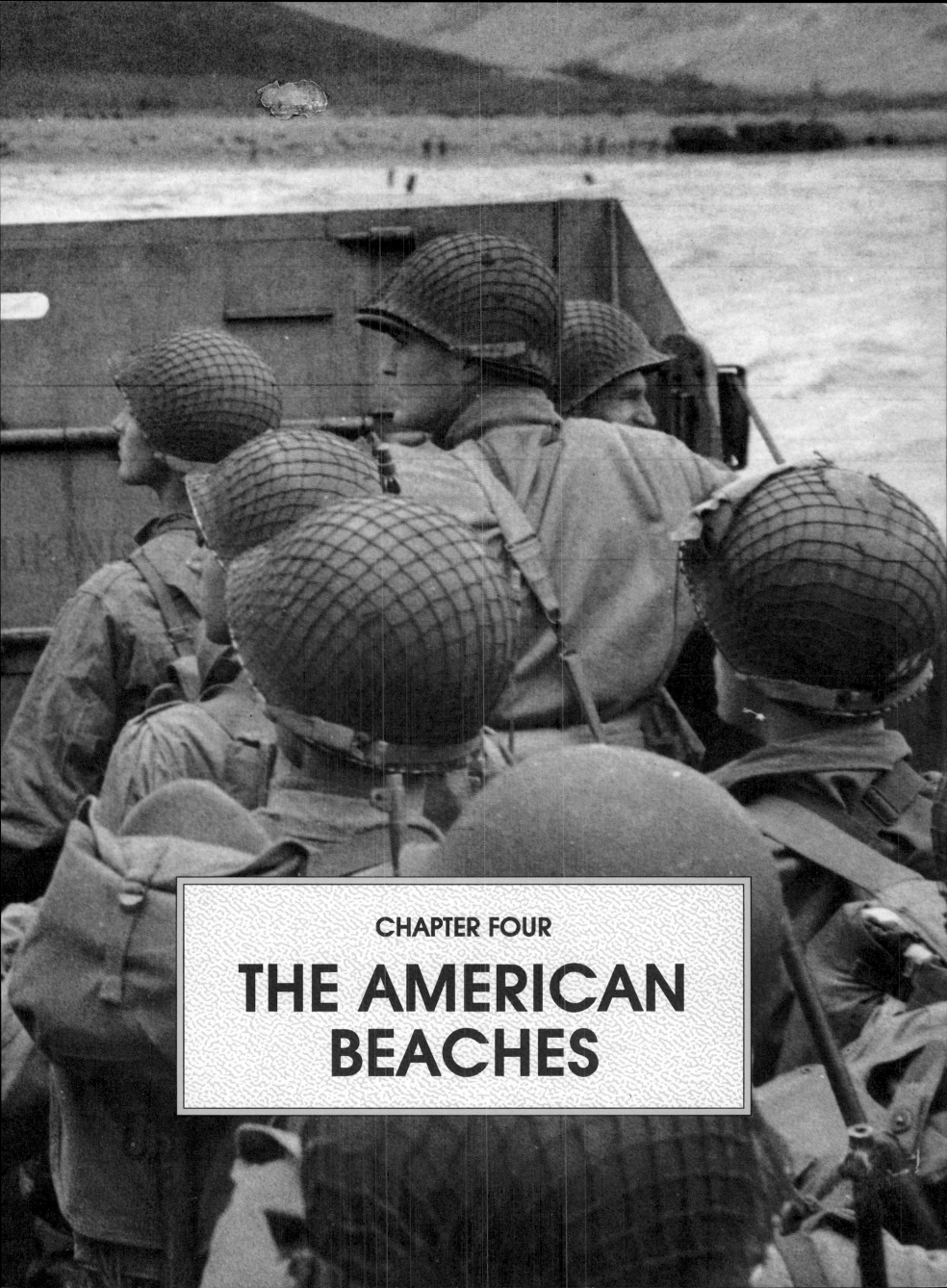

CHAPTER FOUR
THE AMERICAN BEACHES

The Vire estuary separating the beaches designated Utah and Omaha turned the American landings into two distinct battles. The main objective for the landing forces on D-Day was to get far enough inland to link the two beachheads together at the estuary. Otherwise, by keeping the landings separate, the Germans might be able to destroy them in isolation. The main air attack started just after three AM, with the largest German coastal batteries each receiving 500 tons of bombs. As the light improved, the big ships of the Western Task Force under Rear-Admiral Alan G. Kirk began their gunnery duel with the surviving batteries, while General Bradley watched from Kirk's flagship, the USS *Augusta*.

At 4:30 AM the first Allied troops to land from the sea on D-Day, 132 American troopers of 4th Cavalry Group under Lieutenant-Colonel Edward Dunn, captured the Isles St-Marcouf, two tiny islands lying three miles off Utah beach, where German troops had been spotted a month before. Instead of the feared gun emplacements, the cavalry found the islands unoccupied, but still lost two men killed and seventeen wounded to mines and German shellfire.

The regimental combat teams bound for Utah and Omaha were each based on an infantry regiment of three battalions with added troops, including combat engineers with special equipment, armored tankdozers for clearing the beach obstacles, and Navy underwater demolition teams. The final 300 yards to the beach were covered by rocket bombardment from special support craft, each with 1,000 high explosive 5-inch projectiles. Going in with the assault were 105mm self-propelled guns and tanks carried in landing craft so that they could fire on the approach, and special amphibious DD (Duplex Drive) Sherman tanks. On the assault craft each man, wearing a cumbersome invasion wader or life preserver, carried nearly seventy pounds of arms and equipment. Waiting further out were more specialized support craft, including perhaps the strangest vessels taking part in the invasion, the Landing Barges (Kitchen), each capable of serving 700 hot meals a day once the troops were ashore.

Previous page: *Seconds to go before hitting the beach.*
(Fox Photos)
1 *The first letter of the alphabet on its insignia symbolizes US First Army.*
2 *The US Air Medal was usually awarded after five successful combat missions.*

3 *LCI(L)s (Landing Craft Infantry, Large) manned by the US Coast Guard move towards the beaches. Each trails a barrage balloon to deter low-level air attacks; but the Allies had established, and maintained, air supremacy and the depleted Luftwaffe was able to offer little resistance to the Normandy landings.*
(The Bettmann Archive)

6 *Rear-Admiral Alan G. Kirk, USN, commanded Western Task Force on D-Day.*
(US National Archives)
7 *Blowing in the wind off Normandy: the promise of liberation for Europe.*
(US National Archives)
8 *To minimize confusion on the beaches immediately after landing, every man was issued with guidance notes.*

4 *If air attack came, the Allied armada was ready for it. A flak-jacketed gunner strapped into his swivel seat tests out his 20mm anti-aircraft weapon aboard a US escort warship.*
5 *In tubs on deck, twin-mounted 40mm anti-aircraft guns are ready to put up a wall of fire to deter close range air attacks. Note the single-mounted 20mm A.A.A. to left and in foreground.*
(US National Archives)

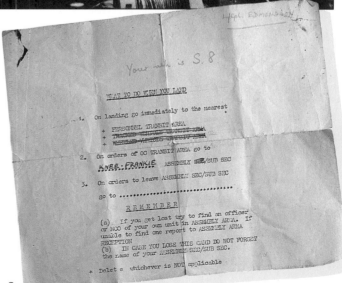

THE ATLANTIC WALL

In December 1941 Hitler ordered the creation of an Atlantic Wall, stretching from Norway to the Spanish border, as a defense against invasion. Work began in earnest in 1942, concentrating on the major ports and harbors of France, particularly after Dieppe. Over 17 million tons of concrete and 1.2 million tons of steel were used to build coast defenses comparable to the Maginot Line, parts of which were demolished and incorporated into the Wall. But few German generals had much faith in the Atlantic Wall. One described it as a "thin, in many places fragile, piece of cord with a few small knots." Where it was finished it was a formidable obstacle, but it was not a continuous line. The strongest parts were in the Pas de Calais, with ninety-three heavy gun emplacements and thirty-nine mobile heavy guns in total, compared with twenty-seven emplacements and twenty mobile heavy guns in Normandy.

Apart from gun positions, pillboxes and strongpoints, the Wall also included several rows of steel girders set up to eighteen feet above the low-tide mark to rip open or obstruct landing craft, and minefields up to 300 yards deep inland from the sand dunes. Rommel, taking over the defense of northern France in late 1943, worked hard to improvise additional defenses further inland as the main part of the Wall. Two belts of mines, each 1,000 yards deep, were laid stretching all the way down the Atlantic coast, a total of over 2 million mines. Rommel planned to add a third belt of mines 8,000 yards deep, and by D-Day the number of mines laid along the French Atlantic coast had increased to 4 million or more. These included what the Germans called "Rommel's asparagus": mines set on poles as anti-glider defenses.

By June, 1944, the Atlantic Wall in Normandy consisted of beach defenses, pillboxes and strongpoints at the water's edge, belts of mines and strongpoints further inland and occasional well-defended seaside villages or hamlets. But it is a common military axiom that an obstacle which is not covered by fire is no real obstacle at all. Rommel's main problem was the numbers and quality of troops to man those defenses, and the need for armored reserves should the Allies break through.

1 *A German sentry stands guard at a 155mm gun emplacement.* (Bundesarchiv)
2 *An Axis cartoonist shows Roosevelt and Churchill as "pipsqueaks," pitting their puny blasts against the Wall.*
3 *Rommel (center) lacked faith in the Wall but worked hard to strengthen it.* (Bundesarchiv)

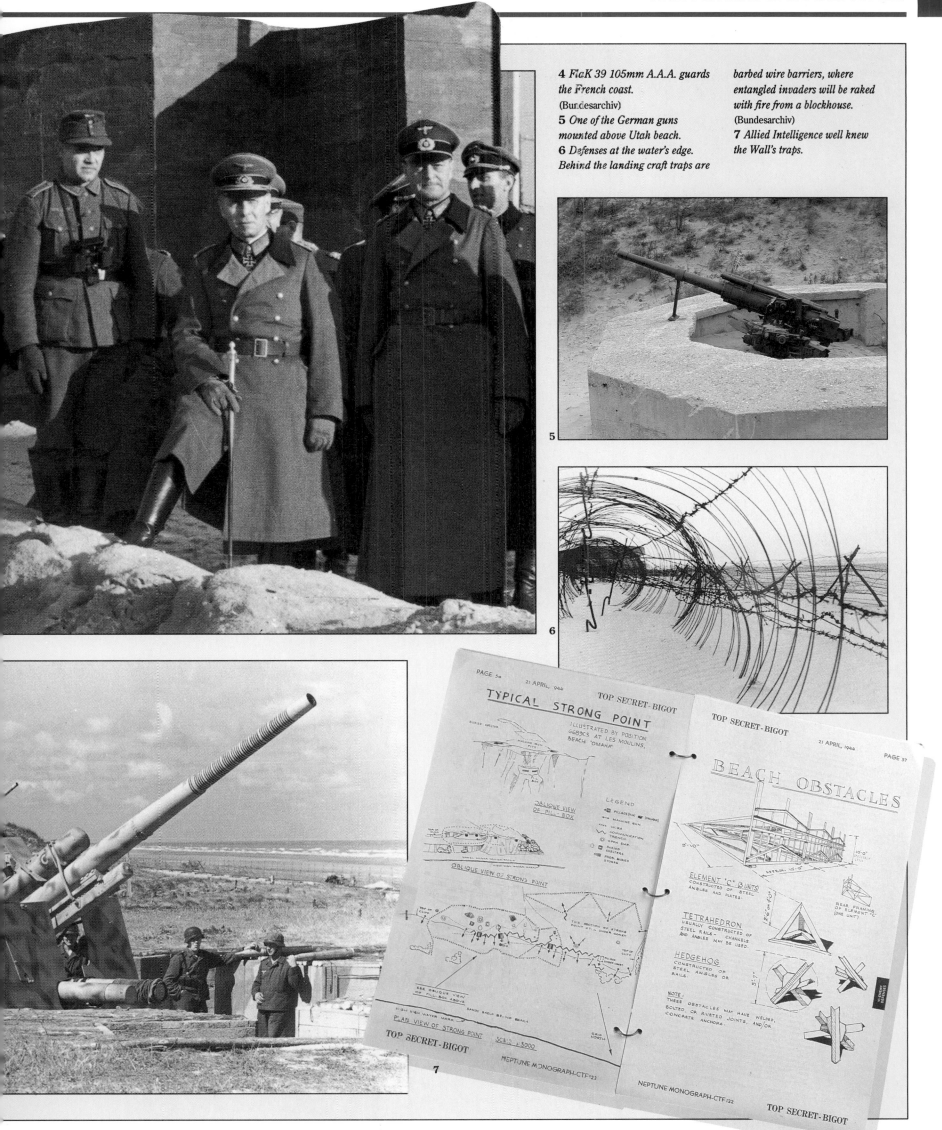

4 *FlaK 39 105mm A.A.A. guards the French coast.*
(Bundesarchiv)
5 *One of the German guns mounted above Utah beach.*
6 *Defenses at the water's edge. Behind the landing craft traps are* barbed wire barriers, where entangled invaders will be raked with fire from a blockhouse.
(Bundesarchiv)
7 *Allied Intelligence well knew the Wall's traps.*

UTAH BEACH

The first wave to assault Utah beach was 8th Regimental Combat Team of 4th Infantry Division, led by the assistant divisional commander, Brigadier-General Teddy Roosevelt, son of the late President Theodore Roosevelt. Although 57 years old and troubled with arthritis, Roosevelt had demanded to go in with the first troops "to steady the men." The only general to land with the first wave, he knew that his son, Captain Quentin Roosevelt, would be landing on Omaha Beach at about the same time.

With bombing and naval gunnery forcing the Germans to keep their heads down, the first landing craft were only minutes from the beaches when an escorting destroyer, USS *Corry*, hit a mine and sank. Next, one of the patrol craft with the crucial task of taking the soldiers to the right beach was hit by a lucky German salvo and also went down. Remarkably, this accident fell in the Americans' favor. Had they come ashore as planned, 4th Division would have stumbled onto one of the most heavily defended parts of the beach. But without a guide, the assault craft, pushed by the heavy tidal current, landed opposite La

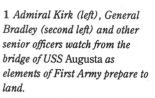

1 *Admiral Kirk (left), General Bradley (second left) and other senior officers watch from the bridge of USS* Augusta *as elements of First Army prepare to land.*
(US National Archives)
2 *On the flanks, escort carriers' planes flew anti U-boat patrols.*
(US National Archives)
3 *This P-47 Thunderbolt did not make it back to base.*
(US National Archives)

US First Army planned to land its first troops on the beaches just after 6:30 AM, after a final forty-minute drenching naval bombardment and blitz from the air. Allied Intelligence identified the defenders of Utah as 709th Static Division and those of Omaha as 716th Static Division, both of poor fighting quality. The much better 352nd Infantry Division was believed to be twenty miles inland near the town of St Lô. The Americans deliberately chose an earlier landing time and much shorter bombardment than the British, to land in front of the German beach defenses, which were covered by the sea at high tide. In order to be out of range of the German coastal batteries, the Americans also started their landing craft from much further out than the British, up to eleven miles in places. But the bad weather and rough sea raised the tide and considerably reduced the amount of beach exposed for the landing, and gave the troops a dangerous and seasick three-hour trip in which more than one landing craft swamped and sank.

4 *Landing craft hang ready for launching from davits on the British troop transport* Empire Lance, *off Normandy.* (US National Archives)

5 *Insignia of 90th Infantry Division combines initials of Texas and Oklahoma: signifying, said its soldiers, "Tough 'Ombres."*

5

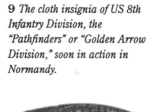

9 *The cloth insignia of US 8th Infantry Division, the "Pathfinders" or "Golden Arrow Division," soon in action in Normandy.*

6 *Some grin; some are lost in thought; many probably say a silent prayer, as GIs file from their transport into a landing craft. Adverse weather and sea conditions meant that for some the rough, nerve-stretching run-in to Utah beach would last up to three hours.* (UPI Bettmann)

7 *An aerial photograph of Utah beach reduces landing craft and vehicles ashore to toy-like proportions. Even though German resistance at Utah was comparatively light, the beach was not quite as peaceful as it looks here.* (Smithsonian Institution)

8 *In a choppy sea, landing craft keep on their inshore course past heavy cruiser USS* Augusta, *flagship of Western Task Force.* (US National Archives)

1

2

3

1 *A Martin B-26 Marauder heads for home after a tactical bombing mission. Choppy seas off Normandy are apparent even when viewed from this height.* (Smithsonian Institution)

2 *The fog of war: a landing craft creates a smoke screen to shield it from German gunners during the final approach run.* (US National Archives)

3 *A plume of smoke and sand marks the detonation of a shell on Utah beach. By happy accident, when strong tidal currents pushed the landing craft more than one mile south of their intended landfall, most of US 4th Infantry Division came ashore in a lightly defended sector.* (US National Archives)

4

5

James Arnold, to send the following waves of landing craft over to his new position. German artillery, firing blind at the landing, took three hours to realize that the Americans were turning south at the last moment, and continued to shell an empty beach. Roosevelt's work on Utah that day won him a Medal of Honor that he did not live to collect, dying of a heart attack two months later.

As the second American wave approached, the infantry worked to overcome the German defenses, while engineers and demolition parties cleared the beach of obstacles. Within an hour, the approaching landing craft had a clear run up to the shore. By mid-morning the divisional commander, Major-General Raymond Barton, had landed and given the order to press inland, against an enemy who showed little inclination to fight. The men of 4th Division pushed up the beach exit roads, linking up with the paratroopers of 101st Airborne Division. In the north, the chief difficulty was the marshes themselves, which made movement off the causeways very difficult and prevented

4, 5, 6 *Survivors from a sunken landing craft are buoyed up by lifejackets as they await rescue by their buddies. Some landing craft foundered on the long run-in to Utah, or, nearing the beach, were sunk by shell fire. Of 4th Infantry Division's remarkably light casualties on D-Day (43 dead; 63 wounded), nearly half were caused by drowning at sea or in the marshes that flanked the landing zone.*
(US National Archives)

Grande Dune, nearly 2,000 yards south of their intended position. Not expecting a landing next to the worst of the marshes, the Germans had left this sector lightly defended. The first men landed almost without loss, followed a few minutes later by thirty-two DD tanks, of which all but four got ashore. Intended to land in front of the infantry on all the beaches, the tanks were held up in the heavy seas. Roosevelt, striding around with his walking stick and flicking sand from shellbursts off his uniform like a man at a beach party, decided that this was good enough, and ordered the senior naval officer on Utah, Commodore 6

12th and 22nd Infantry Regiments reaching their final D-Day objectives. They came to a halt for the night, reinforcing 502nd Parachute Infantry and holding the northern shoulder of the Utah lodgement. In the center, 8th Infantry Regiment reached Les Forges, about a mile south of Ste Mère-Eglise. German resistance to the north prevented the landing force making contact with the main body of 82nd Airborne Division, still holding on to Ste Mère-Eglise itself. The D-Day objectives on the west bank of the Meredet could not be reached before nightfall, and there was still a gap across the Vire estuary between 101st Airborne and the Omaha lodgement area.

Nevertheless, the Utah landing had been a major success. German defensive positions had been sited on the assumption that the Americans would land at high tide, but by coming ashore an hour after low water many heavier guns were left with nothing to shoot at. In the course of D-Day, 4th Infantry Division, backed up by 90th Infantry Division, put ashore 23,250 men, 1,742 vehicles and 1,695 tons of stores for the loss of forty-three dead and sixty-three wounded, lighter casualties than in their last Slapton Sands exercise. Nearly half the division's losses had been men drowned in the sea, or falling into the treacherous marshes while loaded down with equipment. After all the preparation, many who came ashore found the invasion an anti-climax. One paratrooper greeted the new arrivals in France, "Where the hell have you guys been?"

1 *The Bronze Star for gallantry or meritorious achievement, a medal awarded only to personnel of the US Army, is a comparative newcomer to the roll of honor, instituted only in 1944. Far more of the men who landed on the Normandy beaches on D-Day must have deserved this award than actually received it.*
2 *The Navy's role in the invasion did not end at the tideline. Men of the US Navy's 2nd Beach Battalion "take five" after digging themselves a shelter.*
(US National Archives)

3 *Useful for signaling at fairly close range, the AN-M8 Pyrotechnic Pistol fired colored flares.*

4 *While awaiting the order to advance inland, GIs shelter in foxholes dug in the sand of Utah beach, as communications vehicles and armor deploy along the shoreline. More than 23,000 men and 1,700 vehicles were put ashore on Utah on D-Day.*
(UPI/Bettmann)

5 *Utah was quickly secured, and the comparative lack of opposition is reflected in this photograph. Some men fill sandbags to build a strongpoint, but others sit or stand in full daylight, seemingly without fear of shells or sniper fire.*
(Fox Photos)

6 *A mortar crew prepares to lob high angle shells onto a suspected German position.*
(Keystone)

7, 8 *Long after the battle, the remains of a German gun position still look out to sea and barbed wire coils among the sand dunes.*

5

7

6

8

SPECIAL FEATURE: G.I. UNIFORM

Unlike the British soldier with his all-purpose battledress, the American GI, whose nickname was said to come from the letters "G.I." ("Government Issue") stamped on his gear, had both a smart uniform for parade and similar use and a wide variety of specialized combat clothing. As the illustrations here show, the infantryman's major requirement was carrying capacity: packs, pockets, and pouches. For the Normandy landings, GIs were issued with a special "assault pack" comprising a pack, a haversack, and a vest – shown here at (8) – with four sewn-on pouches. Many soldiers found this equipment too bulky, and discarded it in favor of a mix of standard equipment soon after landing.

1 *Most GIs have their steel helmets in place as they near the beach. The Pattern 1941 wool knit cap ("beanie") worn by the man in the foreground was intended to be worn beneath the helmet: it could be rolled down to protect the ears in cold weather.* (US National Archives)

2 *Insignia of US 4th Infantry Division, the "Ivy Division," incorporates a visual pun: its four ivy leaves represent Roman numeral four: "IV."*

3 *Not smart but practical: the D-Day gear of one GI. Model wears MI steel helmet; cotton field jacket with insignia of 29th Infantry Division; olive drab wool trousers. Ammunition for his M1 Garand rifle is in a cotton clip bandolier.*

Note "walkie-talkie" radio receiver/transmitter; waterproof map case; and smoke or chemical grenade.

4 Across the field jacket is the M1910 entrenching tool; vital on a beach under fire. Note cotton duck leggings (left) and two-piece metal mess kit ("meat can").
5 With the web belt is the pouch that holds an aluminum canteen with a cup fitted around its base.
6 A lifebelt helped the laden GI wade ashore. This is shown inflated around the waist of the soldier at center (**7**), who administers artificial respiration to a colleague.
8 A vest – part of the GI "assault pack."

OMAHA BEACH

1 *Smoke from the attackers' naval bombardment and the defenders' artillery and small arms fire shrouds the beach as GIs wade ashore at "Bloody Omaha."* (US National Archives)

Expecting little opposition at Omaha, 1st Infantry Division (the famous "Big Red One" division) and 29th Infantry Division had been given ambitious objectives. By nightfall on D-Day they were to secure an area six miles deep and nearly eighteen miles long, from the base of the Vire estuary at Isigny eastwards almost to Bayeux, linking up with British forces from Gold beach. What the Americans did not know was that the German 352nd Infantry Division had come forward to reinforce 716th Static Division, and many of its troops were dug in along the bluff which, rising to a height of 170 feet, dominated the landing beaches. Between the sand of the beach and the bluff lay a strip of shingle impassable to vehicles, and the only exits from the beach were five draws or gaps in the bluff, all easily defended. To add to the American problems, the bad weather forced many of their aircraft to bomb on instruments only, missing their targets. Holding their fire to disguise their positions, the German batteries left the naval gunners without a target, and in several places the final rocket salvoes fell short. Together with the landing conditions and limited beach area, this was a recipe for disaster.

2 *The sinister shoots of "Rommel's asparagus," as the German defenders of the Atlantic Wall generically nicknamed the beach obstacles the Field Marshal had them build. The heavy metal constructions seen here were called "Czech hedgehogs." Positioned so that they would be submerged as the tide came in, they were intended to rip out the bottoms of Allied landing craft – and at Omaha beach they proved effective.* (Bundesarchiv)

3 *Patterned on an ancient oriental symbol of good luck, the patch of 29th Infantry Division embodied the colors blue and gray, indicating that it was raised in states that had fought on opposing sides in the Civil War.*
4 *Half-tracked field artillery tractors and DUKW ("Duck") amphibious trucks are seen at the water's edge as more men go ashore. Inland, troops deploy towards enemy positions presently hidden by the smoke of the Allied naval bombardment.* (The Bettmann Archive)

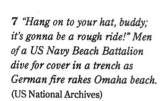

The first assault troops, 16th Regimental Combat Team of 1st Division and 116th Regimental Combat Team of 29th Division, ran into the Omaha beaches just after 6:30 AM, as at Utah. That was about the only point of comparison between the two beaches. Some DD tanks could not be launched because of the weather and surf. Others, launched from 6,000 yards offshore, sank like stones, and only five made it to the beach. Nearly all the 105mm guns being ferried to the shore also went down, as did all but six of the armored tankdozers. At least ten infantry landing craft floundered miles out from the beach, and underwater obstacles ripped the bottoms out of others, leaving the infantry to drown. As at Utah, the current pulled the surviving assault craft eastward, putting troops ashore up to two miles out of position, with the regiments intermingled and without tank support or engineers, in the teeth of the almost untouched German defenses. Within minutes of landing, the entire first wave was pinned on the beach.

5 *This US Army Landing Craft Infantry (Large) has run so close inshore so that men can file down its bow ramps only a few yards off Omaha.* (US National Archives)
6 *The obstacles that have claimed their landing craft now provide shelter for men struggling under heavy fire towards the beach. Many cluster behind an armored tankdozer of 10th Engineer Assault Team: only six of these made it to the beach.* (IWM: AP 25726)

7 *"Hang on to your hat, buddy; it's gonna be a rough ride!" Men of a US Navy Beach Battalion dive for cover in a trench as German fire rakes Omaha beach.* (US National Archives)

6

As more troops hit the beach the confusion and the losses grew worse, with units hopelessly mixed and huddled together. Radios and signalling equipment were lost in the surf, and those waiting offshore had little clear picture of what was happening. At nine AM, Bradley, watching from the *Augusta*, started preparations for abandoning Omaha altogether. This was the moment, familiar in almost every battle, in which the issue comes down to firepower, determination and brute force. American and British destroyers ran in so close that they almost beached themselves, blasting German pillboxes with their guns. A 7

1 *Once the beachhead is established and the area inland cleared, supply ships lie close in and materiel pours ashore. But the cost has been high: on shell-scarred Omaha, cranes clear the wreckage of landing craft and armored vehicles.*
(UPI Bettmann)

lucky hit from the battleship USS *Texas* silenced one of the guns in the heaviest German battery. On the beach itself, leadership was strictly from the front. Brigadier-General Norman (Dutch) Cota, assistant divisional commander of 29th Division, walking upright and flourishing his pistol, took command of the division's eastern sector, and Colonel Charles Canham, commanding 116th Infantry, the western half. "They're murdering us here," Canham yelled at his men, "let's move inland and get murdered!" The sentiment was echoed by Colonel George Taylor commanding 16th Infantry, "Two kinds of people are staying on this beach, the dead and those who are about to die. Now let's get the hell out of here!"

Collecting themselves together, the troops began to fight their way through the German blocks, up the draws and off the beach. It was a matter of companies, platoons, a few brave men making the first movements, gradually bringing others with them. Inspired by Canham and Cota, C Company of 1/116th Infantry fought its way to the top of the bluff at Les Moulins by 8:30 AM, supported by 5th and part of 2nd Ranger Battalions, which had come ashore at the western end of Utah. At the same time, other men

1

2

3

of 3/116th Infantry pushed out toward St Laurent. By mid-morning, Taylor also had most of 16th Infantry on top of the bluff and pressing toward Colleville, a mile inland.

Meanwhile, as delays and the weather made nonsense of the landing timetables, commanders held up less critical reinforcements to let the assault infantry through. Just after ten AM, the second wave of troops began its landing, suffering the same losses and problems as the first. The Big Red One's 18th Infantry Regiment came ashore to the east. Two landing craft beached themselves with all guns firing opposite the Colleville draw, the troops storming

4

5

6

2 *Burned out trucks, a wrecked tank, and the scattered bodies of GIs are strewn on Omaha immediately after the landings.*
(US National Archives)
3 *Many hundred men got no farther than this, but were cut down by intensive fire at the water's edge.*
(US National Archives)
4 *Only five tanks reached Omaha beach on D-Day; and this one stayed there.*
(US National Archives)
5 *Tactical communication on Omaha: a signaler uses a lantern to flash Morse messages, while behind him a captain (two bars on steel helmet indicate rank) checks over his orders.*
(US National Archives)
6 *American wounded: between 2,000 and 3,000 men were casualties on Omaha on D-Day.*
(US National Archives)

Just as the railroad and telegraph profoundly changed the nature of war in the 19th century, so did the development of efficient, portable radio transmitters and receivers influence modern warfare. In World War I, field communications largely depended on easily-broken land lines. But in World War II the introduction of multi-core cable (carrying up to 100 lines) and compact, high-frequency radio equipment established durable and direct links between headquarters and front lines. Such equipment meant that commanding officers could maintain unbroken contact with all their forces; unit commanders could quickly receive intelligence from forward troops and transmit tactical orders; and with "walkie-talkie" radios even the smallest combat units could keep in touch. In amphibious operations, of which D-Day was the greatest, swift and reliable inter-arm and inter-unit communications were essential if beachheads were to be secured and an advance inland begun as swiftly as possible.

2 Having disposed of its German defenders, an American unit has transformed this former gun emplacement into a headquarters post, from which the unit commander can communicate through a field telephone exchange. Note telegraph wires strung above, aerial to right, and cable drums in right foreground
(US National Archives)

1 A German squad leader's gear includes weatherproof case for maps and clipboard; pencils and eraser; compass and identification pennant.

3 Mounted in a motorcycle sidecar, a German signaler reels out cable.
(Bundesarchiv)
4 German field telephone and cable drum; such a linkage was easily cut, or broken under artillery fire.
5 "What do you mean: invasion?" News from the beaches, or maybe

just a poor line, makes a German yell into his field telephone.
(Bundesarchiv)
8 With equal urgency, but less excitement, a US Navy signaler uses a "walkie-talkie" to direct fire onto a German position at Omaha.
(US National Archives)

6 *Shown here is some of the equipment an American signaler might have carried ashore on D-Day. It includes a "walkie-talkie" type radio, the range of which varied considerably according to terrain and atmospheric conditions; a portable coding machine and message pad; and, of course, invasion maps and a wrist compass.*

7 *German forces used this small torch with a hooded beam for close-range battlefield signaling. US and British troops often carried similar torches with movable colored lenses.*

1, 2 *The air-land-sea cloth sleeve badge worn by US Army Amphibious Forces features on the memorial to them later raised at Omaha beach.*

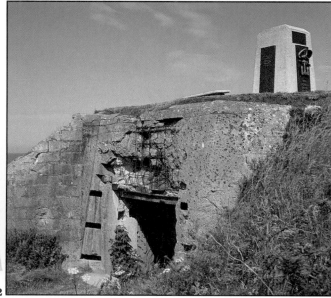

3 and 4 *Part of the cost of securing Omaha. Much of the armor and artillery intended for Omaha was swamped and sank before reaching the beach. Many of the vehicles that did make it were quickly reduced to scrap metal by the concentrated fire of German artillery, heavy mortars,* *and automatic weapons.*
(US National Archives)
7 *But the losses were not all on one side: German prisoners carry one of their wounded.*
(Associated Press)

5 *After the battle: a US Coast Guard inspects a German artillery piece above Omaha.*
(US National Archives)
6 *The Medal of Honor (shown* *here with its Army pendant; the ribbon is the same for all arms) is America's highest award for gallantry: a quality displayed by so many at "Bloody Omaha."*

8 *Medics treat a lightly wounded GI: one of perhaps 2,000 wounded on Omaha on D-Day. Some men were incapacitated before reaching the beach, violently seasick aboard landing craft.* (US National Archives)

9 *D-Day plus one on Omaha. Only a fraction of the materiel* necessary to establish the beachhead could be landed on June 6, when the invaders came close to defeat, but within 24 hours trucks and armored vehicles were rolling inland. (US National Archives)

9

through before the defenders could recover. In the confusion, 18th Infantry became mixed up with 115th Infantry of 29th Division, which took some time to sort itself out before reaching its first objective at St Laurent. At the same time, the rest of 116th Infantry landed near Vierville at the western edge of Omaha, and Canham secured the village in an hour. Fighting was still tough, but well before noon the battle had swung in the Americans' favor.

In the face of the unexpectedly strong German defenses the troops at "Bloody Omaha" had done an incredible job, for which many were decorated, including Canham and Cota. Even so, the landing was still very precarious. Although more infantry were landed during the afternoon, all suffered heavy losses, and it proved virtually impossible to land artillery. Lacking guns and tanks, the Americans' progress inland was both slow and painful. By nightfall, 116th Infantry and 5th Rangers held a position about 1,000 yards inland from Vierville, separated by a long gap of nearly two miles from St Laurent and a more-or-less continuous front 2,000 yards inland and surrounding Colleville, which was still in German hands.

In the chaos, official American accounts admit that estimates both of troops landed and of casualties for Omaha are little more than guesswork. The intention was to land 34,000 men and 3,300 vehicles on Omaha, and of these something between 2,000 and 3,000 men became casualties. For a while during mid-morning, German commanders reported that they had stopped the invasion on the beaches as Rommel had intended. Many who landed on Omaha also believed that their landing had failed, and that they would be wiped out the next day.

10

10 *"Duck" amphibious trucks were widely used on D-Day: each could carry about 50 men, or the equivalent weight in stores, from landing ships and across the beaches. Aptly nicknamed from its technical designation DUKW (D: 1942, year of design; U: utility; K: all-wheel-drive; W: dual rear axles), the 36-foot-long Duck had a top speed of about 5 knots at sea and up to 50mph on land. Some 21,000 were built during World War II.* (US National Archives)

1

2

THE POINTE DE HOC

Before D-Day Allied intelligence identified a German battery of six 155mm guns well dug-in on top of the Pointe de Hoc three miles west of Omaha beach (given as the Pointe de Hoe in all American official accounts), a sheer cliff 100 feet high with a stretch of beach twenty-five yards wide beneath it. The whole of Omaha lay within range of these guns, and neither bombing nor shelling could be guaranteed to silence them. A special task force of two Ranger battalions trained in cliff assaults, using rocket-guns to fire rope grapnels to the top of the cliffs and extension ladders borrowed from the London Fire Brigade, was selected to silence the German guns.

The plan called for the first wave, three companies of 2nd Rangers under Lieutenant-Colonel James Rudder, to land at the same time as the main American assault. A fourth company – Charlie Company – would land at the westernmost point of Omaha and capture the German strongpoint at Pointe de la Percée, then advance to cover the flank of the Pointe de Hoc landing. The remaining two companies and the whole of 5th Rangers formed the second wave. If the first landing at Pointe de Hoc succeeded they would land there, and advance inland toward Isigny

1 *In a pre-D-Day strike, A-20 Havoc bombers blast the suspected German clifftop battery at Pointe de Hoc.*
(Library of Congress)

2, 3 *Men of the US Army's 2nd Ranger Battalion scaled these sheer, 100-foot cliffs under fire on D-Day, to attack casemates believed to house six 155mm guns threatening Omaha beach. The casemates proved empty, but the guns were located inland and quickly destroyed.*

4 *Rangers climb the cliffs with the aid of sectional ladders and rocket guns firing rope grapnels.*
(US National Archives)

5 *"Bigoted" (top secret) intelligence documents describe the Pointe de Hoc emplacement in detail.*

THE RANGERS

The US Army's Rangers were founded in May, 1942, at the instigation of General Marshall, based on the British Commandos and named after Rogers' Rangers, the irregular American raiders of the French and Indian War. The 1st Ranger Battalion under Major W.C. Darby, trained by the British at their Commando school, proved a success in raiding operations, and a few of its men fought with the Commandos at Dieppe. In early 1943 the Rangers were expanded to six battalions, two for the Mediterranean, two for the Pacific and two for Europe, in order to provide a spearhead force for major amphibious assaults. A battalion designated 29th Rangers was also formed from 29th Infantry Division to continue the raiding tradition.

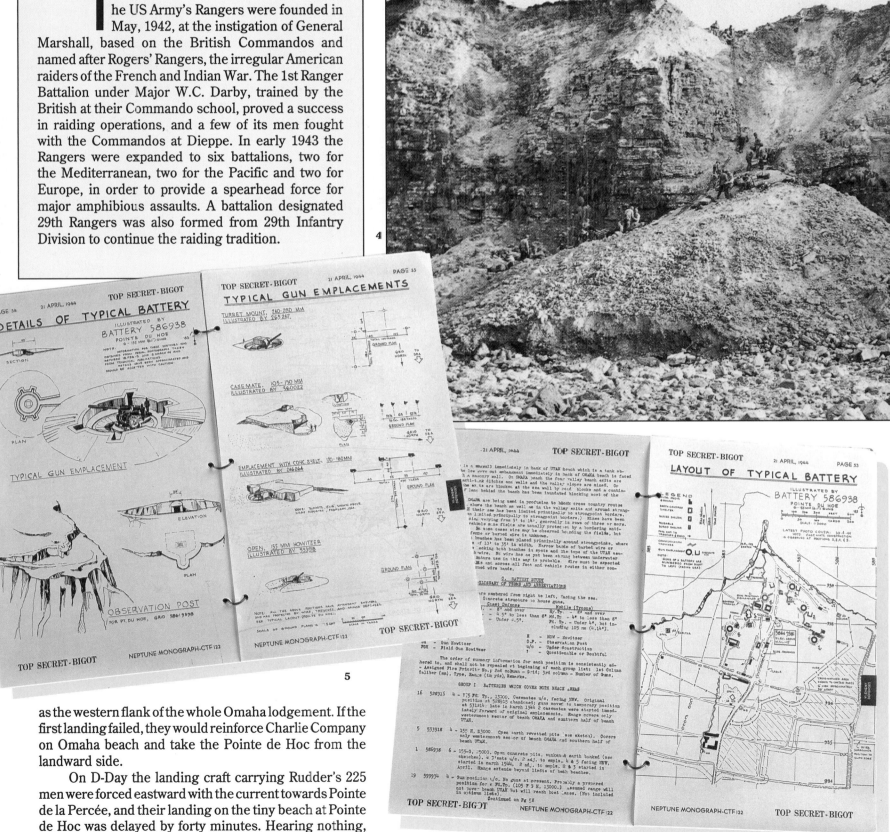

4

5

as the western flank of the whole Omaha lodgement. If the first landing failed, they would reinforce Charlie Company on Omaha beach and take the Pointe de Hoc from the landward side.

On D-Day the landing craft carrying Rudder's 225 men were forced eastward with the current towards Pointe de la Percée, and their landing on the tiny beach at Pointe de Hoc was delayed by forty minutes. Hearing nothing, the remaining Rangers under Lieutenant-Colonel Max

1 *DUKWs fitted with turntable extension ladders borrowed from the London Fire Brigade failed to get across the cratered beach at Pointe de Hoc, so the Rangers climbed with the aid of ropes and with ladders made by fitting* *together sections of light metal tubing.* (US National Archives)

2 *Awaiting invasion, a German gunner checks his range.* (Bundesarchiv)

1

2

3

4

3 *German gunners shroud their piece with camouflage netting against air surveillance. Many such guns threatened the invasion beaches and needed to be taken out by Allied air attack or raiding parties.* (Bundesarchiv)

4, 5 *The remains of their tough concrete emplacements are still to be seen along the Channel coast.*

Schneider assumed that the assault had failed and landed at Omaha, where they joined in with 116th Infantry.

Meanwhile, coming ashore with fire support from the destroyers USS *Satterlee* and HMS *Talybont*, the Rangers climbed the Pointe de Hoc under German fire, the first troops reaching the top within five minutes. Only a handful of men were lost, and the Germans gave ground once the Rangers were on top of the cliff. To their surprise they found that the casemates, partly wrecked by repeated Allied air and naval bombardment, were empty. The French Resistance had been unable to get the information to London that the guns had not yet been installed.

Patrolling forward, at nine AM, the Rangers found the battery a few hundred yards inland in a camouflaged firing position but deserted by the Germans. They destroyed it.

For the rest of the day the small Ranger force was pinned down in the heavily-cratered ground at the Pointe de Hoc, surrounded and intermingled with Germans and under counterattack from further inland. It was not relieved until June 8. Casualties on D-Day were about forty men, plus another ninety-five over the next two days. Rudder, who was wounded twice, was decorated for his achievement.

6 Rest and medical treatment for Rangers who have reached the clifftop.
7 Aftermath of two days' fighting in the rubble of the batteries at Pointe de Hoc, where "Old Glory" now reigns. Some Rangers break for chow; others bring in prisoners.
(US National Archives)

8 The battlefield grave of a GI is a reminder of the price paid by many for success on D-Day. Rommel is said to have predicted: "... the first twenty-four hours will be decisive ... for the Allies, as well as Germany, it will be the longest day ...."
(US National Archives)

Upon his appointment as inspector of coastal defenses, Rommel told Hitler bluntly that the invasion would have to be repulsed on the beaches, as all the pillboxes and other grandiose fortifications would be rendered useless by intensive Allied bombing. His idea was to install a chain of barriers and obstacles along the coast which would make any landing so difficult that the Germans could counter-attack at their ease. To this end he laced the beachheads with underwater obstacles – mined wooden posts and steel "Hedgehogs" that would destroy landing craft – and row after row of landmines. Over 5 million mines of all types were planted along the "Atlantic Wall." For maximum effect, the mines were scattered in belts of varying thickness on the beaches, across fields and roads. The Allies had developed simple electro-magnetic mine-detectors, but to counter this, the latest German mines were made of non-metallic materials such as wood, bakelite, and even glass – making them ruthlessly efficient and responsible for many of the casualties suffered in the Normandy campaign.

1, 2 One of the commonest types of anti-personnel mine was the "S" mine, two examples of which are seen here, one in cross-section. Activated by foot-pressure, this would launch a salvo of steel balls up to waist height before exploding, earning the nickname "de-bollocker." Also shown with the standard warning sign are a captured and re-utilized French anti-tank mine and a Schumine. The Schumine was of wooden construction and therefore invisible to Allied mine-detectors, which operated on electro-magnetic principles.

1

2

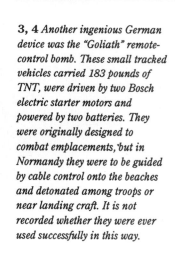

3

3, 4 Another ingenious German device was the "Goliath" remote-control bomb. These small tracked vehicles carried 183 pounds of TNT, were driven by two Bosch electric starter motors and powered by two batteries. They were originally designed to combat emplacements, but in Normandy they were to be guided by cable control onto the beaches and detonated among troops or near landing craft. It is not recorded whether they were ever used successfully in this way.

4

5 *A Sherman "Crab" (or flail) tank in action on one of the British beaches. The Crab was another of the "funnies" developed by Major-General Hobart of 79th Armoured Division. This type of tank cleared a path through minefields by carrying a rotating "carpet-beater" of chains on a frame ahead of its own tracks. This process greatly assisted the early British advance from the beachhead.*

6 *An assortment of German mines and grenades. Back row: Two 'S' mines, one in its carry-case; a 6.6-pound magnetic demolition charge or "sticky-bomb." Center row: "Mushroom" Tellermine 43 (anti-tank); Schumine 42 (anti-personnel); Pot Mine A200 (anti-personnel); Tellermine 35 (anti-tank). Front row: Panzerwurfmine hollow-charge anti-tank hand grenade (containing 18½oz of TNT); Glasmine 43.*

CHAPTER FIVE

THE BRITISH BEACHES

On the British sector, like the American, the main aerial bombardment of the Atlantic Wall and the inland German defenses began at three AM, before first light. But the amphibious landings were not to start until 7:30 AM, giving the Eastern Task Force under Admiral Sir Philip Vian an hour longer than the Western Task Force to make sure of the heavy German guns before the troops hit the beaches. The British placed the assembly areas for their landing craft closer in than the Americans, about seven miles offshore, but they also had two main beaches to assault, together with one for the Canadians. The three British and Canadian beaches ran in a continuous line for twenty-four miles, but the first landings would secure only five one-mile sections of beach, to be joined together during the day as the beachhead expanded. Unlike the almost deserted American beaches, those chosen by the British and Canadians were dotted with small seaside villages, hamlets and individual houses, making the character of the fighting on their sector very different.

Coming ashore at Gold beach, the westernmost of the British beaches, the troops of 50th (Northumberland) Division were expected to reach Bayeux, seven miles inland, and link up with the Americans coming off Omaha at Port en Bessin, between the two beaches. East of Gold came Juno beach, the Canadian target. But the most difficult, and most important, task on D-Day went to the men landing on Sword beach, opposite Caen. The brigade groups of the veteran 3rd Infantry Division (Montgomery's old division, usually known as 3rd British Division to distinguish it from Canadian 3rd Infantry Division), were to capture Caen itself, linking up with 6th Airborne Division east of the River Orne. Caen was seen as a vital prize on D-Day. If the British could reach it they could stop the German 21st Panzer Division, which Allied Intelligence placed south of the city, from charging forward onto the landing beaches.

Drawing on the lessons of Dieppe and amphibious operations in the Mediterranean, the British planned to use commandos and assault engineers to help their divisions ashore, together with specialist armored vehicles for clearing obstacles. These included the specially designed "Funnies" of British 79th Armored Division under Major-

3 *A pillbox cleverly camouflaged to resemble a beach-front cafe, on the harbor at Le Havre.*
(U.S. National Archives)
4 *The British Army standard issue 'Very' flare pistol.*
5 *An example of the invasion brief handed to all members of 21 Army Group upon embarkation. This copy has been personally signed by General Montgomery.*

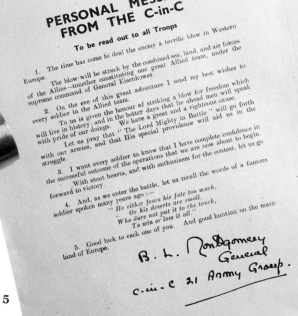

1 *HMS* Warspite *and HMS* Ramillies *direct their deadly fire against the coastal batteries situated at Villerville and Benerville, east of the main British task force.*
(Keystone)
2 *German troops rush from the security of their blockhouse to man the forward defenses of their bunker system.*
(Bundesarchiv)

7

8

6 *This exceedingly rare photograph gives us the German view of the invasion fleet as it appeared at the mouth of the Orne river, at Lion-sur-Mer.* (Bundesarchiv)

7 *The capture of the La Breche strongpoint covering Sword beach took nearly three hours, during which the waves of troops coming ashore were exposed to vicious machine-gun and mortar fire.* (Bettmann)

8 *Despite the ferocity of the Allied bombardment, the German coastal batteries could not be prevented from directing their concentrated fire against Sword. Their accuracy accounted for many Allied losses on D-Day.* (Bundesarchiv)

THE BRITISH BEACHES

1 Cap badge of the Hampshire Regiment. As part of the 50th (Northumbrian) Division, the 1st Hampshires landed on Gold beach on D-Day.

2 Royal Navy AAA mounts scan the sky as landing ships head for the British beaches.

General Percy Hobart, an early pioneer of tank warfare brought out of retirement for the purpose. Hobart's vehicles were interspersed throughout the assault divisions. Including their Commandos and armor, both 3rd British Division and 50th (Northumbrian) Division had no fewer than five brigade groups each for the D-Day landings. Midget submarines surfacing and showing lights were used to mark the landing beaches for the approaching assault craft, and despite the current the British had less difficulty finding their beaches than the troops landing an hour earlier at Omaha and Utah. With a harder and more ambitious task to perform on D-Day than the Americans, the British were more experienced, more thorough, more cautious, and less urgent in their approach, all a reflection of Montgomery's influence and determination not to take risks with his men's lives. Dempsey, as British Second Army commander, was still in England when the landings started, only taking up position offshore in the afternoon, in marked contrast to Bradley.

3 An aerial view shows apparent chaos, with landing craft struggling ashore through heavy surf to join the milling throng on the beach.

4 At Gold beach, naval bombardment had knocked out many – but certainly not all – of the German coastal guns.
(US National Archives)

5 Field postcards gave no information away: but folk waiting anxiously at home must have been grateful even for such basic information.

GOLD BEACH

To the thunder of the last rocket salvoes, the two brigade groups of 50th Division reached Gold beach at 7:25 AM. By this time, the bombardment had put many of the German coastal guns out of action, and the approach went well. The beach itself was a gentle slope up to the sand dunes and farmland beyond. But immediately to the west of Gold beach, from Arromanches-les-Bains to Port en Bessin, the shore was protected by a rocky shoal and the start of a cliff which would become the bluff at Omaha. As the Allies expected, German 716th Static Division covered the British landing areas all the way east to Sword beach. But dug in along the cliff were also the defenders of 352nd Infantry Division, of far higher fighting quality. Several of the German guns, positioned to enfilade the landing

HOBART'S FUNNIES

In March 1943, General Alan Brooke brought Major-General Percy (Peter) Hobart out of retirement to command a special formation, known as 79th Armored Division. Instead of fighting as a division, it was to develop a variety of armored vehicles and explosive devices to cope with the defenses of the Atlantic Wall. Some early ideas, like the "Great Panjandrum" – a giant Catherine wheel used for mine clearance – were notorious failures at the experimental stage. Other designs proved successful, and made a contribution to D-Day out of all proportion to the division's size.

Hobart's men produced and operated a wide variety of equipment. The Crab, a giant flail on a roller fitted to the front of a Sherman tank, was used to clear minefields by exploding the mines harmlessly in front of the vehicle. The AVRE (Armored Vehicle Royal Engineers) was a Churchill tank fitted with a 40-pounder petard mortar for clearing obstacles at very close range. A flamethrower fitted to a Mark VIII Churchill made the Crocodile tank for burning out strongpoints, a weapon particularly feared by the Germans. Another Churchill tank was modified to carry a 40-foot box girder bridge for spanning obstacles, while Bobbin tanks laid a canvas path for vehicles across soft sand, and Facine tanks dropped bundles of metal rods into ditches or trenches, or in front of sea walls, making them easier to cross. Nearly all the Funnies also had their normal tank guns and machine guns.

The most famous of the Funnies were the DD amphibious Shermans, also used by the Americans and based on an original American idea. By the time of Overlord these were no longer officially part of 79th Armored Division but had been allocated to armored brigades attached to other divisions. Although offered other Funnies to support the landings on Omaha and Utah, Bradley declined the offer. The elderly Centaur tanks of the Royal Marines Armored Support Regiments, fitted with a 95mm howitzer, were also not part of 79th Armored Division but performed a similar role on D-Day.

6

8

7

6, 7 *A Sherman DD (Duplex Drive; from the twin screw propulsion unit fitted at the rear, visible at 7) tank with its buoyancy screen lowered (6), and raised (7) in the "swimming" position.*
8 *The Crocodile flame thrower tank, towing 400 gallons of fuel in an armored trailer, burned out strongpoints from a range of 80-140 yards.*
9 *The Bobbin tank could lay a 10-foot-wide canvas path for vehicles across soft sand.*
(IWM: H 37886)

9

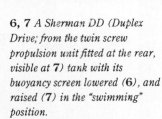

5

1

2

1 One of the typical machine-gun strongpoints positioned along the length of the Normandy coastline.
2 The view across Gold today, with the remains of the Mulberry Harbor at Arromanches still visible in the distance.

approaches, had been missed by aerial reconnaissance or could not be hit from offshore. Facing a high tide and a force five wind in addition to the German defenses, the British lying off Gold decided not to risk launching their DD Shermans but to bring them in by assault craft onto the beaches. Many of the Funnies which got ashore with the first wave were employed as ordinary tanks, and several times during the day these specially adapted armored vehicles meant the difference between success and failure in the struggle to overcome German strongpoints and press inland. Without them, the British at Gold could have faced the same casualties as the Americans on Omaha.

At the western end of Gold, 231st Brigade Group landed next to the small seaside village of Le Hamel, which the Germans had turned into a company strongpoint, still almost intact despite the bombing and shelling. It took fifteen minutes for the first tanks to join the infantry on the beach, while the shelving sand meant that assault

3

3 Gold beach as it appeared on the morning of June 6, 1944. The "funnies" of 69th Brigade Group pick their way ashore through the lines of "Rommel's Asparagus" and other obstacles, under the withering fire of the heavy batteries at Longues-sur-Mer.
(Bettmann)

craft often grounded early, leaving the men with a difficult wade to dry land. The battalion assaulting Le Hamel, 1st Battalion, The Hampshire Regiment, lost its commanding officer and second-in-command within minutes, and the firefight to take the village lasted until late afternoon. Meanwhile, the rest of the brigade bypassed Le Hamel and moved inland to secure the beachhead. A few minutes behind the first wave, Commandos of 4th Special Service Brigade came ashore west of Le Hamel, wrecking all but one of their assault craft in the process. "Perhaps we're

intruding," one observed in true British fashion, "this seems to be a private beach!" Pushing overland behind Arromanches by the clifftop paths, the leading troops of No. 47 Royal Marine Commando reached the line of Port en Bessin by nightfall and took it in the early hours of the following day.

To the east of 231st Brigade Group, the first wave of 69th Brigade Group came ashore with their Funnies and beach-clearing engineers. Landing close to the seaside village of La Riviere, they pushed about a mile inland to

4

4 *The assault brigade groups of 50th Division, part of XXX Corps, come ashore supported by Sherman DD tanks of the 4/7th Dragoon Guards and the Nottinghamshire Yeomanry, at around 08:15 hours, Gold beach.* (IWM: MH 2021)

5, 6, 7 *Two examples of German gun emplacements and an observation post, part of the Atlantic Wall defenses at Longues-sur-Mer known locally as "Le Chaos."*

8 *The London* Evening Standard, *reported the first day's events as accurately as possible, but the initial press releases from SHAEF were deliberately vague. This meant that Fleet Street had to use additional but inaccurate material from the German-controlled press agencies based in neutral countries.*

9 *Allied losses were lighter than expected on D-Day itself – less than 2,000 men – but the real battle had yet to begin.* (U.S. National Archive)

5

6

7

8

9

1 *Cap badge and shoulder flash of The Green Howards (Princess of Wales's Own Yorkshire Regiment).*
2 *Sergeant-Major Stanley Hollis, 6th Green Howards, won the first Victoria Cross of the Normandy campaign for his gallantry on Gold beach.*
(Keystone)

3 *The smoke of conflict drifts across a British-held beach as materiel continues to pour ashore.*
(IWM: CL 25)
4 *The White Ensign denotes the post of a Royal Naval Beach Party, whose task is to ensure that the landing of men and supplies goes as smoothly as possible.*
(IWM: A 24012)

their first objective, a German battery near Mont Fleury. In clearing a German pillbox at Hable de Heurtot during the first minutes of the landing, Sergeant-Major Stanley Hollis of 6th Battalion The Green Howards captured twenty-five prisoners and won the Victoria Cross, the only man to do so on D-Day. It took several hours before La Rivière was cleared, but all the time troops were moving off the beach and further inland. At eleven AM the third brigade of the division, 151st Brigade Group, came ashore and pushed up through the division's center, now securely held although Le Hamel still had not fallen. An hour later the division's final infantry brigade, 56th Brigade Group, also came ashore, together with the divisional commander, Major-General D.A.H. Graham. The 231st Brigade Group, still partly entangled at Le Hamel, secured the flank of the

beachhead by taking Arromanches with support from naval gunfire. The rest of the division could now advance as a single body, against light opposition as many of the defenders of 716th Static Division had already fled. Nevertheless, 56th Brigade Group came forward cautiously, taking five hours to advance three miles, and was still a mile short of Bayeux by nightfall. To the east of this brigade, 151st Brigade Group pushed out a little faster, and just reached the Bayeux-Caen road by the end of the day. Linking up with the Canadians from Juno, 69th Brigade Group made the division's deepest advance of the day, a distance of about eight miles, despite a sharp firefight late in the afternoon. While this was going on, the beaches were secured and cleared, troops of 7th Armored Division (the famous "Desert Rats") were coming ashore behind 50th Division.

Although 50th Division was held short of its D-Day objectives, it was firmly inland on a continuous front, and its position was secure. Some 24,970 men had come ashore on Gold beach, and casualties were under 1,000 killed and wounded. A landing which had threatened to be as bloody as Omaha had turned, like Utah, into something that felt to many who took part like an exercise with casualties added. As night closed in, the men stopped and began to make tea.

SECRET.

LANDING INSTRUCTIONS.

If there is anything in these instructions which you cannot understand, see your section Officer at once.

1. You are about to take part in the invasion of Europe. The operation will be known by the codeword 'OVERLORD'. Do not disclose this codeword nor any of those which follow, to anybody and do not use them in conversation among yourselves. You have all been told them and there is no point in discussing them. You never know who may overhear you.

2. You will be landed on one or other of 3 beaches. The code names of these are ITEM, JIG and KING. Wherever you land, carry out the following instructions.
(a) Go at once to the Beach Transit Area, which will be marked. Go straight-there do NOT hang about looking for your friends or your own section. If you are on foot go to the personnel Park, if you are with a vehicle go to the Vehicle Park and carry out the first stage of dewaterproofing i.e. sparking plugs, breather holes etc. DO NOT wait for orders- get on with it. SPEED in clearing the ships and beaches is essential. WASTE NO TIME.

(b) In this Transit Area, collect yourselves into your sections and then move off to the Assembly Area and go to the section marked TENNYSON. If you know your section has landed but you cannot find them in the Transit Area, go straight to TENNYSON independantly.

(c) On arrival at TENNYSON, you should find a guide from the unit who will tell you where to go. If you cannot find the guide, go to Army Troops Report Centre and ask where your unit is.
(NOTE. Army Group Troops Report Centre is NOT the same thing. Do NOT go there)

3. If you have any difficulty, look for H.Q.Army Troops, one of their vehicles or their report centre. Their sign bears the number 844 and this is on all their vehicles. DO NOT bother other HQs. or vehicles; they will have problems enough of their own and will not be able to help you anyway.

4. As soon as you have joined the unit in the TENNYSON area, burn these instructions. DO NOT keep them as a souvenir and DO NOT screw them up and throw them away- BURN them.

5. Remember that speed is essential and that beaches and ships must be cleared. Get to TENNYSON area as quickly as you can. There will be hundreds of things which may tempt you to stop and have a look. DON'T stop GET CRACKING- there will be plenty for you to do.

6. It is possible that you may be landed on a beach other than those mentioned in para 2 above. If this should happen, go to the assembly area for that beach and make enquiries at the Army Troops Report Centre as in para 2 (c) above. DO NOT start looking for TENNYSON Area in this case.

Major.
O.C.Serial 43193.

5

6 *"Very Pistol," used by British forces to fire pyrotechnic signal flares.*

7

8

5 *Instructions issued to men due to land on Gold Beach stress the need for swift and well coordinated assembly once ashore.*
7 *A British Cromwell cruiser tank leaves its landing craft off Gold beach.*
(IWM: MH 2014)
8 *A memorial commemorates 47 Royal Marine Commando's savage fight to secure Port-en-Bessin harbor, Gold beach.*

THE COMMANDOS

The British Commandos came into being at the start of the Second World War as volunteers from the Army and Royal Navy, who were given special training to carry out minor raids on occupied territories. The units formed for these raids had various names, and most men kept the uniforms and badges of their parent units. Like all private armies, the Commandos provoked their share of jealousy and obstruction, and it took a prolonged fight before they were all allowed to wear the same green beret (which became as distinctive as the red beret of the British airborne troops) and the Combined Operations shoulder flash. The term "Commando," which at first had little official meaning, came from the Boer *Commandos* (commands) against which Winston Churchill had fought in South Africa, and throughout the war he was the Commandos' principal champion.

From July, 1940, the Commandos were known officially as Special Service troops, a title disliked by the men because of its initials (or because other troops took to calling them "Suicide Squads"). A Commando unit was, on paper, the equivalent of a weak battalion, with about 400 men in four troops and a heavy weapons troop, but in practice, organization and composition varied greatly. By 1943 the Army had twelve separate Commandos, including No. 10 (Inter-Allied) Commando, with one French troop, one Dutch, three Belgian, one Norwegian, one Polish and one troop of "enemy aliens," including Germans. No. 14 (Arctic) Commando, formed later for raiding in northern waters, included British, Canadian, American Indian and Norwegian members. The first Royal Marine Commandos were formed from their raiding forces in 1942, and there were eight Royal Marine Commandos (Nos. 40 through 47) by 1944.

1st Special Service Brigade on D-Day was composed of Nos. 3, 4, 6 Commando and 45 Royal Marine Commando, with the addition of the French from No. 10 Commando. The 4th Special Service Brigade was composed of Nos. 41, 46, 47 and 48 Royal Marine Commando. Although used as first wave troops for Overlord, the Commandos were given specific objectives to seize rather than being employed as assault infantry, and retained their principal role as small-scale raiders throughout the war.

2 Frenchmen of No.10 Commando formed part of 1st Special Service Brigade on D-Day. (IWM: B 5281)

3 Commandos embark for Normandy. Although they were among the first to land, the Commandos did not form part of the main assault: they had specific tasks, including the seizure of strongpoints and bridges, and scouting and raiding missions. (IWM: BU 1181)

4 The letters "SS" have a sinister significance in the context of World War II. Here, however, they appear on the cloth insignia of Brigade Headquarters personnel of 1st Special Service Brigade.

5 Men of 4 Commando are supported by Sherman DD tanks as they prepare to assault the German battery at Ouistreham on D-Day. (IWM: MH 2012)

1 *Heavily laden Commandos advance up the beach.* (IWM: BU 1185)

6 *The Combined Operations badge worn by British Commandos symbolized their readiness to fight by air, land, or sea. A badge of near identical design was worn by their American counterparts.*

6

1 *Cap badge of The Lovat Scouts, a Scottish regiment raised by the then Lord Lovat for service in the Boer War (1899-1902). Lord Lovat's Commandos of 1st Special Service Brigade were led onto Sword Beach by His Lordship's personal piper.*

SWORD BEACH

The first troops of the leading brigade of 3rd British Division, 8th Brigade Group under Brigadier E.E.E. (Copper) Cass, hit the beach at the little seaside village of La Brèche at 7:25 AM, with at least one officer reading speeches from Shakespeare's Henry V through a mega-phone to his seasick men. Lying between Ouistreham a mile to the east and an offshore shoal a mile to the west, Sword beach at La Brèche, which had been turned into a formidable strongpoint by the Germans, had room for only one brigade to land at a time. But air and naval bombardment, and the landing by 6th Airborne Division hours before, had done a good job of reducing the defenses, and the first wave came in together and on time. Of 40 DD Shermans all but six were successfully launched, and twenty-eight survived the landing and the first few minutes on the beach. As at Gold beach, the first wave also included Hobart's Funnies, Centaur tanks of the Royal Marine Armored Support Regiment, and self-propelled guns. The engineers arriving to clear the beach defenses

2 *Only aerial shots like this can come near to conveying the apparent (occasionally real) chaos off the beaches, where the sea, said one US observer, was "like Broadway in rush hour."* (IWM: EA 25992)

3 *High tide at about 1:00 PM on D-Day: empty landing craft are littered along the beach; vehicles move off inland, where fires set by the pre-invasion bombardment are still burning.*

4 *British infantrymen prepare to advance from Sword. Congestion on the narrow beach delayed the deployment of armor, so some infantry moved inland unsupported.* (IWM: B 5091)

5 *La Brèche, site of British 8th Brigade Group's landing on Sword beach at 7:25 AM on D-Day, as it is today: a peaceful seaside resort. Pre-invasion bombardment, and Sherman DD tanks and other armor landed in the first wave, were able to minimize casualties here.*

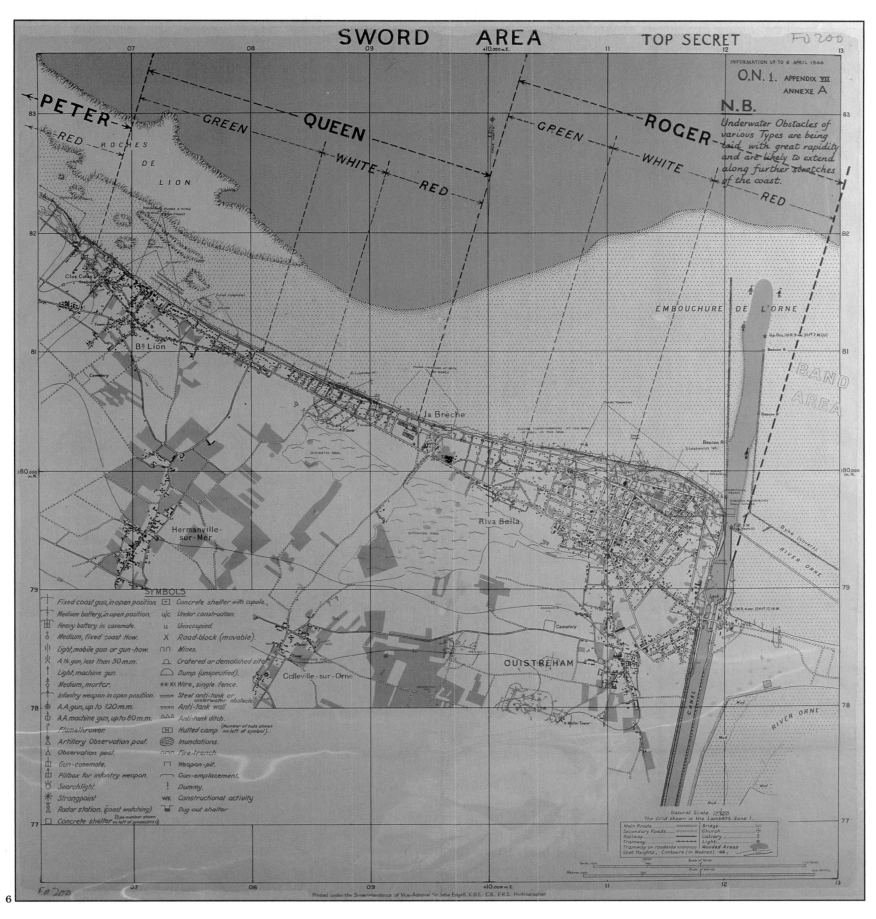

SWORD AREA — TOP SECRET — FO 200

INFORMATION UP TO 6 APRIL 1944

O.N. 1. APPENDIX VII ANNEXE A

N.B. Underwater Obstacles of various Types are being laid with great rapidity and are likely to extend along further stretches of the coast.

were hit by German machine-gun fire as they landed, but within minutes the armor had dealt with the enemy. The first two infantry battalions, expecting to be virtually wiped out by German fire, landed almost without a casualty. Soon they were heavily engaged with small parties of defenders further inland. Following them within minutes were the rest of the brigade and the Commandos of 1st Special Service Brigade, under Brigadier Lord Lovat, complete with piper.

While fighting for La Brèche continued, 8th Brigade Group and the commandos fanned out to secure the landing. The center of Ouistreham, a fashionable resort complete with hotels and a casino, was captured by French troops of No. 10 (Inter-Allied) Commando. Lovat reached Pegasus Bridge two minutes behind schedule, apologizing to the tired paratroops for the delay. But by the time La Brèche fell at ten AM, the bad weather and fast rising tide had reduced the strip of beach to barely fifteen yards of sand. Meanwhile, two miles inland near Colleville, a regimental headquarters strongpoint of 716 Static Division, codenamed Hillman by the British and defended by over 270 men, kept the leading battalion of 8th Brigade Group,

6 *"Top Secret" map of the Sword landing area, on the extreme left of the Allied line and bounded by the estuary of the Orne River (where airborne landings on the night of June 5-6 had secured vital bridges).*

1 *The Browning .50in Caliber M2 (HB) machine gun was the standard heavy support weapon of US forces in World War II and for years afterwards. Often vehicle mounted, its uses included anti-aircraft and even anti-tank roles.*

2 *Sherman DD tanks prepare to jettison their buoyancy screens (sometimes blown off by a small,* built-in explosive charge) before moving up the beach in support of British infantry. (UPI/Bettmann) 2

3 *Men of Germany's "Indian Legion" man an MG-34 machine gun on the Atlantic Wall. Many Indians who opposed British rule in their homeland volunteered to serve Germany or Japan.* (Bundesarchiv)

4 *The basement of the German blockhouse at Port-en-Bessin.*

1st Suffolks, pinned down all day. The last defenders at Hillman surrendered only on the following morning.

Within hours of the first landing at Sword the British timetable began to slide, as the beach became a jumble of landing craft, men and equipment. Although the infantry of 185th Brigade Group came ashore successfully with the commandos, the narrow strip of sand made it much harder for armor and specialist equipment to get ashore. Only about half the intended number of vehicles and stores reached dry land by the end of the day, and there were terrible traffic jams as tanks maneuvered past La Brèche. The division's main armor, 27th Armored Brigade, took until midnight to land the last of its troops, and most of its tanks were tied down in the fighting at La Brèche and Hillman.

Having little choice but to go forward alone, at 12:30 PM the first infantry of 185th Brigade Group set off inland, leaving the armor to catch up. Skirting Hillman, the brigade came under fire from enemy guns and infantry, and had only pushed as far as Pegasus Bridge by mid-afternoon. By four PM, as the leading battalions reached Bieville, just three miles short of the outskirts of Caen, they found that they had left their advance too late. Emerging toward them from out of the city were the tanks of 21st Panzer Division, which the Allies had believed to

be still at least ten miles further south. Hastily calling for armored support to be moved up past Hillman, 185th Brigade Group destroyed sixteen German tanks and stopped the panzer division's counterattack, but Bieville remained the limit of 3rd British Division's advance. Although the leading battalion of 185th Brigade Group, 2nd Battalion The King's Shropshire Light Infantry, got two companies into Lebisey Wood and a mile closer to Caen than anyone else, they had to retreat during the night.

The remaining brigade of the division, 9th Brigade Group, was meanwhile moving westward to complete the

5 *The camouflage netting that has protected its cliff-top position from Allied air reconnaissance has been thrown aside, and a German 105mm howitzer opens fire on the invasion beaches.* (Bundesarchiv)

6 *Royal Navy Commandos undertake the hazardous chore of uprooting "Rommel's Asparagus" – clearing beach obstructions, many of them incorporating mines or boobytrapped with explosive charges, ahead of the main assault waves.*

7, 8 *Interior of the German blockhouse below the Vauban Tower at Port-en-Bessin. Taken by 47 Royal Marine Commando – see (8) on page 105 – it is now preserved as one of the many memorials to the D-Day battles.*

link-up with the Canadians on Juno beach. The brigade's intended target for D-Day was Le Carpiquet airfield, two miles west of Caen and ten miles from Sword beach. Instead, facing a growing threat from the German armor, the divisional commander Major-General T.G. Rennie ordered the brigade to reinforce the line of the Orne and Pegasus Bridge. A few minutes later a German mortar bomb wounded the brigade commander and killed most of his staff. The brigade group was employed to provide additional security for the existing lodgement, rather than driving forward.

At seven PM, 21st Panzer Division put in a major counterattack from Caen onto the Sword landing area, a charge led by fifty tanks of 22nd Panzer Regiment. "If you don't push the British back into the sea," the regimental commander, Colonel Hermann von Oppeln-Bronikowski, was told, "we will have lost the war." Rushing down into the three mile-wide gap between the British and the Canadians to their west, the armored drive almost reached the sea at Lion-sur-Mer. But well prepared British defenses and anti-tank fire knocked out thirteen of Oppeln-Bronikowski's tanks and stopped the drive literally in its tracks just short of the cliffs. By an amazing stroke of luck for the British, this moment coincided with the arrival of the gliders of

1 *Inter-service cooperation played a vital part in the efforts to delay the advance of the German panzer divisions. Here, a Royal Navy wireless post relays information from a reconnaissance aircraft to warships off the beaches, enabling them to lay down fire from their big guns against the armored columns.*
(IWM: B 6631)
2 *Shoulder flash of 10 (Inter-Allied) Commando. Two Fighting French troops of 10 Commando landed on D-Day with 4 Commando and helped secure the Casino at Ouistreham.*

6th Air Landing Brigade, coming down on their landing zones on either side of Pegasus Bridge and directly over the heads of the astonished German armored troops. The Germans pulled back hurriedly, and by nightfall the gap between Juno and Sword was unoccupied by either side.

In the day's fighting, 21st Panzer Division lost a total of fifty-four out of 124 tanks, and had failed in its main objective, to defeat the invasion on the beaches and push it back into the sea. The 3rd British Division had put 28,845 men ashore at Sword beach and suffered about the same number of casualties as their fellows at Gold, including some men drowned in the rising tide when they fell wounded on the beach. But having failed to reach Caen, the division was on the defensive, needing to close the gap to its west and to reinforce 6th Airborne Division east of the Orne. While Allied aircraft deep behind the front lines tried to delay the advance of the panzer divisions, the question was whether the British on Sword could survive long enough to gain a secure position, or whether they would be pushed into the sea.

3

1

2

equipment is battered, but Britain's "PBI" ("poor bloody infantry") slog onward, advancing from Gold beach towards Caen through a town showing the scars of battle.
(IWM: B 5266)
5 *Having taken the Ouistreham battery, men of 4 Commando move out from Sword beach towards the Orne River line and the positions established by 6th Airborne Division.*
(IWM: BU 1178)

3 *Although the British invasion forces on Sword beach were hard pressed on the evening of June 6, units were already moving inland – like these infantrymen assaulting a German position in a Normandy village.*
(UPI/Bettmann)
4 *The men look weary, their*

4

6

6 *It was too early for the cheering crowds – but on D-Day itself some French people were already on the streets to give a warm welcome to the liberators of Europe.* (IWM: BU 1188)

Infantry tactics during World War I were increasingly dominated by the heavy machine gun. Later in that war, and thereafter, armies sought to counter this by conferring greater fire power on the individual soldier and the small unit. Thus, the World War II period saw a huge increase in the development and use of personal and "squad" automatic weapons: the light machine gun, sub-machine gun, and "assault rifle." These weapons were designed to be mass-produced quickly and cheaply and used efficiently after the most basic instruction. They look what they are: utilitarian killing tools.

1 *Seen here in cut-away, the German MG–42, "Spandau" to the Allies, was a fine light machine gun. It fired 7.92mm cartridges from 50-round belts at a rate of up to 1,200 rounds per minute.*
3 *British infantryman (center) with Bren light machine gun in hip-firing position. Although*

slower firing (500 rpm; .303in cartridges from a 30-round box magazine) than the "Spandau," it was more durable and versatile.
(IWM: B 6184)

4 *Ugly, sometimes unreliable: the British 9mm Sten Mark 2 sub-machine gun. It was very cheap to produce and, with a 32-round box magazine, a useful close-quarter arm.*
5 *Britain's 9mm Lanchester Mark I SMG (with 50-round box magazine), was basically a copy of the German Bergmann MP-28, hurriedly put into production in 1940. Few saw much service.*
6 *Made entirely of metal and plastic, the 9mm German MP-40 "Schmeisser" SMG was perhaps the best arm of its kind. More than one million were produced in 1940-45.*
8 *Cheap but reliable: the .45in M3A1 "grease gun" was the US Army's standard SMG by early 1945.*

2 *The Browning Automatic Rifle 1918A2 fired .30in caliber cartridges from a 20-round box magazine. The BAR was a standard squad weapon for the US Army.*

7, 9 *Once refused by the British Army as a "gangster gun," the Thompson M1A1 SMG served the Allies well and was especially favored by Commandos and other Special Forces for the stopping power of its .45in rounds.*

4

5

6

10 *Effective but expensive, the 7.92mm FG-42 assault rifle was designed for use by German paratroopers.*

11 *The first* Sturmgewehr *("Assault Rifle") to bear the name, Germany's 7.92mm MP-44, entered service in 1943. Its excellent design greatly influenced such later arms as the AK-47 "Kalashnikov."*

10   11

CHAPTER SIX

THE CANADIAN BEACHES

As a Dominion of the British Empire, without even their famous Maple Leaf flag in 1944, the Canadians in Normandy were often viewed as part of the British forces. For their achievements on D-Day alone, they deserve independent recognition. Canadian 3rd Infantry Division landed on Juno beach as part of British I Corps alongside 3rd British Division on Sword, supported by British troops of 4th Special Service Brigade and British Funnies; and throughout the campaign the Canadians gave an outstanding example of cooperation in Montgomery's plans. But they were also heirs to a distinct Canadian identity and tradition, the only all-volunteer national force on either side on D-Day. Some were Americans who had gone to Canada to enlist before the US became involved in the war. Many were Irish, Scots or French Canadians returning to fight for France, and more than one Canadian of Polish origin found that the "German" opposite him in battle was a Pole, conscripted unwillingly into the German Army.

Previous page: A Sherman tank and Bedford trucks roll ashore from a US landing ship at a "Mulberry" harbor.
(US National Archives)
1 *Battledress jacket of a sergeant of the Royal Winnipeg Rifles ("Little Black Devils"), who landed on Juno beach.*

THE PLAN

Juno beach, like Sword and Gold, was gentle sands and holiday Cottages, with four strongpoints at the hamlets of Vaux, Coucelles sur Mer, Bernières sur Mer and St Aubin sur Mer. A fifth hamlet, Langrune sur Mer on the easternmost point of Juno beach, was the target for No. 48 Royal Marine Commando, meant to link up with No. 41 Royal Marine Commando coming from Sword to Lion sur Mer a bare mile away. Offshore from Juno, with the exception of a one-mile gap at Courcelles, lay the rocky shoal and potentially treacherous shallows which also constricted the Sword landing area. Rather than try to hit this narrow gap, the Canadians chose to land ten minutes after the British with two brigades side by side, letting the higher tide take them over the shoal. Their objective for D-Day was the Bayeux-Caen road, linking up with British

2 *Allied aircraft marked by "invasion stripes" overfly a troop transport.*
(Keystone)
3 *Cap badge: The North Shore (New Brunswick) Regiment.*

9th Brigade Group at Le Carpiquet. The role was given to Canadian 3rd Infantry Division, while the rest of the Canadian forces waited in Britain for the next stages of the Normandy campaign, part of the complex equation of alliance warfare. The Canadians were given no major objective to capture on D-Day, but they were made the vital link between the British forces aimed at Bayeux and Caen.

THE ALLIED NATIONAL CONTINGENTS

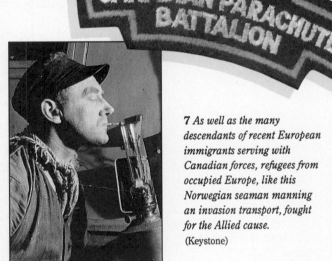

Although only a single Canadian division took part on D-Day, the Canadian forces in Normandy eventually grew to three infantry divisions and an armored division. Canadian 1st Parachute Battalion served with British 6th Airborne Division throughout the Normandy campaign. Also attached to the Canadian First Army for most of the campaign was the Polish 1st Armored Division, made up of volunteers who had escaped from Poland in 1939.

While many who served in the Canadian and American forces were first or second generation European immigrants, the British had many refugees from Hitler's Europe serving with them either as individuals or in units, apart from the men of 10th (Inter-Allied) Commando. An armored division was furnished for Normandy by the Free French (renamed the Fighting French in 1944) as French 2nd Armored Division. Two French parachute battalions served with the British Special Air Service on clandestine operations in Normandy. One Dutch parachute company also served with the Special Air Service, while the Dutch Princess Irene Brigade, a composite force of infantry and armor, and 1st Belgian Infantry Brigade, fought alongside the British 6th Airborne Division in the later stages of the Normandy campaign.

Apart from individuals or mixed crews from Europe and most parts of the British Empire, British tactical air forces for the Normandy battle included twenty fighter squadrons of the Royal Canadian Air Force, ten Polish squadrons, five Fighting French, four of the Royal New Zealand Air Force, three of the Royal Australian Air Force, three Czech, two Norwegian, two Dutch, two Belgian, and one from Newfoundland. The naval task forces under Ramsay that made the D-Day landings possible included warships serving with the navies of France, Canada, Poland and Norway.

7 As well as the many descendants of recent European immigrants serving with Canadian forces, refugees from occupied Europe, like this Norwegian seaman manning an invasion transport, fought for the Allied cause.
(Keystone)

6 Marker buoys chart the path to the beaches for invasion shipping. As well as "Channel chops," shoals and shallows provided potential hazards at the Canadians' landing area.
(Keystone)

8 These smiles must have been a welcome sight for the Canadians in Normandy. Newly arrived nurses of No. 10 Canadian General Hospital are seen at Arromanches soon after D-Day.
(National Archives of Canada)

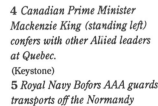

4 Canadian Prime Minister Mackenzie King (standing left) confers with other Allied leaders at Quebec.
(Keystone)

5 Royal Navy Bofors AAA guards transports off the Normandy beaches.

1 *On the East Front the German Army encountered an impressive Soviet weapon it nicknamed the "Stalin Organ": a railed assembly, often mounted on a truck, for the simultaneous launching of from 30-50 solid-fuel, fin-stablized, 82mm rockets, with a range of some 7,000 yards. Germany adopted the weapon in a number of forms, notably as the Fohn ("Spring Storm") AAA installation, to launch 35 73mm rockets. The assembly seen here is in use as field artillery in Normandy.*
(Bundesarchiv)

2 *Allied rocket salvos at the ready: a Canadian-crewed LCS(R) support craft mounts massed launching tubes.*
(US National Archives)

JUNO BEACH

As the Canadians began their run-in covered by fire from offshore, the importance of even a few minutes' difference in the timetables showed as the worsening weather began to have a major effect on their landing, and the strong current and waves pushed many of the smaller bombardment or landing craft out of position. The difficulties in assembling the landing force in the rough sea took the landing a further ten minutes behind the planned schedule, and into trouble. The tide had risen over the first lines of beach obstacles, and instead of landing in front of them 7th Brigade Group landed at 7:45 AM and 8th Brigade Group ten minutes later right on top of the submerged girders and mines. The infantry were also coming ashore without the tank support they had expected. Given the rough sea no risks were taken with launching the DD Shermans. On 8th Brigade Group front they came in by landing craft behind the infantry. The same was to have happened on 7th Brigade Group front, but at the last minute they were launched from 4,000 yards, and lost six tanks before the shoreline. Only about half of the surviving tanks got ashore before the infantry as planned. Of forty Royal Marine Centaur tanks, only six got ashore.

As on all the beaches at D-Day, the infantry were dismayed to see the German defenses still intact, their own landing craft wrecked, and the first men dying as they

1

2

3 *A landing vessel that helped put the Canadians ashore sits high and dry on Juno beach: a scene of calm very different from that of the morning of June 6, when rough seas delayed the landings and denied many Canadian infantrymen the armored spearhead they had expected.*
(National Archives of Canada)

3

4

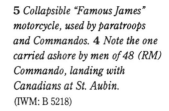

5 Collapsible "Famous James" motorcycle, used by paratroops and Commandos. **4** Note the one carried ashore by men of 48 (RM) Commando, landing with Canadians at St. Aubin. (IWM: B 5218)

6 Like that of The Queen's Own Cameron Highlanders, its "parent" in the Old Country, the cap badge of The Cameron Highlanders of Ottawa shows St. Andrew, Scotland's patron, with his Cross. The regiment's 107mm mortars helped keep down defenders' heads on Juno beach.

jumped from the assault craft. More than one soldier believed that the landing had failed and would become a bloodbath. Le Regiment de la Chaudière became briefly convinced that it had lost all its weapons when its landing craft were hit, and came ashore prepared to fight with knives only. But although only a fraction of the German defenses were destroyed by the Allied bombardment, it had succeeded in its main objective of keeping the defenders' heads down on the approach. On each of the three Anglo-Canadian beaches about a third of the landing craft were wrecked, mostly in collisions or damaged after they had discharged their troops, and few weapons were actually lost. It may not have felt like it to its participants, but the Canadian landing was the most successful of D-Day.

The 7th Brigade Group under Brigadier H.W. Foster landed on either side of the River Seulles estuary at Courseulles, but with all the delays it had suffered it was nearly 8:15 AM before all the first wave of troops got ashore. With the assault engineers and some of the tanks late, the brigade had a tough fight for the first few minutes, and in taking its designated strong point one company of the Royal Winnipeg Rifles was reduced to twenty-seven men. But Allied Intelligence work before the landing had been very good, and almost every one of the major German defenses or guns had been identified correctly. Although fighting and sniping at Courseulles and Vaux continued until five PM, most of the brigade was able to bypass the German defenses and press inland.

To the east, 8th Brigade Group under Brigadier K.G. Blackader, also without its tanks for the first few minutes, found German resistance just as hard, and clearing Bernières without armor cost the Queen's Own Rifles 143 men. In house-to-house fighting at St Aubin, also little damaged by the bombardment, AVREs were brought up to help

1 *Men of the North Nova Scotia Highlanders and Highland Light Infantry of Canada splash ashore at Bernières with bicycles – on which it was hoped they would speed down the road to Caen!* (National Archives of Canada)
2 *Cap badge of The Queen's Own Rifles of Canada.*
3 *The British .45in De Lisle Silent Carbine (note bulky barrel housing for silencer) was used by Commandos.*
4 *An abandoned German machine gun post provides cover for men of Le Régiment de la Chaudière as they wait to move off Juno beach.* (National Archives of Canada)

Canadian Soldiers!

For over five years you as auxiliary troops have been fighting and dying for the ambitions of English politicians and the fattening of war profiteers and racketeers.

For years you have not seen your families. You don't know whether you will ever see them again.

Many Canadian soldiers who are fighting in Europe thousands of miles away from their country are already being asked to volunteer in the Pacific War in spite of the fact that in Canada there are tens of thousands of men in uniform who have not yet seen any fighting.

From volunteering to being compelled to go is only a short step.

Canadians! England wanted war and declared war on Germany, dragging your country into it although the relations between the German and Canadian peoples had already been friendly. The German soldiers know that they are fighting for the security of their homes and the future of their children.

What are YOU fighting for?

A1-136-10-44

5 *Assault landing craft of Le Régiment de la Chaudière hit Juno beach.* (IWM: MH 4505)
6 *A German propaganda leaflet exhorts Canadians not to fight for "the ambitions of English politicians."*
7 *More bicycles are brought ashore by Commandos. They proved to be of little use.* (IWM: BU 1184)

WEAPONS FILE: GAS AND GRENADES

The fear that poison gas might once again be used as a weapon was common to both sides in 1944. For the Allies, fears of gas attack prompted the production of some 60 days' supply of gas shells for retaliatory use. In addition, aircrew were specially trained in gas-bombing techniques and all invasion troops were issued with gas masks. On the German side, intelligence sources wrongly anticipated that the Allies would use gas in their preliminary attack, so they too stockpiled gas shells and all troops were required to carry gas masks. Grenades were used in great numbers in the close fighting among the hedgrows. The Germans used their familiar explosive "stick" grenade, while the Allies used "Pineapple" shaped fragmentation types. Other close-combat weapons included the German "Panzerfaust" rocket projector and "Panzerschreck" rocket launcher – similar to the American "Bazooka" – and the British PIAT spigot mortar launcher.

1, 2, 5 *The German* Panzerfaust *was the best infantry anti-tank weapon of the war. Basically, it was a small, one-shot hollow charge rocket fired from a throwaway tube and capable of penetrating 200mm (8 inches) of armor plate at 30, 60 and later 100 meters (98, 196 and 328 feet). Of the two shown here (**2**) one carries the early 3¼lb bomb* *while the other carries the later standardised 6¾lb unit. They terrorized the Allied tanks (**5**), which were virtually defenseless against them in the tight hedgerow country.*

3 *A selection of infantry weapons: German stick grenade; British "Airborne" 2-inch mortar and round; Hawkins No.75 anti-tank grenade (converted from a talcum can); a Mills No.36 grenade and an M2A1 "Pineapple" grenade.*

4 *A standard-issue German gas mask and case showing the replacement filter kit in the lid.*

6 *An excellent example of German anti-gas equipment as stored in a chest from an observation bunker on the Atlantic Wall. Contents include gas masks and cases, mask holders (to assist drying after use), filters, decontamination fluid, spare filters, gas goggles and a maintenance kit. The yellow "skull" pennant is a minefield warning.*
8 *This photo serves to show the usual method of carrying the gas mask case in action.*

7 *German stick grenades on a carrying frame, itself usually transported in a pressed-steel case (1). To prime the grenade, the cap at the base was unscrewed and the pin (which was on a length of string) was then pulled. The fuse gave approximately five seconds delay before exploding. German grenades relied on their explosive effect, while Allied grenades used fragmentation to kill.*

1

1 *Perhaps a victim of the big naval guns of the pre-landing bombardment, a German soldier is partly entombed in the wreckage of his position on the Atlantic Wall.*
(US National Archives)
2 *The terrific strain of holding a field command at a crucial moment of the war is evident in* the face and gestures of Major-General Rod Keller, commander of Canadian 3rd Infantry Division. Keller, seen here at his headquarters outside Bernières, was faced with potential disaster as the swiftly rising tide narrowed the beach on which his men and vehicles clustered.
(National Archives of Canada)

2

3

4 *As befits a French-Canadian unit, the cap badge of Le Régiment de la Chaudière, part of the 8th Brigade Group that landed at Bernieres, incorporates a fleur-de-lis.*
5 *A Canadian LCI(L) off Juno beach appears to carry more bicycles than men! Early in the war, both the Germans, in their attack on the Low Countries in 1940, and the Japanese, in Malaya and elsewhere, had made good use of bicycles to speed the advance of infantry.*
(UPI/Bettmann)

3 *The gun of a Cromwell tank traverses Juno beach at St. Aubin, where the North Shore Regiment of Canada landed on D-Day. Under its protection, men begin* the urgent and dangerous task of detecting and clearing the extensive German minefields. Minefields up to 300 yards deep lay just inland; it is estimated that by D-Day more than 4,000,000 mines had been laid along the French Atlantic coast.
(IWM: B 5224)

4

5

blast through the strongpoints, although it was not until six PM that the last Germans gave up. Coming ashore at St Aubin at 8:45 AM, No. 48 Royal Marine Commando with 4th Special Service Brigade headquarters fought its way through to Langrune, but was held up further east by another German pillbox. Although the landing had gone well, the gap through to Sword beach could not be closed.

By 11:40 AM the division's last brigade, 9th Brigade Group, was ashore, with the distant Le Carpiquet as its objective. Although the leading troops from the first landing on Juno were already two or three miles inland, the Canadians suffered the same difficulties which were slowing down the British on either side: a rapidly-narrowing strip of beach and traffic jams in getting vehicles ashore quickly. In the race against time, the sea wall at Bernières and Courseulles became a major obstacle.

In the early afternoon the divisional commander, Major-General Rod Keller, set up his headquarters outside Bernières for a concerted advance through the minefields of the Atlantic Wall. Except for those troops still clearing the village strongpoints near the beach, 7th Brigade Group pressed out to the southwest, linking up with 50th (Northumbrian) Division from Gold beach at Creully, about four miles inland. Both 8th Brigade Group and 9th Brigade Group coming through the center reached about the same distance inland, but increasing German resistance

6

6 *Many of the German strongpoints along the beaches mounted the fast-firing* Maschinengewehr *42 (MG–42)* *light machine gun; shown in cutaway form at (1) on page 114, and seen here on a tripod mount.*

1 *Speeding Sherman tanks kick up a dust storm as they spearhead a Canadian advance into Normandy.*
(UPI/Bettmann)

2 *Temporarily pinned down by sniper fire, Canadians of 8th Brigade Group take cover at St. Aubin, where the defenders have improvised anti-tank obstacles by jamming the streets leading up from the sea front with logs.*
(IWM: B 5228)

3 *Another reason to proceed with caution: Canadian engineers sweep for mines on the road towards Caen.*
(National Archives of Canada)

4 *Anticipating close-quarter action, the Canadian on the left has his bayonet fixed.*
(Keystone)

3

4

to the east nearer Caen brought the Canadian drive to a halt three miles short of Le Carpiquet at dusk. Most of the forward defenders of 716th Static Division near the beaches had fled, and patrols of 1st Hussars (6th Canadian Armored Regiment), just reached across the Bayeux-Caen road, the division's main objective for D-Day, before pulling back for the night.

Expecting a counterattack on the following day, the Canadians dug in at nightfall on a rough line about four miles inland from Juno beach, three miles short of their planned D-Day objectives. The evening attack by 21st Panzer Division into the gap between Sword and Juno prevented the link-up with 3rd British Division, but the line with 50th (Northumbrian) Division was continuous and solid. During the day about 21,400 men had come ashore on Juno beach, to very mixed experiences. There had been some hard fighting, and the division's losses were 340 killed, 574 wounded and forty-seven taken prisoner. But many men, particularly those landing later, had seen more Frenchmen and women than Germans, mostly overjoyed or astonished to find French Canadians among their liberators. It hardly seemed like a war.

5 This German anti-personnel mine could not be detected by electro-magnetic gear.

5

6

7

6 A cigarette against firing pin and detonator shows the scale of the boobytrap at (5). When laid, the lid of its wooden box was held up by a twig. An unwary footfall closed the lid, displacing the firing pin and priming the detonator to set off a half-pound explosive charge.
(Keystone)
7 Canadian jeep ambulance: note the distinctive pattern of the Canadian steel helmet.
(National Archives of Canada)

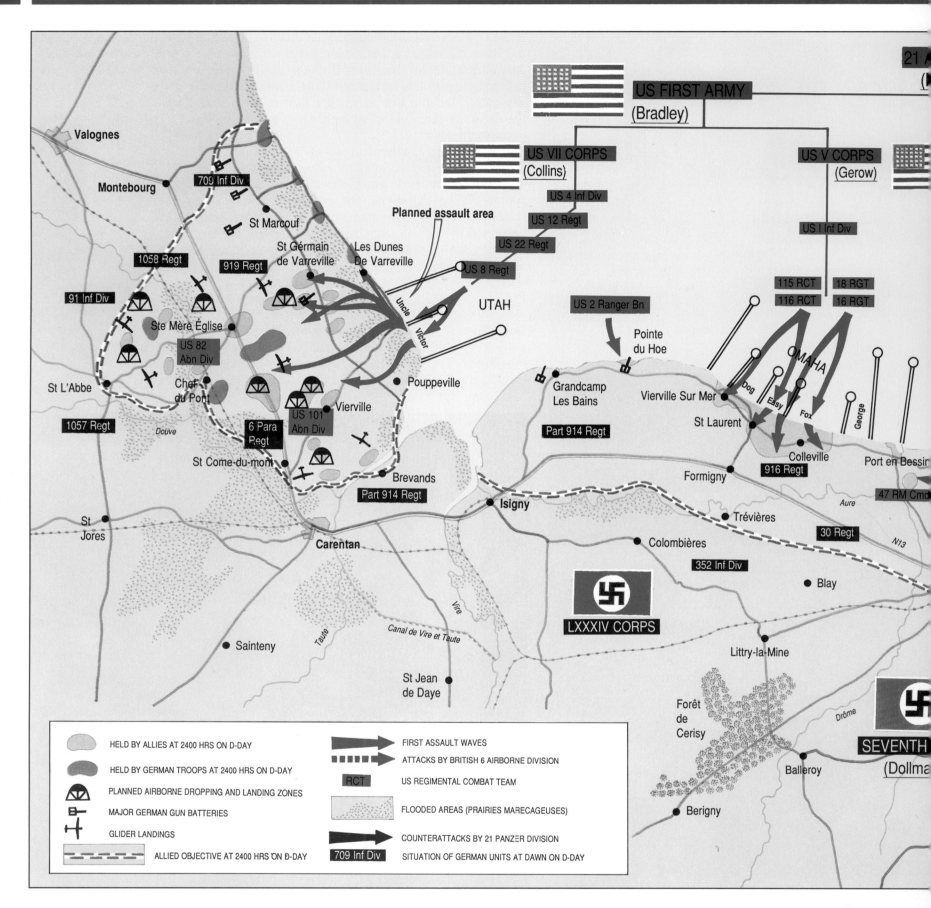

Map legend:

- HELD BY ALLIES AT 2400 HRS ON D-DAY
- HELD BY GERMAN TROOPS AT 2400 HRS ON D-DAY
- PLANNED AIRBORNE DROPPING AND LANDING ZONES
- MAJOR GERMAN GUN BATTERIES
- GLIDER LANDINGS
- ALLIED OBJECTIVE AT 2400 HRS ON D-DAY
- FIRST ASSAULT WAVES
- ATTACKS BY BRITISH 6 AIRBORNE DIVISION
- RCT — US REGIMENTAL COMBAT TEAM
- FLOODED AREAS (PRAIRIES MARECAGEUSES)
- COUNTERATTACKS BY 21 PANZER DIVISION
- 709 Inf Div — SITUATION OF GERMAN UNITS AT DAWN ON D-DAY

1 As the map shows, the Allies' ideal aim on D-Day – a continuous front about 60 miles long and 10 miles deep – was not achieved. The Germans now might push into the gaps between the secured areas and split up the Allied forces.

THE END OF THE DAY

If everything had gone perfectly for the Allies on D-Day, they would have been ten miles inland on a continuous front of nearly sixty miles, from Quineville to the west through to Cabourg in the east, including both Bayeux and Caen. Montgomery's most optimistic pre-landing forecasts included tanks from Gold and Juno reaching Villers-Bocage, seventeen miles inland southwest of Caen, together with armored car patrols from Sword closing on Falaise, thirty miles due south from Sword,

while the American airborne divisions pushed across the Cotentin to St Sauveur le Vicomte, fourteen miles west of Utah. Measured against this ideal position, the D-Day landings had hardly been a success. On none of the five beaches had the troops reached the objectives set for them. The only division to carry out its mission completely was British 6th Airborne, and even then the Merville battery had only been silenced, not destroyed. The greatest and cheapest Allied success had been at Utah, which although useful for widening the lodgement area was also the least important of the beaches in terms of Montgomery's plans. Even at Utah, the line of the Meredet was not

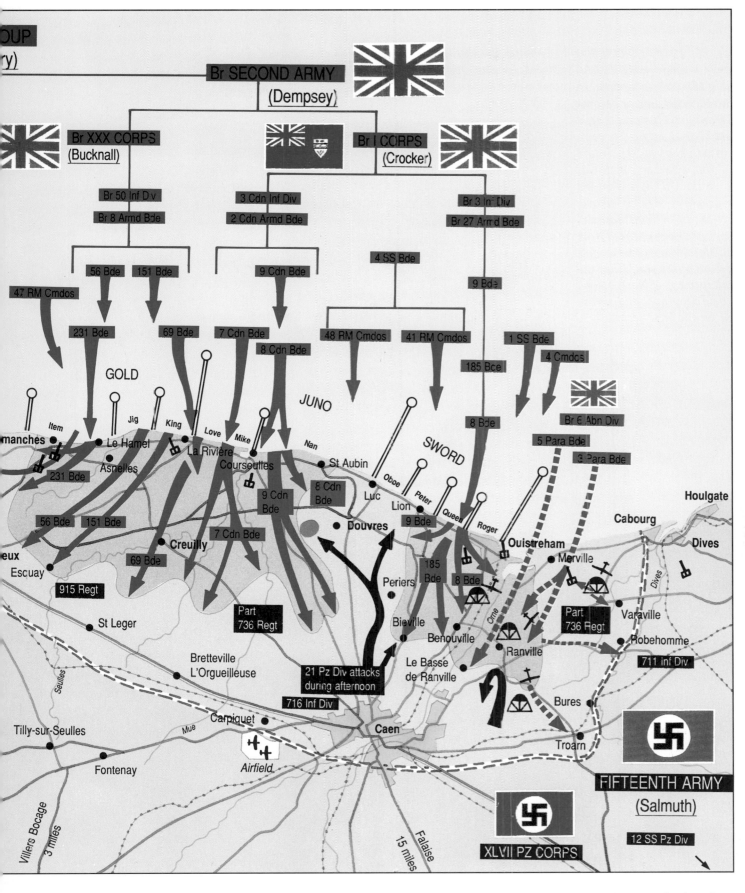

By midnight on June 6, 1944 the Allies had landed some 155,000 men in Normandy (including some 26,000 by air), with more than 1,000 vehicles and guns. They took around 10,000 casualties – the greater proportion on "Bloody Omaha." German losses on D-Day have been estimated at 6,000.

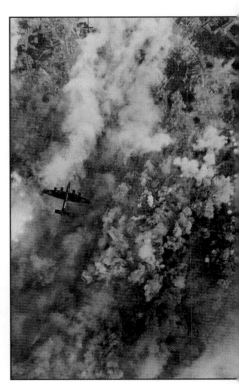

2 On D-Day Allied aircraft flew some 14,000 sorties: reconnaissance, transport, reduction of defenses, and interdiction of deployment. Here, on a later vital mission, a British Lancaster flies over the cauldron of Caen on July 7, when 450 heavy bombers dropped some 2,500 tons of ordnance. The city was devastated; the damage inflicted on its German defenders allowed British and Canadian troops to enter on July 10. The Allies had hoped to take Caen within 24 hours of landing in Normandy, but the area of this key communication center on the road to Paris was not fully secured until the last week in July.
(IWM: CL 347)

secure, and 82nd Airborne was still cut off at Ste Mère-Eglise. The situation at Point de Hoc and Omaha, separated from the other beaches by gaps of between five and ten miles on either side, verged on the critical. In the British sector, with Bayeux still in German hands, Gold beach was threatened from the west, and the failure to take Caen made the airborne lodgement east of the Orne extremely vulnerable. If the Germans could exploit the gaps between the beaches they could reduce the landings to four small pockets unable to support each other.

Against that, the Allies were ashore and completely through the Atlantic Wall in all places except Omaha. The Germans had failed to stop the landing on the beaches, and in trying to do so they had taken heavy casualties. The 709th and 716th Static Divisions had been virtually destroyed and 352nd Division and 21st Panzer Division severely mauled. Although exact casualties cannot be established, the Allies had lost about 10,000 men from all causes, which for the generals came as a relief and was nothing like the bloodbath they had feared. Each individual Allied soldier, sailor and airman had his own perspective on that. But D-Day was over, and the Battle for Normandy had begun.

SPECIAL FEATURE: BATTLEFIELD MEDICAL AID

Between June 6 and September 15, 1944, c.2,000,000 Allied personnel arrived in France – where some 40,000 were killed in this period and c.160,000 wounded. In earlier wars many of the latter would have died or become permanently disabled. In World War I, c.54 per cent of men with chest wounds died; in World War II only 6 per cent. Further, in every major conflict in history up to 1914, more men died of "battlefield diseases" like dysentery, malaria, and typhus than died of wounds: in the US Civil War, the Union armies lost about twice as many men to disease (c.185,000) as were killed in action. US official statistics show that the number of deaths per 1,000 wounded fell from 8.1 in 1917-18 to 4.5 in 1941-45. Major reasons for the fall included the introduction of antibiotics like penicillin; the discovery of plasma and the establishment of blood banks; increased provision of surgical field hospitals; and speedy air evacuation of badly wounded men to base hospitals.

1 Sterile wound dressing packs carried by British Army medical orderlies.
2 US medics put a wounded man aboard a landing craft for evacuation from the beaches.
(US National Archives)

3 Allied personnel evacuated from a combat zone were "tagged" so that their arrival in a rear area could be recorded.

4 Wounded early in the D-Day landings, a GI receives treatment from a US medical corpsman. Working in the front line, medics – most of them enlisted men with only the most basic medical training – were sometimes called upon to perform miracles of "foxhole surgery." Their duties meant that they often had to expose themselves to fire when "fighting" troops could remain under cover: in some campaigns, proportionately more medics were killed in action than "fighting" troops. More than 3,000 US Army medics were killed in action in World War II. (UPI/Bettmann)

5 Stretchers pack the deck of a transport as wounded Allied soldiers are evacuated.
(US National Archives)

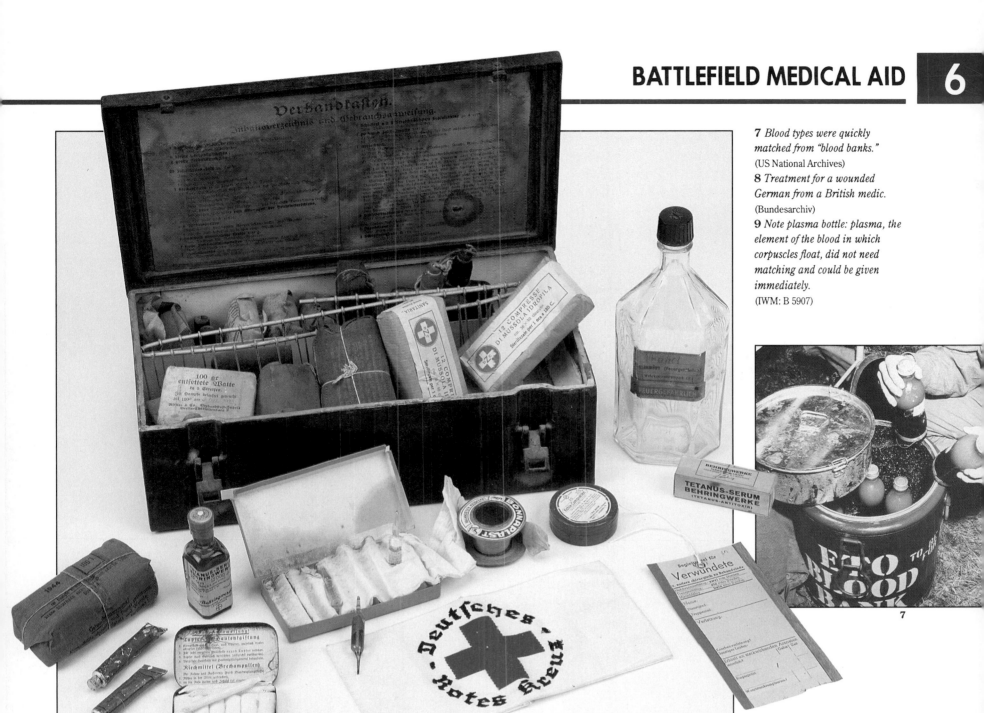

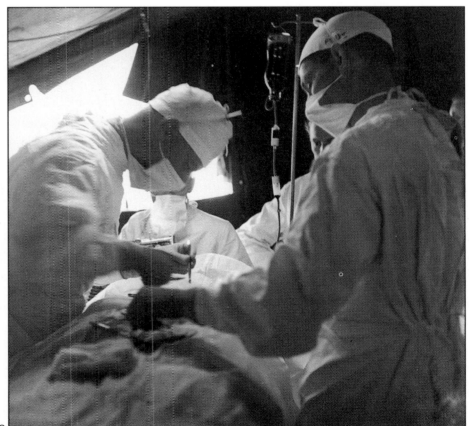

7 *Blood types were quickly matched from "blood banks."* (US National Archives)
8 *Treatment for a wounded German from a British medic.* (Bundesarchiv)
9 *Note plasma bottle: plasma, the element of the blood in which corpuscles float, did not need matching and could be given immediately.* (IWM: B 5907)

6 *Dressings, drug syrettes, and anti-tetanus serum equip a German Red Cross medic.*

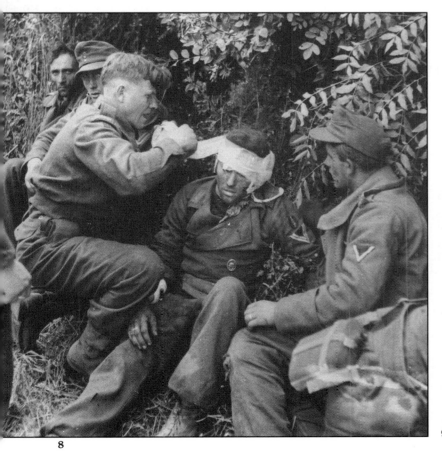

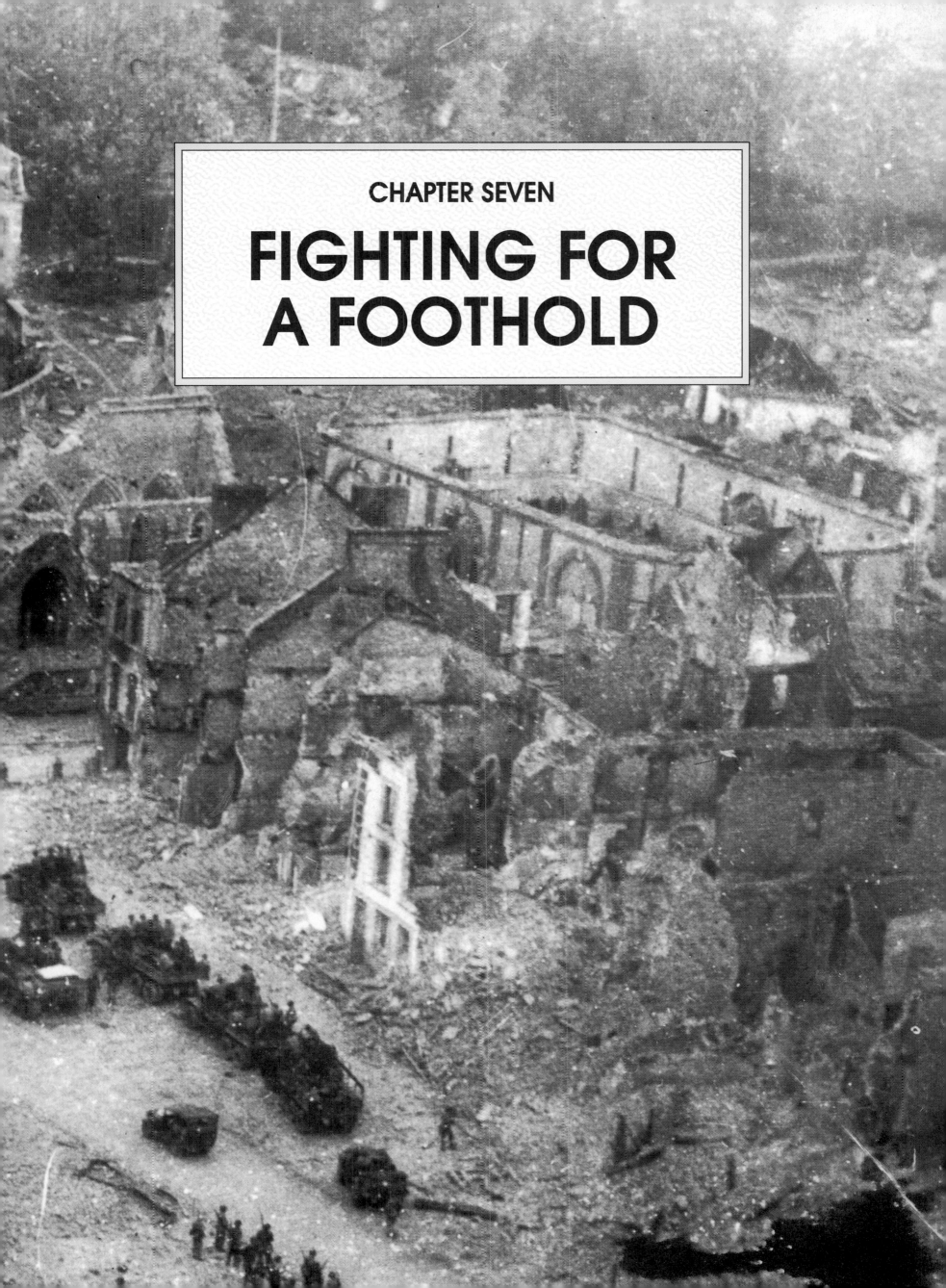

CHAPTER SEVEN
FIGHTING FOR A FOOTHOLD

I t was said by those who fought in Normandy that it had been impossible before D-Day to imagine what the day after would be like. The danger, drama and risks of the landings had taken too much thought and emotion. No-one knew exactly what was going to happen, and whatever the result there was no choice for both sides but to press on from whatever D-Day had to offer. For most of the Allied soldiers ashore and inland it was a surprisingly quiet night which led to the dawn of D+1, broken only by the sound of aircraft and occasional Luftwaffe bombing raid on the beaches. Others experienced local counterattacks, but in most cases both sides seemed briefly stunned by the impact of D-Day itself. There was little time for sleep. The first of the wounded had already been evacuated back to southern England, and the first of the dead had been buried. Tented hospitals and aid posts were set up, patrols pushed out into the darkness, and on the beaches themselves work continued to clear obstacles and land the men, equipment and tons of supplies still coming in from across the Channel.

Early in the morning, Montgomery conferred with Bradley and Dempsey on board their command ships before going ashore to set up his 21st Army Group tactical headquarters. Eisenhower arrived later in the day for a briefing. The immediate priorities, as Montgomery saw them, were to link up the existing beaches, still widely separated, and to keep driving forward to retain the initiative. Typically, Montgomery also had a third priority, to avoid any possible setbacks and to "get the whole organization sorted out and working smoothly." When a risk might have led equally to triumph or disaster, it was Montgomery's style to prefer caution.

Field Marshal Rommel, who had been at home in Germany celebrating his wife's birthday when he learned of the invasion, had arrived back at his own headquarters at La Roche-Guyon (on the River Seine north of Paris) after dark on D-Day. Like the other side, Rommel had at most another day in which to change the verdict of the D-

Previous page: *The price of liberation: a US armored column advances through a shattered town in Normandy.* (Keystone)

1, 2 *From D+1, transports poured supplies onto the beaches while thousands more GIs, seen at (2) disembarking from a US Coast Guard craft, waded ashore.* (UPI/Bettmann; both)
3 *"Charging Boar" insignia of British XXX Corps.*
4 *A British newspaper's montage of Normandy area.*

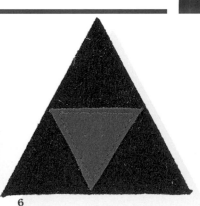

5 *General Omar Bradley, USA.*
(US National Archives)
6 *Insignia of British 3rd Infantry Division.*

Day landings. If the Allies could capture Caen, link up their beaches and stake out enough territory deep in the Normandy countryside before the German defense could coalesce, then Rommel would have little choice but to fall back. On the other hand, major German counterattacks driving between the forces coming ashore from the beaches might still throw the Allies back into the sea. If neither side succeeded in pushing the other back, then Normandy would become a battle of attrition and transport systems, in which the side which could bring the greatest firepower

and numbers into the area would, eventually but surely, overwhelm the other. Neither Rommel nor Montgomery had any doubts as to which side that would be.

On the American beaches and landing zones it was a question of hanging on to what had been gained, and joining together the still fragmented forces, rather than exploiting inland. The 82nd Airborne at Ste Mère-Eglise linked up at last with 4th Division coming off Utah beach in the early hours of June 7. Later in the morning, Ste Mère-Eglise was attacked by a mixed German battlegroup,

7 *An RAF reconnaissance pilot "scrambles" to his Typhoon.*
(Keystone)
8 *Counterattack: 12 SS Panzer Division moves through Caen.*
(Bundesarchiv)
9 *GIs dig in, ready to meet the German counterthrusts.*
(US National Archives)

1 *A sign in Bayeux, secured June 7, points to tough battles ahead, including Villers-Bocage and Caen.*
(IWM: B 3276)

2 *Note metal cowls over exhaust system, part of the "wading" gear of the Sherman tank.*
(US National Archives)

1

2

3 *Tilly-sur-Seulles, southeast of Caen, was devastated by tank battles.*
(IWM: B 5776)

4 *Shermans of British XXX Corps roll into Bayeux.*
(IWM: B 5685)

3

4

scraped together from different formations during the night and led by Seventh Army's reserve Storm Battalion, an elite assault unit. With help from 4th Division's armor, the paratroopers and glider troops repelled the attack, which lasted most of the day. The other main action was against some "German" soldiers caught in a pocket south of Ste Mère-Eglise, who turned out to be a battalion of native Georgians from the Soviet Union and were talked into surrender by a Russian-speaking American. Meanwhile, 29th Division and 1st Division pushed out east and west from Omaha beach, reaching the Vire estuary at Isigny and making contact with the British from Gold beach at Port en Bessin by the morning of June 8. Neither American move was seriously threatened, but the Germans continued to deny them even their original D-Day objectives.

The Germans abandoned Bayeux, the old medieval capital of Normandy, on June 7, and the British 50th Division moving off Gold beach occupied the town almost without incident, one day late. Bayeux fell into Allied hands virtually undamaged, in marked contrast to many other towns and villages of Normandy which were to be almost destroyed in the campaign. Further east, the British airborne troops, like their American counterparts, were fighting against German counterattacks and trying to clear pockets of resistance within their original landing area. The Germans had reoccupied the Merville battery, which came back to life shelling Sword beach and had to be silenced once again. The last German pocket at Bréville was not eliminated until six days after D-Day.

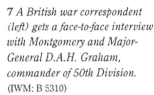

5 British headlines make the inland thrust sound simple.
6 Insignia of a correspondent for Yank magazine, which was written for and by American enlisted soldiers.

7 A British war correspondent (left) gets a face-to-face interview with Montgomery and Major-General D.A.H. Graham, commander of 50th Division. (IWM: B 5310)
8 Staff of the Air Delivery Letter Service, tasked with expressing correspondent's reports. Note "Press" dispatch bags; also at (9). (IWM: CL 197)

Although the British and Canadians joined up their lines between Sword and Juno beaches on June 7, their attempt to push on to Caen ended once more in failure. The 185th Brigade of 3rd British Division, attempting once more to reach Lebisey wood, was thrown back again by 21st Panzer Division. Meanwhile, help had arrived in the night for the Germans, in the shape of the leading elements of 12th SS Panzer Division (Hitler Jugend), under its charismatic deputy commander (and later commander) Colonel Kurt (Panzer) Meyer. Announcing that the British were "little fish" to be thrown back into the sea, Meyer started his attack that morning with the landing beaches as his objective. Although he failed, his armored attack rode over and shattered the Canadian 9th Brigade, itself advancing on Le Carpiquet airfield. This brought British Second Army's whole advance to a halt until more troops could be landed. With the attacks on both sides stalled, Normandy was set after all to become a slogging match.

10 Horsepower and manpower: an improvized rack on this jeep carries both a motorcycle and a pedal bike. (US National Archives)
11 Two-way traffic: supply-laden DUKWs move inland from the beachheads while empty ones return to reload.

WEAPONS FILE: RIFLES AND BAYONETS

The rifle was as important to the infantry in the Second World War as it had been in the first. Technology had changed the weapon very little since 1918, although science had greatly improved the reliability and efficiency of the ammunition. In Normandy, American research discovered that in many regiments, only 15 percent of riflemen actually fired their weapon in action. In the dense hedgerow country, it seemed, what mattered most to the troops in the front line was the ability to saturate the battle area with the weight of your own fire – and automatic weapons were much better suited to that function. As an easy comparison, the German MG42 machine-gun (invariably a "Spandau" to the Allies) could pour out some 1,200 rounds a minute, against the average 16-20 rounds per minute of the American Garand M1 semi-automatic rifle. Little wonder then, with an estimated 63 percent of Allied casualties being riflemen, that for most infantrymen, the desire to take cover until the unseen opposition had been flushed out by heavy fire caused such lengthy delays to the Allied advance.

1, 9, 10, 11 *The classic image of a German rifleman advancing, with a Mauser Kar 98K rifle. The bolt-action Karabiner 98K was the standard-issue German rifle of the Second World War, with some 11.5 million produced between* 1935-45. *The Kar 98K was 7.92mm caliber and the internal box magazine carried five rounds. The tangent-leaf sight was graduated to 2,000 meters and the muzzle velocity was 2,800 feet per second.*

*A selection of the bayonets issued for these rifles: (***7***) US M1 Sword bayonet; (***8***) UK No.4 Spite bayonet; (***10***) German S.84/98 bayonet fitted to the Kar 98K and (***11***) detached.*

4, 5, 9 *Two examples of grenade-launcher adapted from standard rifles: a Lee-Enfield No.4 with a No.36 Mills Grenade Launcher and a Mauser Kar 98K with launcher and an anti-tank grenade fitted. Both had an effective range of around 100 yards.*

2, 3 *A youthful rifleman of the 6th Royal Scots Fusiliers positions himself to fire through a hedge opening near St. Manvieu on 26 June. His rifle is the ubiquitous British Lee-Enfield No.4. Approximately 3.6 million of these were produced between 1940 and 1944 in Britain, Canada and the US. The bolt-action No.4 rifle was .303 caliber and the external, detachable box magazine carried ten rounds. The standard rifle had a leaf sight graduated to 2,000 yards (the effective range) and the muzzle velocity was 2,440 feet per second.*

6 *The Garand M1 semi-automatic rifle was probably the best rifle of the Second World War. Of .30 caliber with an eight-round internal box magazine, it had a gas-operated reloading action, was sighted to 2,000 yards and had a muzzle velocity of 2,740 feet per second. Over 4 million were produced.*

THE BATTLEFIELD

1 *A German soldier takes aim with a Fallschirmjägergewehr 42 (FG-42) 7.92mm assault rifle. Largely a specialist weapon for paratroopers, the FG-42 could fire either single rounds or bursts.* (Bundesarchiv)

The waters, rich pastures and heavy soils of Normandy produce apple and pear orchards, beef and dairy cattle, and of course seafood. The Allied soldiers found themselves in the land of oysters, cider and Calvados (apple brandy) and Camembert cheese. It was good country for farming, but not for fast movement. The Germans had marked the flanks of the battlefield by the deliberate flooding from

the medieval campaigns in Normandy, knowing that the old routes once considered suitable for ox-carts had to mark the easiest going through the region.

The Americans had the worst of the hedgerow country, which from St Lô southward becomes rising ground, leading to what the locals call the "Suisse Normande" between Vire and Falaise. The supposed resemblance is to Alpine valleys and pasture rather than a mountain range, but Mont Pincon, rising to 1,200 feet west of the town of Falaise, is a respectable obstacle for

1

2

2 *Well concealed by luxuriant undergrowth at the edge of a grove, a German 75mm field piece is prepared to engage Allied armor. Note the ready supply of ammunition at foot of tree in foreground.*
(Bundesarchiv)
3 *More low-key than most German propaganda leaflets – even with a trace of dry humor – this message promises the men of the Allied Expeditionary Force "a hot party" the next time they attack … and the next time … and the next.*

which the paratroopers had suffered on the night of D-Day. To the east, the flooding of the Dives worked for the British once they had secured the area in providing a defense against the Germans, but it also made a direct advance eastward difficult. Throughout the battle, the Germans feared and guarded against a second landing just east of Cabourg to extend the British line. On the American flank the flooding along the line of the Douve and its tributaries was far worse, almost cutting across the base of the Cotentin peninsula. For the attacking troops, a green and open water meadow could too easily turn out to be a treacherous swamp.

Just inland from the beaches, the Allied soldiers hit the main farm country of Normandy, which Bradley called the "damndest country I've seen." Cow pastures and orchards ran for miles inland, divided into small irregular green fields by earthbanks, each topped by thickly twined hedgerows. A maze of sunken, overgrown country lanes with steep banks or stone walls led to villages or farmhouses with enclosed courtyards and solid stone walls, built for defense in medieval times. The hedgerow country, known locally as the bocage, was a map-reader's nightmare and a defender's paradise. The main road nets ran (and still run) through six choke points at towns or large villages. Closest to the landing beaches were Bayeux, which became a main objective for planned German counterattacks, Carentan, which lies between Utah and Omaha beaches, and Caen itself. Approximately ten miles further inland is Villers-Bocage, where the road southwest from Caen meets another coming south from Bayeux. The main road runs due west from Villers-Bocage to St Lô, and continues slightly north of west to Lessay on the west coast of the Cotentin peninsula. Patton in particular made a study of

Hello A.E.F.

We know that you must attack us again. Soon!

You know this too.

We know this will be a Hot Party.

You know this too.

We know that this will be just another of a long series of attacks.

You know this too.

We know that after the forthcoming attack again large numbers of tanks and other equipment as well as many brave British soldiers will lie shattered in front of our lines.

You know this too.

We don't know whether you will survive or not.

You don't know either.

A word of advice : You'd better drop a line home right away.

3

4 *Summer foliage in Normandy: these GIs might almost be on New Guinea or Guadalcanal!*
(The Bettmann Archive)
5 *As a "going map" shows, the bocage, with its tangle of narrow lanes, streams, and high hedges, was certainly not tankers' terrain.*

4

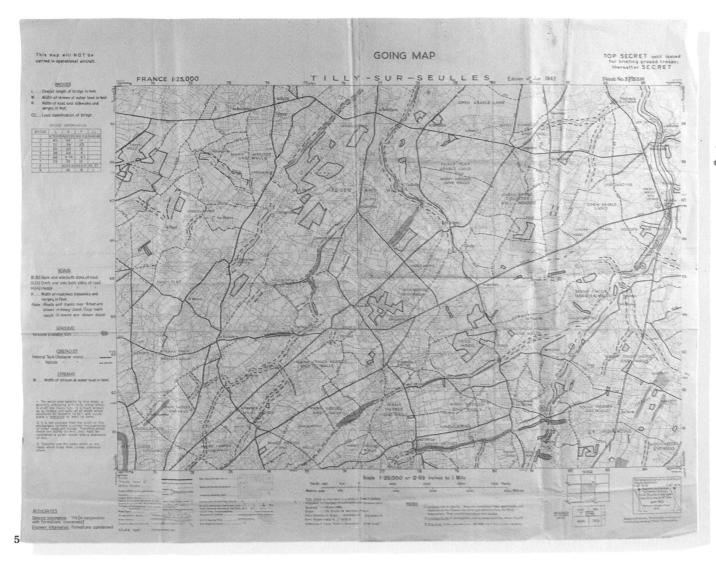

6 *Cap badge of the The Lincolnshire Regiment, an element of the 9th Brigade of 3rd British Division.*

climbers. The word Falaise itself means "cliff," and there are several deep cliffs and gorges in the region. From the swamps of the Cotentin through to the Suisse Normande, the battle was for the Americans a succession of hedgerows, hills, streams and villages, among which the enemy could often move without being seen. Advancing inland, the American soldiers were overlooked either by rising ground or by German observation posts in the characteristic Norman tower or steeple of each village church. In the first weeks of the battle, the costly and bloody experience of fighting in the hedgerows was made doubly frustrating

7 *A US unit commander maps out his next move.*
(US National Archives)

8 *Near Villers-Bocage, June 1944: men of an SS Panzer unit with their well-camouflaged Tiger heavy tank.*
(Bundesarchiv)

BOCAGE TACTICS

The structure of the hedgerow country offered the Germans a natural system of defensive lines like an old First World War trench system, and the tactics that they used to defend Normandy were very similar to those which they had developed in the First World War. A thin line of riflemen and machine-gunners would hold a forward position, falling back to a battle position in which the Germans would try to trap the attackers, bringing in pre-registered artillery, mortar and anti-tank fire from all sides. Tanks and self-propelled or assault guns were often dug-in and used as armored strongpoints, but if possible an armored counterattack would be put in just as the attackers faltered. Particularly at close ranges, the heavier armor and guns of the German tanks made a considerable difference. Very often, it was impossible for the Allies to know where the main position was, and the Germans could hold a front with very few troops since the Allies often assumed that this was the forward position of a much stronger force.

The chief problem for the Allies was finding their way through the hedgerows. Artillery and air support were vital for defeating German strongpoints, and often this could not be coordinated since the troops on the front line could not report their positions accurately. Armor and infantry coordination in this blind country was equally difficult. Tanks, moving down predictable narrow tracks between the earth banks of the hedgerows, offered excellent targets to German gunners or infantrymen with panzerfaust

rockets. In mid-July the American adopted the "Rhinoceros," a set of heavy steel prongs like tusks fitted to the front of a tank. Invented by Sergeant Curtis G. Culin of 2nd Armored Division, this enabled tanks to drive straight through the hedgerows, considerably easing the problem.

For both sides attacking in the hedgerows was a case of planning well, and watching the plan fall to pieces as coordination broke down into a series of firefights. A rate of advance of 2,000 yards a day was considered good going on the Allied side. Overwhelming firepower to blast away the enemy was often the only solution.

1 *A US patrol fights its way through a leafy wall.* (US National Archives)
2 *British infantry face the same conditions.* (IWM: B 5751)
3 *Both need this Sherman "tankdozer" to clear the way.* (Keystone)
4 *British infantrymen ready to fire a PIAT (Projector Infantry Anti-Tank).* (IWM: B 6185)

by the belief that it should not be happening at all, that according to Montgomery's plans the Germans should have already withdrawn further inland.

The British and Canadians faced a rather different problem, that of the city of Caen. Fighting in built-up areas is notoriously difficult and costly, and the outlying villages and Le Carpiquet airfield (which could not be taken for a month, despite several attempts) became major challenges in themselves. The tall towers of the steelworks of Colombelles, northeast of Caen, provided the Germans with excellent observation all the way back to the beaches. To the west and southwest of Caen, the difficult bocage country runs up to the apparently insignificant slope of Hill 112 (metres), from which the whole of the battlefield can be overlooked. To the east of Caen the countryside changes to more open farmland, a smooth and gently sloping plain dotted by little farm villages and crossed in 1944 by two railway lines running east from Caen, but otherwise almost devoid of feature, leading up to

4

5

6

8

5 *The Mauser 98K, standard rifle for German infantry.*
6, 7 *The PIAT anti-tank mortar with its 2.5-pound bomb; an infantry squad weapon effective against armor up to about 115 yards.*

7

Bourguébus ridge behind the city. On the far side of Bourguébus village the ground slopes away again down to Falaise, and the tactical significance of the ridgeline was obvious to both sides.

To the west of Caen, therefore, the British and Canadians faced the same easily defended hedgerows as the Americans. To the east of the city they faced an open killing ground, and head-on they faced a potential blood-bath, for themselves and for the people of the city, in the streets and rubble of Caen. But between Caen, the Dives and the sea, the British were squeezed into a narrow strip of territory which gave them little room to maneuver and barely enough space to land and deploy their troops and equipment. Once the lines solidified, Caen was the key to the battle, the "anvil of victory" as one veteran put it. Instead of a rapid push inland, Montgomery would try to capture Caen, drawing the Germans into an attrition battle while the Americans fought through the hedgerows. Rommel also had seen the obvious significance of the city, and was diverting reinforcements to its defense, still in the hope of launching a counterattack down onto the beaches, only a few miles away.

9

8 *Typhoons hit German installations near Caen: the RAF's Typhoon fighter mounted eight 3-inch rockets in its ground-attack role.*
(IWM: C 4460)
9 *Cap badge of The Queen's Royal Regiment, in hard fighting at Villers-Bocage.*

The Waffen-SS pioneered the use of camouflage clothing, which went into general issue in time for their participation in the German invasion of France in 1940. The first items in use were mottle-patterned smocks with matching helmet covers. They were reversible, with predominantly green colors on one side for spring/summer wear and yellow/ browns on the other side for autumn/winter wear. The German Army favored its own reversible camouflage uniforms, whose "splinter" patterns were quite distinct from those of the SS. The Allies were not as advanced as the Germans in the production of specialized camouflage outfits. The Americans did issue some of their Pacific "blotch" camouflage suits, but quickly recalled them again as their wearers were frequently mistaken for SS troops, and shot at by their own men.

3 Allied air supremacy over Normandy made the concealment of men and machines essential. Here, local foliage has been utilized in the camouflage of a German Flak 38 20mm anti-aircraft piece mounted on an SdKfz 10/4 half-track. The infantry have also made some effort with their hedgerow!

1 The Waffen-SS camouflage smock, with the spring/summer color side showing. SS rank was displayed on the collar – hence the smock itself did not have a collar, but a draw-string fastening. Note also the vertical access slits for pockets.
2 A German Army sniper in his two-piece camouflage suit takes aim from a vantage point overlooking the Allied lines.

1

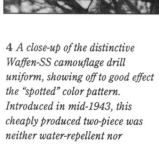

2

3

4 A close-up of the distinctive Waffen-SS camouflage drill uniform, showing off to good effect the "spotted" color pattern. Introduced in mid-1943, this cheaply produced two-piece was neither water-repellent nor reversible and was therefore often worn in conjunction with other items such as the smock (1). Also displayed here are the MP44 automatic assault rifle, two triple magazine pouch sets, gas mask case and helmet with cover.

4

5 A Schütze (Private) of the Hitlerjugend Division, resplendent in camouflage smock and helmet cover, helps to manhandle a howitzer into position outside Caen.

6 The US Army issued a number of troops with these one-piece camouflage tunics for the Normandy Campaign, but they quickly withdrew them because soldiers wearing them were often mistaken for SS men and shot at by their own troops. Other items on display here are the standard issue helmet, cartridge belt, M1 Garand rifle and bayonet, water bottle and entrenching tool.

7 Rudimentary front-line camouflage, demonstrated here by German infantry with grass and straw tied to their helmets and **(8)** a Group leader of the Hitlerjugend Division crawling forward over rough ground.

1 *Cap badge of The Royal Ulster Rifles, who took part in the Caen campaign as part of the 9th Brigade of the British 3rd Division.*

1

2 *The massive turret of a German Tiger VI (Model E) heavy battle tank.*
(Bundesarchiv)

4 *Villers-Bocage: a German communications car and Panzer Mark IV converge on a wrecked British Cromwell Mark IV.*
(Bundesarchiv)

2

3 *With men of his command, 2nd Company of Waffen-SS 101st Heavy Tank Battalion, Lieutenant Michael Wittmann (facing camera, leather coat) confers with his battalion commander, Lieutenant Colonel von Westernhagen (facing camera, camouflage suit).*
(Bundesarchiv)

VILLERS-BOCAGE

For the first few days both sides worked furiously to reinforce the battlefield. Allied airpower delayed and attacked the eight German divisions ordered toward Normandy after the landings, while the Allied navies and armies struggled in vain to keep their own build-up of troops over the Channel and across the beaches on schedule, in the face of setbacks on D-Day and steadily worsening weather. By June 10 the British believed that they held the advantage, with the 7th Armored Division ready to go into action south of Bayeux. Against tough German opposition the Desert Rats made a good start, hooking past the German armor covering Caen to the west and driving south and southeast towards Villers-Bocage. The plan, if everything had worked perfectly, was for a spectacular double-envelopment of Caen, with the equally famous 51st (Highland) Division attacking from the east of Caen and also driving southward, and British 1st Airborne Division, still held in reserve in England, dropping just south of the city to complete the encirclement. In this way, Montgomery hoped to take Caen early, and with few casualties. It depended on 7th Armored holding, and keeping, the road junction at Villers-Bocage and the nearby high ground.

4

3

WITTMANN

Michael Wittmann was the greatest of the tank aces of Nazi Germany, accounting in his career for 138 enemy tanks and assault guns together with 132 anti-tank guns, a record which has never been equalled in warfare. Born in 1914, he joined the German Army in 1934, serving in the infantry. In 1937 he transferred to the Leibstandarte Adolf Hitler, Hitler's SS bodyguard, which grew to become the 1st SS Panzer Division during the Second World War. Wittmann commanded an armored car for the campaigns in Poland and France, and an assault gun for the invasion of Greece and Yugoslavia. Getting his first tank in 1941, Wittmann made his reputation on the Eastern Front against the Russians, earning the Iron Cross during Operation Barbarossa. Notching up kill after kill, he was given one of the first Panzer VIE Tiger tanks to command, and in early 1944 was awarded the Knight's Cross with Oakleaves. In April he transferred to the new Waffen-SS 101st Heavy Tank Battalion in Normandy, again commanding Tigers. For Villers-Bocage he was awarded Swords to go with the Oakleaves on his Knight's Cross, and promoted to captain. He was killed in action along with his crew when surrounded by Canadian tanks fighting south of Caen on August 8, 1944.

5

6

7

7 *Pennant of 7th Armoured Division ("Desert Rats").*
8 *Sign of a hard road for Allied and German tankers!*
(IWM: B 8485)

5 *Panzer "ace" Michael Wittmann: promoted captain after Villers-Bocage, but soon afterwards killed in action near Caen.*
(Bundesarchiv)
6 *A tank commander of 12th SS Panzer Division enjoys the Normandy sunshine in the turret of his Panther.*
(Bundesarchiv)

8

Led by 22nd Armored Brigade, under its brave and eccentric commander Brigadier Robert (Looney) Hinde, the British armored division began its advance on June 12 into the gap between the defenders of Caen and the German troops to the west facing the Americans. In the early hours of June 13 a squadron of the brigade's leading regiment, 4th County of London Yeomanry (Sharpshooters) in their Cromwell tanks, with infantry of 1st Battalion, The Rifle Brigade, in support, stormed into Villers-Bocage almost without opposition. The advance was going well, and it appeared that Caen was set to fall. At this moment, the Sharpshooters and Riflemen had the sheer bad luck to run into a small force of four or five German Tiger tanks (and one Panzer Mark IV) commanded by the most

formidable tank fighter of the Second World War, Lieutenant Michael Wittmann of the Waffen-SS, who held the record for the most enemy tanks destroyed on either side. Wittmann's attack at Villers-Bocage was so swift and so stunning that accounts, even from eye-witnesses, differ as to what exactly occurred. It appears that after driving through Villers-Bocage along the road to Caen the British squadron halted and relaxed to wait for the rest of the brigade. Leaving his other tanks to watch this column, Wittmann took his own Tiger across the fields and around the British tanks, entering Villers-Bocage from the northeast. There he surprised and destroyed the four tanks of the regimental headquarters before anyone quite knew what had happened, pulled back in the face of British return fire, and rejoined the rest of his unit. The British, with their command gone, and possibly thinking Wittmann had been destroyed, took no action until the Tigers suddenly opened fire on them from hiding, knocking out most of the squadron.

While the German tanks withdrew to rearm and refuel, the British worked to recover from this sudden attack. When Wittmann came forward again in the afternoon into the narrow streets of Villers-Bocage his attack fared slightly less well. An anti-tank gun blew a track off Wittmann's own tank, causing the Germans to fall back with another Tiger lost. But in return the British had lost twenty-seven tanks, and with German pressure growing there was little chance of reinforcements getting through. That night the squadron pulled back from Villers-Bocage. Wittmann and his tank crew escaped unharmed.

1 *The bodies of German riflemen lie in a lane in the bocage. Fighting on the defensive, German infantry used the lanes and hedgerows as a "trench system," firing and falling back in the hope of luring attackers into a zone commanded by the fire of pre-registered artillery.*
(US National Archives)

2 *Among the equipment left behind when the Germans pulled out of Villers-Bocage was this 280mm "Kurze Bruno" railroad gun.*
(IWM: B 8752)

Wittmann's action had stalled the whole advance of 7th Armored Division, which could otherwise have driven almost unopposed to the outskirts of Caen. On June 14 the first elements of 2nd (Vienna) Panzer Division arrived to fill in the gap west of the Caen defenses, recapturing Villers-Bocage and threatening the British with being squeezed in a vice from two sides. Dempsey called off the attack, and the Desert Rats pulled back to a more easily defended position. Once more, the line in front of Caen resisted British attempts to find a cheap way forward.

3 *The 25-ton Panzer IV made up about half the strength of panzer divisions in Normandy.*
(Bundesarchiv)
4 *A crew of five was cramped into* the Panzer IV.
(Bundesarchiv)
5 *The British Cromwell tank mounted a 75mm gun.*
(Bundesarchiv)

6 *Villers-Bocage, briefly occupied by British 7th Armoured Division from June 13, was retaken when the division withdrew. This was how the town looked on August 5, when it was secured by British 50th Division. A burned-out Sherman (note 7th Armoured's "Desert Rat" insignia), memorial to the savage tank battles fought here, sits among the ruins.*
(IWM: B 8632)
7 *An aerial view of Villers-Bocage conveys the full extent of its devastation.*
(IWM: CL 193)

The great tank battles of the Normandy campaign may be broadly described as a clash between Allied quantity and German quality. Although the number of tanks involved throughout the campaign cannot accurately be stated, it is safe to say that the Allies normally had an advantage of at least two to one: for example, attacking towards Caen from June 10, Montgomery initially deployed some 1,350 tanks against about 670 German machines. The workhorse of the Allied armored units, accounting for about two-thirds of their total strength, was the American-built M4 Sherman. The Sherman engaged the lighter, but better armored and better gunned, Panzer Mark IV, which accounted for about half the German strength, on roughly equal terms, but, like the British Churchill and Cromwell tanks, was outclassed by the German Panther and Tiger machines. The bocage terrain of Normandy favored defensive tactics, in which the superior guns and protection of the heavier German tanks outweighed Allied tanks' advantages in numbers, speed, and mobility.

1 *A British Churchill (Infantry Tank Mark IV) crosses an embankment. The 40-ton Churchill, normally mounting a 75mm gun, was the most numerous British tank used in Normandy. It was slow (with a maximum road speed of 15 mph), and although heavily armored, with 6-inch frontal plates, proved vulnerable to the high-velocity 75mm gun of the lighter Panzer Mark IV in the short-range actions common in the bocage. It was valuable as a basis for several specialized armored fighting vehicles, for bridging, mine-clearing, armored recovery, flame throwing, and other tasks.* (IWM: B 6122)

3 *Gear worn by a US tanker in Normandy includes one-piece overall and web belt with ammunition pouch and first aid pouch (right) and pistol holster. Note the leather crash helmet, pierced for ventilation, and goggles.*

2 *The US M7 Self-Propelled Howitzer – nicknamed the "Priest" because of the pulpit-shaped tub housing its 0.5in AA machine gun – mounted a 105mm M2 howitzer on an M3 or M4 tank chassis.* (US National Archives)

4 *In the Churchill Mark VII Crocodile, a flame projector replaced the hull-mounted machine gun. The armored trailer contained 400 gallons of flame fuel and five cylinders of compressed nitrogen, used to pump fuel to the projector. It threw a jet of flame to 80-120 yards.* (IWM: B 9682)

5 *The 55-ton Tiger I (Panzer VI) heavy battle tank won a fearsome reputation in Normandy. Its relative lack of mobility and liability to mechanical failure were not great handicaps in the short-range defensive actions it most often fought there – and in such actions its high-velocity 88mm gun proved effective against the armor of all Allied tanks.*
(Bundesarchiv)

6 *Four of its five crewmen take the air as a Tiger I (Model E; VIE) rolls towards Villers-Bocage in June 1944. The Tiger had a maximum road speed of 24 mph. Only about 1,350 of these powerful machines were completed.*
(Bundesarchiv)

7 *Weighing nearly 70 tons, the massive Tiger II ("Royal Tiger" or "King Tiger"), slow and clumsy but hard-hitting with its long, 88mm gun, entered service around the time of D-Day. Only about 485 were built; many served on the Eastern Front.*
(Bundesarchiv)

8 *A German heavy tank lies in ambush. The Normandy bocage was ideal for such tactics: most tank actions there were probably fought at ranges of no more than 120-350 yards.*
(Bundesarchiv)

9 *Both sides used "tank hunters"* or *"tank destroyers": powerful anti-tank guns mounted on tank chassis. This German example comprises a 75mm PaK40 anti-tank gun on the chassis of a French Hotchkiss H-39 tank.*
(IWM: MH 390)

1 The German SdKfz 250 Light Armored Personnel Carrier was made in several variants. Weighing about 12 tons, it could carry four fully-equipped men, as well as its driver and commander.

4 Dashboard of the SdKfz 250 halftrack. It had a maximum road speed of 37 mph.

3 The versatile SdKfz 251. It was also built with a fully-enclosed armored body, for service as an ammunition carrier or artillery observation vehicle.

2 A camouflaged SdKfz 251 Armored Personnel Carrier. Germany used halftracked vehicles in many roles. As an infantry carrier the 20-ton SdKfz 251 could carry up to 10 men, as well as its driver and commander. It was also used as a mobile mount for anti-tank or anti-aircraft guns or rockets; and as a bridging, flame throwing, or engineer vehicle.
(Bundesarchiv)

CARENTAN

Meanwhile, the American priority was to link up the forces from Utah and Omaha beaches by capturing the small town of Carentan at the base of the Vire estuary, held by the tough German 6th Parachute Regiment. The task of capturing Carentan was given to the parachute and glider infantry of 101st Airborne Division, advancing at times in single file over the causeways and footbridges of the Douve and the nearby Carentan Canal. This under-rated small action was one of the most important of the battle, since this was the last place at which the Battle of Normandy could have been decided quickly, and in the Germans' favor. The 17th SS Panzergrenadier Division was on its way to reinforce the town, and if 6th Parachute Regiment could hold Carentan, the Americans in the Cotentin peninsula would be cut off from the rest of the landing force.

Attacking through the hedgerows, the men of the Screaming Eagles came within reach of Carentan by June 10, and on the following night put in a grim attack supported by mortars, artillery, naval gunfire and tank destroyers (American self-propelled assault guns). By the early hours of June 12 the first American paratroopers and glider infantry had forced their way around and into the town, only to find that most of the Germans had withdrawn and set up a new defensive position to the south. While the American airborne troops were

5 *A machine gunner brings up the rear as GIs advance along a country road in Normandy.*
(US National Archives)

6 *"Old Glory" flies in triumph above a memorial to the dead of World War I in Carentan, secured by US forces on June 12-13.*
(UPI/Bettmann)

4

5

6

8

consolidating their position, Allied intelligence, including Ultra signals, told Bradley of a build-up by 17th SS Panzergrenadier and two other German divisions to the south and west, prepared to retake Carentan. The German attack came on the morning of June 13 and drove the paratroopers back to within 500 yards of Carentan, but was unable to break through, while American armor and artillery support rushed to join in the defense. By the evening of June 13 the American line in front of Carentan was secure.

7 *Some of the equipment of a GI of 2nd Infantry Division.*
8 *The German* Nebelwerfer, *a six-barreled rocket launcher, was nicknamed "Screaming Meemie" from the sound made by its missiles.*
(IWM: B 7785)

7

1 *Back to the horse-and-buggy age: folk in the battered towns of Normandy had no fuel – and often no homes.*
(US National Archives)
2 *Later in June storms temporarily grounded aircraft. Here a British Seafire is maneuvered across a waterlogged airstrip.*
(Keystone)
3 *A breakwater of sunken transports shields Normandy shipping during the great storm of June 19-21.*
(UPI/Bettmann)

1

2

3

The main American objectives were now Cherbourg and St Lô, but neither proved an easy task in the hedgerows. By June 17, despite valiant American efforts to push down toward St Lô, the front was showing signs of stalemate. "The tanks kept trying to move forward, but got stuck," complained one battalion commander, "the infantry withdrew and took up defensive positions." They were unable to break through. Less than five miles from St Lô the Americans came to a halt which would last for more than a month.

THE GREAT STORM

In war, bad weather is a test of a good plan. On June 19, as both sides began to look once more for a way to force a decision in Normandy, the already poor summer weather broke into a three-day storm. For the British, chiefly responsible for the sea transport, this was a major event, "the worst storm in living memory," which sank or damaged more ships than the Germans managed to hit in the whole campaign in northwest Europe. The Americans gave it much less attention. Although it wrecked the Mulberry harbor that they were building off Omaha beach, this was already proving unsatisfactory (being poorly built according to the British, or built slowly and with more care according to the Americans), and was abandoned altogether after the storm.

As long as the storm lasted, Allied schedules fell apart as rates of landing were reduced to a third of those planned. Convoys were driven back to their home ports, and small craft were lost out in the Channel. Over 800 craft were beached in Normandy and could not be floated off until the next high spring tide a month later. It says much for the thoroughness of the Allied approach that the impact of the storm did not seriously endanger their position in Normandy, and it is perhaps fair to suggest also that Montgomery's caution had been justified. It is also a reflection on how badly the Germans were losing the build-up battle that they were unable to take advantage of the grounding of Allied aircraft in Normandy and southern England to launch a counterattack. After the battering of the "Great Storm," both sides were in a position only to pause and take stock.

CHERBOURG

As the storm had underlined, supplies and transport were becoming the key elements in the Normandy battle, and the Allies badly needed a major port. This need produced the last fast-moving action of the battle for some weeks, the drive across the Cotentin by US VII Corps, commanded by the peppery, adventurous, Lieutenant-General Lawton J. Collins. On June 14 "Lightning Joe" Collins attacked westward through the already stunned German defenders, reaching the coast at Barneville on June 17 and cutting off three German divisions to the north. The marshes and flooding of the Cotentin now acted as a prison for the escaping Germans. Switching northward within a day, Collins opened his assault on the outer defences of Cherbourg on June 22. This was the sensible way to take a sea fortress, from the landward side, supported by an air and naval bombardment. Even so, with apparently nothing to fight for, the defenders still put up a hard contest, and two Medals of Honor were won that day by Corporal John

4 *A civilian in Cherbourg sports the American flag. The vital port was taken by US VII Corps at the end of June.* (Keystone)
5 *Support from the sea: the British cruiser Glasgow lobs 6-inch shells into Cherbourg.*
6 *En route to Cherbourg, an M7 "Priest" rolls down the remains of a village street on the Cotentin peninsula.* (US National Archives)

1 *Field jackets: (top) staff sergeant, US 1st Infantry Division; (bottom) sergeant, VII Corps, US 1st Army.*
2 *A German soldier sets a demolition charge. Cherbourg was thoroughly sabotaged.*
(Keystone)
3 *Royal Navy divers begin mine clearance at Cherbourg.*
(US National Archives)
4 *The Cherbourg garrison surrendered on June 26-27.*
(US National Archives)
5 *GIs with a "liberated" German communications car.*
(US National Archives)

"Commando" Kelly and Lieutenant Carlos Ogden. Despite repeated orders from Hitler that no ground must be given up, and that Cherbourg must hold to the last man, the commanding officer, Lieutenant-General Karl-Wilhelm von Schlieben, surrendered on June 26 together with most of his force. As von Schlieben himself mournfully observed, "You can't expect Russians and Poles to fight for Germany against Americans in France." Von Schlieben refused, however, to order a general surrender, and it was not until July 1 that all resistance in the peninsula ceased. Bradley, who had mildly entertained thoughts of inviting von Schlieben to dinner in the manner of commanders of an earlier era, dropped all ideas of chivalry on hearing of this.

The capture of Cherbourg, although a considerable feat of arms which removed the last real threat to the Allied position in Normandy, didn't provide the benefit that had been expected. The port had been so thoroughly sabotaged by the Germans that it was virtually useless for the next month. "A masterful job," reported the American engineer who rebuilt the port, "beyond a doubt the most complete, intensive and best-planned demolition in history." Meanwhile, the Mulberry and the beaches remained the only supply link for the Allied forces.

6 *German troops surrender.*
(Keystone)
7, 9 *Jubilant civilians help tear down the sign of the Todt Organization, which used slave labor for military construction work … and Allied flags take its place.*
(US National Archives)
8 *Lieutenant-General Karl-Wilhelm von Schlieben surrenders at Cherbourg.*
(Planet News)
10 *Insignia of US VII Corps.*

1 *One of Hitler's "foreign legionnaires," a member of a Turkmen volunteer unit from Eastern Europe, is questioned by an officer of British 51st (Highland) Infantry Division.*
(IWM: B 6267)

PLANS AND ACHIEVEMENTS

There is an old military saying that no battle plan survives contact with the enemy. Before the invasion, the planning staff at 21st Army Group had drawn up a set of "phase lines" as a general guide to the territory that they expected to liberate at each phase of the battle. These were professional planning estimates rather than a fixed time-table, but they did show reasonable expectations for the battle. If everything had been on schedule, by D+25 the Allied armies would have reached a line beyond the whole of the Normandy peninsula, as far south as St Malo, Rennes and Alencon in the heart of France. Instead, they were pinned within a few miles of their original landing beaches by enemy forces which were growing increasingly stronger, and with no immediate prospect of breaking out. To the east, the D-Day objective of Caen remained firmly in enemy hands. In the center, the attacks on both Villers-Bocage and St Lô had been stopped dead. To the west Cherbourg had turned out to be useless. It took considerable optimism, or considerable vision, to believe that Montgomery was winning his battle. His armies were

2, 3 *By rail to battle: German tankers in summer dress relax as their camouflaged Panthers are freighted to Normandy. A vital task of Allied tactical air forces was to disrupt the railroad system.*
(Bundesarchiv)
4 *RAF reconnaissance pilots are debriefed in Normandy.*
(Fox Photos)

5 *Pilots of P-47 Thunderbolt ground attack aircraft grab a quick breakfast.*
(Keystone)
6 *Armored reinforcement for the Allies; July 1944. These Shermans would equip the French 2nd Armored Division.*
(IWM: EA 32615)

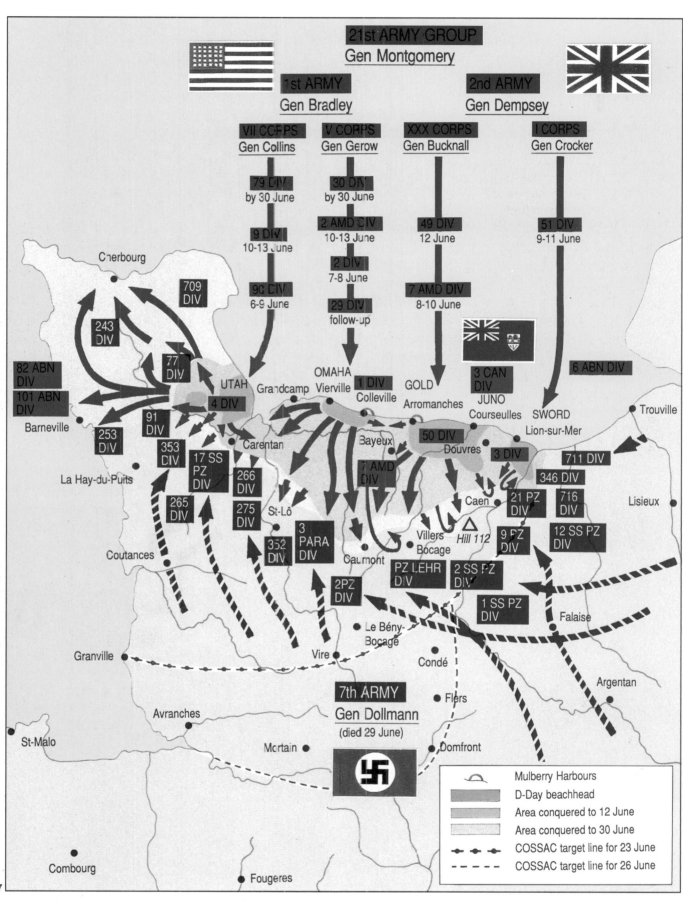

7 *As the map shows, the goals set by Allied planners before D-Day could not be attained. Nevertheless, by late June the Allies had established a continuous, defensible lodgement area from which to strike at the German line.*

firmly ashore, linked up into a continuous defensible lodgement area, and only something close to a German miracle could have now driven them into the sea. He was winning the build-up battle by a considerable margin, as his supplies and troops resumed their flow after the interruption of the great storm, while the Germans found it increasingly difficult to move either reinforcements or supplies to Normandy against Allied air power. Meanwhile, the attrition battle which was developing was doing far more damage to the Germans than it was to the Allies, costing them the equivalent of 2,000 casualties a day more than the replacements they were receiving just to hold their positions. The bulk of the German armor was being pulled in to defend Caen, leaving the Americans in the bad hedgerow country with a slightly easier task than they might otherwise have had. The new month would provide fresh opportunities to strain the German line until it broke. All this was clear to the Germans, but on the Allied side Montgomery's cheerful faith in himself infuriated his critics. Bradley was one of many who feared that the front would never be broken, and that the Allies would still be in the same positions when winter came.

CHAPTER EIGHT

A PLACE CALLED CAEN

1 *Men of a German armored unit, one in Feldmütze side cap, the other, mounted in a halftrack, in steel helmet, consult their maps.*
(Bundesarchiv)
2 *On the defensive: a German machine gunner peers into a caldron of fire.*
(Bundesarchiv)
3 *A 155mm howitzer of the Royal Artillery puts down fire on a concentration of German forces near Tilly-sur-Seulles, west of Caen.*

1

2

3

4 *Lieutenant-General Miles Dempsey took command of British 2nd Army in January 1944. His stalwart work in Normandy won him a knighthood later in that year.*
(IWM: EA 38785)

the last German snipers, many of whom refused to surrender, or were not given the chance. Some of the Hitler Jugend threw themselves on top of British tanks with explosives strapped to their bodies, or held sticky bombs against the sides until they went off. After two more days, by the morning of June 29, the British armor was holding the north slopes of Hill 112 in the torrential rain, with the Germans still clinging to the southern slopes, and both sides bringing down artillery and mortar fire onto the hill. At one point British and German positions were only five yards from each other.

The Epsom offensive was now running out of steam as the Germans began to concentrate newly arrived formations against it. What finally swung the balance in the Germans' favor was the appearance on June 29 of II SS Panzer Corps, two armored divisions which had been traveling by rail and road from the Eastern Front since June 12, and were thrust into the battle without preparation. Despite British attacks, the crucial Rauray spur had remained in German hands, giving the two Waffen-SS divisions space to deploy against the Epsom salient for an attack along a "Panzer run" or rising slope from Villers-Bocage through to Rauray. Advance warning by Ultra gave Allied artillery and airpower a chance to stop the Germans, and on June 30 the heavy bombers of RAF Bomber Command, flying over Normandy in daylight for the first time, unloaded 1,100 tons of bombs onto Villers-Bocage. The Waffen-SS attack was met the following day by more artillery and airpower, and a solid infantry and tank defense. Although the panzers were stopped, Dempsey ordered O'Connor to pull back from Hill 112 and secure the line of the Odon. It had taken troops from five German armored divisions, four of them Waffen-SS, to bring Epsom to a halt. But it was clear that, at least for the moment, there was no way through to Caen from the west.

on top of rifles driven bayonet-first into the earth, each marking a place where a man had fallen.

The night passed in small firefights and sniping, and in the hasty reissue of orders. At dawn on June 27 a sharp Scottish attack secured a bridgehead over the Odon, and the tanks of 11th Armored Division pushed forward against infantry and engineers of the 12th SS Panzer Division. The infantry fought to secure the ground gained and clear

DEMPSEY

Miles Christopher Dempsey was born on December 15, 1896, and was educated at Shrewsbury school and Sandhurst. Commissioned into the Royal Berkshire Regiment, he served from 1916 on the Western Front in the First World War, winning the Military Cross and being slightly gassed in 1918. Recovering, he saw active service with his battalion in Iraq 1919-1920. After an orthodox regimental career (in which he acquired the nickname "Bimbo," which he would never explain) Dempsey rose to command 1st Battalion The Royal Berkshires by 1939. He first distinguished himself in the Second World War commanding 13th Infantry Brigade in the engagement at Arras in May, 1940. Marked as an able soldier, he served in Britain as Chief of Staff to the Canadian Corps, then as commander of 46th Infantry Division, followed by 42nd Armored Division (which never saw action). In December, 1942, he was appointed as the new commander of XIII Corps in Montgomery's Eighth Army, commanding the corps in Sicily and Italy.

Becoming established as Montgomery's leading subordinate, Dempsey was always overshadowed by his flamboyant commander, but achieved a high reputation of his own within the British Army. In January, 1944, he was appointed to command Second Army for the campaign in northwest Europe, advancing from lieutenant-colonel to lieutenant-general in four years. He was knighted in July, 1944. After the end of the war in Europe, he held in rapid succession the commands of Fourteenth Army in the Far East, Commander Land Forces South-East Asia, and Commander-in-Chief Middle East. In 1946, just after being promoted to full general, he retired voluntarily from the Army. He spent the years 1947-1951 with the Racecourse Betting Control Board before retiring once more, dying on June 5, 1969.

5 *German veterans calmly await the Allied onslaught.*
(Bundesarchiv)
6 *Waiting for a possible counterattack: a British Churchill tank takes cover among ruins near Hill 112.*
(IWM: B 8051)
7 *German mortar teams have found the range of Allied armored and soft-skinned vehicles deployed in the Epsom offensive and destroy an ammunition truck with a direct hit.*
(IWM: B 6017)

5

6

7

4

HEAVY BOMBERS

The heavy bombers of the Allied Air Forces in Operation Overlord were the Lancasters and Halifaxes of Bomber Command of the Royal Air Force, and the B-17 Flying Fortresses and B-24 Liberators of the United States Army Air Force's 8th Air Force. The official statistics quote the number of heavy bombers available to the RAF as 1,470 and to the USAAF, 1,970 – a total of 3,440 aircraft. While these forces remained under the control of their respective Commanders – Air Chief Marshal Sir Arthur Harris and Lieutenant General James H. Doolittle – the overall direction of air operations out of England passed to the Supreme Commander.

These forces had been engaged in Operation Pointblank activities for some months before D-Day, (see "Air Power", page 38) during which time they had flown 62,524 sorties and delivered 160,000 tons of bombs. Generally speaking, the RAF's operations had been carried out at night; those of the USAAF during the hours of daylight.

On the night of June 5/6, 1,015 heavy bombers of the RAF attacked ten heavy calibre long range coastal batteries in the invasion area. The aircraft were divided more or less equally among the targets, and about 500 tons of bombs fell on each. There were no reports from the invasion forces that any of the batteries were able to open effective fire during the assault, or for some hours after it.

At the same time, in the Pas de Calais area to the north east, other heavy bomber squadrons were carrying out sophisticated diversionary operations to suggest to the enemy that the invasion was about to take place in that area.

Between first light and H-Hour 1,361 heavies of the 8th Air Force attacked the defenses of three of the four landing beaches. (The fourth was attacked by medium bombers of the Ninth Air Force).

Further day bomber operations on D-Day were intended to block roads at key centers in the Normandy area in order to inhibit enemy troop movements. However, these operations were seriously hampered by the unexpectedly dense overcast in the target areas. The blind-bombing techniques were not sufficiently accurate for such pinpoint targets to be attacked effectively.

Plans for the use of heavy bombers after D-Day included the concept of saturation bombing of tactical targets, such as troop concentrations, immediately in front of the ground forces. The first major operation of this kind was on the evening of July 7 in conjunction with Operation Charnwood, the British assault on Caen. As dusk approached, 450 bombers with a strong fighter escort, passed over the British front line to unload over 2,000 tons of bombs on the defenses. This had a great effect on the morale of the Allied ground forces, but there is little evidence to suggest that the raid had any significant influence on the attack. So great was the fear of "friendly fire" casualties that the bombing line had been fixed 6,000 yards ahead of the British front line, and its main impact therefore had been well behind the enemy's strongly defended forward area.

It was never proved that the heavy bombers could operate effectively against tactical targets, and their main value in the progress of Overlord continued to be against the kind of targets they had attacked during Pointblank operations.

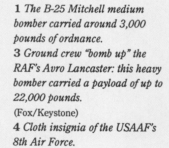

2

2 A Canadian pilot serving with the Royal Air Force.
(Keystone)
5 A B-17 Flying Fortress heavy bomber of 8th Air Force hits a tactical target.
(UPI/Bettmann)

1 The B-25 Mitchell medium bomber carried around 3,000 pounds of ordnance.
3 Ground crew "bomb up" the RAF's Avro Lancaster: this heavy bomber carried a payload of up to 22,000 pounds.
(Fox/Keystone)
4 Cloth insignia of the USAAF's 8th Air Force.

3

1

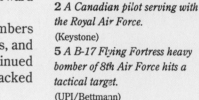

4

6 Field jacket, leather crew jacket (bearing the sobriquet of his plane), flying helmet, and other gear of a USAAF staff sergeant.
7 B-17G Flying Fortresses in formation over Britain, where some 2,000 USAAF heavies were operational in mid-1944.
(US Air Force)

8 *Insignia of the USAAF's 9th Air Force, UK-based tactical striking force in 1944-45.*

Napoleon Bonaparte opined that: "In warfare, morale is to material as three is to one." Allied leaders in World War II recognized the importance of keeping fighting men in good heart. Outside the front line, servicemen in the European Theater of Operations generally fared better than civilians in terms of availability of "luxury" foods (like red meat, eggs, fruit, and candy), cigarettes, and liquor – all strictly rationed, if available at all, in Europe; often in short supply even in the USA. (GIs in Britain were thought to be so well provisioned that "Limey" troops complained the "Yanks" were: "Overpaid, overfed, oversexed – and over here!") The United Service Organizations (USO) set up clubs for US servicemen worldwide and sent top entertainers to give shows even in combat zones; the Navy, Army and Air Force Institute (NAAFI) and Entertainments National Service Association (ENSA) did the same for British and Commonwealth troops.

1 *This linen roll of a type first issued in World War I made a handy carrier for some of a soldier's most essential gear: "eating irons," hair brush – and shaving tackle …*
4 *… which is put to good use by a GI in the field.*
(US National Archives)

2 *Sheet music for British popular songs of the period. "When they sound the last All Clear" (i.e. the siren at the end of the last air raid) was sung by Vera Lynn, hailed as the "Forces' Sweetheart."*
5 *The "liberated" piano may be a few keys short of a concerto – but the GIs still sing up a storm.*
(US National Archives)

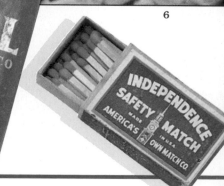

3, 7, 9 *Forgotten brands that once brought comfort. In the World War II period smokers were in a majority, and an ample supply of cigarettes and pipe tobacco was essential to servicemen and women.*
6 *British servicemen – like these*

crewmen of a Royal Navy landing ship, briefly resting ashore at Normandy – called cigarettes "fags," "snout," or "weed" – and were glad of the chance for "a quick drag."
(US National Archives)

8

9

8 *Gambling was another way to relax. An amateur but well-organized bookmaker takes comrades' bets on The Derby, Britain's premier horse race.* (IWM: B 5667)

10 *A groundsheet, a jerrycan of water, and the shelter of a tank – all a British soldier needs for bathtime luxury.* (IWM: B 6152)

11 *With a few exceptions – such as pioneer sergeants of British infantry regiments – regulations required soldiers to be clean shaven!*

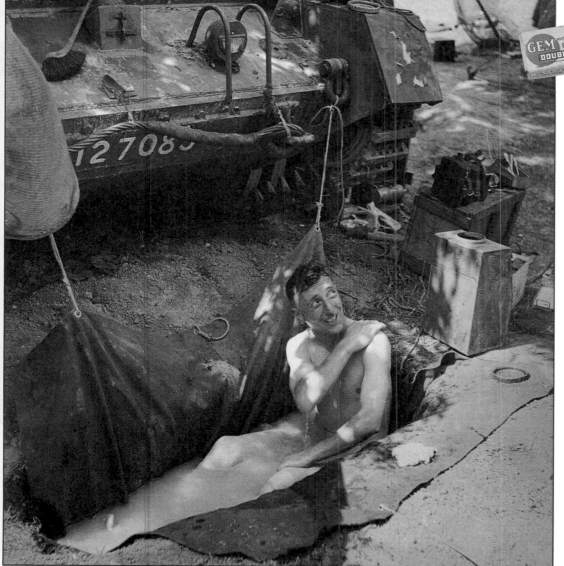

10

11

1 *Cloth formation sign of British 50th (Northumbrian) Infantry Division.*
2 *A British 4.5-inch Gun Mark 2 adds its weight to the massive pre-dawn bombardment on July 8, immediately before the Charnwood attack on Caen.*

from 79th Armored Division and by massed artillery and air support, took on the Hitler Jugend Division (now commanded by "Panzer" Meyer) defending Le Carpiquet and western Caen. Despite the great weight of fire power used, the Canadians were able to secure only Le Carpiquet village and the northern part of the airfield, while taking over 350 casualties during the day. Nearly a third of these came from one battalion, the Royal Winnipeg Rifles, which ended the day back on its starting line in the face of German fire.

For the Allies to break through the German defenses needed the same kind of firepower that had been used for the original D-Day landings, and that meant artillery and bomber support on a massive scale. In order to take Caen itself while holding down Allied casualties, Montgomery (with some prompting from Eisenhower) requested the heavy bombers of RAF Bomber Command to attack the northern part of the city. British I Corps under Lieutenant-General John Crocker, including Canadian 3rd Division, would then attack through the rubble. Although nearly 500 bombers were involved, dropping 2,500 tons of bombs, the resulting plan was confused and worked almost in spite of itself. For safety, the target area for the bombers was set 6,000 yards ahead of the British and Canadian positions, so actually missing the outlying German village strongpoints while falling on French houses. The bombing took place on the evening of July 7, rather than immediately before the ground assault the next day. The greatest contribution of the bombers was the tremendous boost for the attacking troops of watching the bombers. It had, according to one Canadian battalion, "improved their morale 500 percent." As on D-Day itself, that was perhaps the most important thing.

The British and Canadians launched their attack, codenamed Operation Charnwood, at dawn on July 8 with their now standard artillery bombardment, followed by what the Canadians described as "a day of fierce and bloody fighting." It took, in fact, until the following morning for the Allied troops to drive the Germans out of northern Caen, as far as the River Orne which flows through the city. In the process Canadian 3rd Division took more casualties than it had suffered on D-Day. The southern and eastern part of Caen, including the Colombelles steelworks, remained in German hands. Fortunately, since June 12 the Resistance in Caen had been in contact with Allied high command, and had agreed upon refuges in the center of the city which Allied bombing and shelling did not touch. Even so, at least 500 French men and women had died in the fighting, and many more since June 6. On liberation, as one survivor put it, "the joy is great, and yet restrained." As often in Normandy, French-speaking Canadians received an especially warm welcome.

3 Standartenführer (Colonel), later Gruppenführer (Major-General) Kurt "Panzer" Meyer (right) is seen with Fritz Witt (left), then commanding 12th SS Panzer Division. (Bundesarchiv)

4 French civilians retreated underground as Allied bombers and artillery hammered Caen. (IWM: B 7457)
5 A Volkswagen staff car stands at the gate of Hitler Jugend Division's pre-D-Day headquarters near Paris. (Bundesarchiv)
6 Among the defenders of Caen were men of the 16th Luftwaffe Field Division, seen here amid the wreckage caused by Allied bombardment. (Bundesarchiv)

7 Aerial view of Caen shows the extent of devastation.
8 Fritz Witt, seen here as a Standartenführer (Colonel), wearing the Knight's Cross with Oakleaves at his throat, commanded Waffen-SS Hitler Jugend Division until killed by naval shellfire at his headquarters on June 16. (IWM: MH 6106)

1 *A British patrol sweeps Caen for German hold-outs on July 9. Although Operation Charnwood resulted in the city's occupation by British and Canadian troops on July 8-9, strong German forces remained in its southern and eastern environs.*
(IWM: B 6686)

2 *Retreating through Caen, a German infantryman aims his* Maschinenpistole MP-40 *(Schmeisser). The sub-machine gun was an ideal street-fighting weapon, and the Schmeisser was one of the best of its kind: Allied soldiers sometimes discarded their own SMGs in favor of captured MP-40s.*
(Bundesarchiv)

German armor pinned down on the eastern side of the bridgehead. Dempsey's proposal for the offensive tried to solve several problems at once. The British were still being kept desperately short of space by being pinned north of Caen, and needed to break through further to the south. At the same time, the hedgerow fighting had taken a heavy toll of Dempsey's infantry, but left his three British armored divisions fairly unscathed. Dempsey's plan, codenamed Operation Goodwood, was for an armored drive across the open, rolling country east of Caen, up onto Bourguébus ridge and beyond, using the armored divisions grouped together into a single corps, once more VIII Corps under O'Connor. Instead of infantry making the break through the front line for the British armor, the heavy bombers would be used to repeat the same tactic used for Charnwood by destroying the German front-line troops from the air in a saturation bombardment.

Talk of this major offensive to finally break out past Caen drew great enthusiasm from Eisenhower and the SHAEF staff, who were happy to arrange for the heavy bombers of Bomber Command to be used once more. Montgomery, however, was less enthusiastic and toned down the aims of Demsey's plan, limiting the offensive to

into the air like leaves, and overturned by the force of the bombs to land upside down. As 11th Armored Division led the drive forward, the first Germans came out of their foxholes to surrender, in no state to resist. But the further the attack pushed forward, the more the tanks became separated from the infantry, who were pinned down in small firefights to clear the little farm villages which

1

2

4 *Although cooperation between the Allies and French Resistance resulted in the creation of "refuge" zones for civilians during the fighting, several hundred civilians died in Caen. One British soldier aids a senior citizen amid the ruins …*
(IWM: B 6794)

7 *… and another gives a lift to a young survivor.*

clearing Caen and "writing down" the German armor. Even Montgomery, however, expected to capture Bourguébus ridge and get his armored cars out beyond the ridge towards Falaise. Montgomery's caution, and confusion at high and low levels over what Goodwood was supposed to achieve, combined to produce another British disappointment.

At exactly 5:30 AM on July 18 the waiting soldiers of VIII Corps watched as the leading bombers dropped their cascades of flares over the German positions. In the next 45 minutes, more than 1,000 Allied heavy bombers dropped 5,650 tons of bombs onto the German positions. This was followed by a further two hours of bombing and shelling, leaving the German defenders in the front line dead, wounded or stunned by the blast. Tiger tanks were blown

3 *An old-time hand grenade forms the badge of Britain's Grenadier Guards.*

3

4

BRITISH SPLIT CAEN LINE

Reds Cross Bug River, Roll Toward Lwow, Brest Litovsk

DAILY NEWS

Vol. 26. No. 21 — New York, Wednesday, July 19, 1944 — FINAL

5 *New York headline somewhat overstates the success of Operation Goodwood.*
6 *Allies join hands: leaders of the French Resistance in Caen welcome British troops to the city on July 9.*

6

7

8

8 *Ancient battle honors figure on the badge of The Rifle Brigade (Prince Consort's Own).*

1 *The Germans left Caen heavily mined. As these British tankers show, a comparatively safe way of clearing mines was the device known as the "Scorpion" or "Crab." When the drum at the front of the tank is rotated, the flailing chains will detonate mines in its path.*

dotted the slope. Meanwhile, in the rear, a massive dust-choked traffic jam was developing as armored divisions tried to reach the front line from the far side of the River Orne. The last of the divisions, 7th Armored, would spend the entire day in this traffic jam without reaching within shooting distance of the enemy. At the same time, the unsupported tanks of 11th Armored were running into harder opposition as they were ambushed by German tanks, assault guns or anti-tank guns concealed in the villages. "I saw Sherman after Sherman go up in flames," remembered a tank commander with the 3rd Royal Tank Regiment, leading the attack, "and it reached such a pitch that I thought that in another few minutes there would be nothing left of the regiment." Virtually unsupported, the tanks were forced to halt. The Guards Armored Division

3 *Badge of the US XIX Corps.*
4 *An SS Obersturmführer (Lieutenant) with his arm in a sling gets a lift on a motorcycle combination driven by a wounded wearer of the Knight's Cross.* (Bundesarchiv)
5 *Hugging the ground so as not to draw sniper or artillery fire, GIs of US XIX Corps cautiously enter St. Lô on July 18.* (Keystone)

2 *The "Indianhead" patch of US 2nd Infantry Division dated from World War I.*

coming up behind had an equally unpleasant experience, coming under fire from 88mm anti-tank guns from the village of Cagny to their front, thought to be clear of Germans, while Tiger tanks threatened them from behind. One Sherman, commanded by Lieutenant J.R. Gorman of 2nd Irish Guards, surprised a Tiger at only 200 yards range. Gorman's first shot bounced off the Tiger's armor, and on the second his gun jammed. Gorman promptly ordered his driver to ram the Tiger, and both crews jumped clear.

Meanwhile, 3rd British Division was attacking to the east of VIII Corps, while to the west Canadian 2nd Division joined Canadian 3rd Division in finally clearing Caen, including the Colombelles steel works. The Canadians picked up the last German radio transmission from Colombelles, "Battalion headquarters surrounded. Long live the Führer!" But despite the high hopes and promises of Goodwood, clearing Caen was almost all that it achieved. After another day's hard fighting the British secured Bourguébus village and the main slope of the ridge, an advance of barely seven miles at the cost of over 400 tanks and 5,000 men. Montgomery could take some comfort from the fact that the Germans had pushed two Waffen-SS panzer divisions back into the line to stop his attack.

THE AMERICANS AT SAINT LO

Only one major obstacle now prevented an Allied advance, the town of St Lô. Its capture was another small battle which afterward became lost in the larger story of Normandy, but which helped turn the fight the Allies' way. St Lô had already suffered heavily, having been bombed by the Allies from D-Day onward, to turn it from a road junction into a road block for the Germans, and in the expectation that it would be in American hands by D+10. A crucial ridge leading to the high ground of Hill 192, about three miles to the northeast, dominated the

6 *A pall of smoke rolls over German-occupied St. Lô. This photograph must have been taken well before the final American assault on July 17-18 – which would surely have driven the many civilians seen here to seek cover.*
(Bundesarchiv)

6

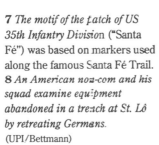

7

7 *The motif of the patch of US 35th Infantry Division ("Santa Fé") was based on markers used along the famous Santa Fé Trail.*
8 *An American non-com and his squad examine equipment abandoned in a trench at St. Lô by retreating Germans.*
(UPI/Bettmann)

8

CHAPTER NINE

"MAKE PEACE,
YOU FOOL!"

When a battle seems to be going badly, good generals try to look at events from the enemy viewpoint, to understand his problems as well as their own. The Allied commanders in Normandy had some understanding of the German position from Ultra and other intelligence sources. But with 21st Army Group still stuck a few miles from the D-Day beaches after two months' hard fighting, even the most optimistic could not have imagined their enemies' bafflement that they did not just walk through the troops defending Normandy, worn almost to nothing by the attrition battle in the hedgerows and around Caen. As far as most of the German commanders were concerned, the Battle of Normandy had been lost within a few days of D-Day, and the war had been lost a long time before.

Although happy enough to claim the credit for their victories earlier in the war, by 1944 most of the German generals believed that increasing interference by Adolf Hitler in the conduct of operations was robbing them of any chance of winning the Second World War, or at least of not losing so quickly. For the liberation of France the Allies had established a system of unified command which, if it took the genius of Eisenhower to make it work, encouraged the cooperation of air, land and naval forces. In contrast, the German system was fragmented, and impossible to make work efficiently. No matter how hard the troops in the front lines fought, they were let down by a Nazi state and war machine which placed them in a hopeless position.

Since 1934 Hitler as Führer had also been Commander-in-Chief of the German armed forces, consisting of the Army, Navy and Luftwaffe. In December, 1941, he had fired the Army Commander-in-Chief and taken that post also, dividing the war into two separate areas. Army headquarters (OKH) controlled the war on the Eastern Front, which occupied most of the German war effort, while Armed Forces headquarters (OKW) took responsibility for all other fronts. In practice, both the Eastern Front and other operations came increasingly under Hitler's personal direction as the war progressed, from his Supreme Headquarters (RFH) at the Wolf's Lair near Rastenberg in eastern Germany. There, basing his judgements on nothing but maps and his own instinct, Hitler would issue orders down to divisional level, often bypassing his own chain of command. The head of OKW after 1941, Field Marshal Wilhelm Keitel, was so subservient to Hitler that he became known behind his back as Lakeitel (Little Lackey).

Previous page: *Outside SS, armored, and paratroop units, German forces in Normandy included many sub-standard troops. The men seen here are certainly not impressive physical specimens of the "master race."*
1 Men sprang to attention and saluted when a vehicle carrying this pennant passed, for it distinguished the staff car of a member of the German high command. The leather case covered it when the vehicle was traveling without its august occupant.

The commander-in-chief for the Western Front (OB West), appointed in 1942, was the elderly Prussian aristocrat, Field Marshal Gerd von Rundstedt. Unlike Eisenhower, however, as an army commander von Rundstedt had no direct control over naval or air forces. The Luftwaffe, under the command of Hitler's deputy Führer, Hermann Goering, was allowed to fight its own war. The Waffen-SS, under Heinrich Himmler, also had its own chain of command and supply independent of the army. Von Rundstedt had very little power to conduct the defense of German-occupied Europe as he wished. Fixated with the Eastern Front, and with little understanding of seapower or the growing strength of the United States, Hitler gave the west a low priority. According to von Rundstedt, he would be told that a new division would be arriving from Germany, Russia or Norway, only to find that "it would consist in all of a divisional commander, a medical officer, and five bakers."

Von Rundstedt also complained repeatedly about the weakness of the Atlantic Wall, in which he had little faith. Even in 1944 he had sixty divisions to defend 3,000 miles of coastline, and he could not understand why the Allies had not invaded in 1942 or 1943. The idea that they

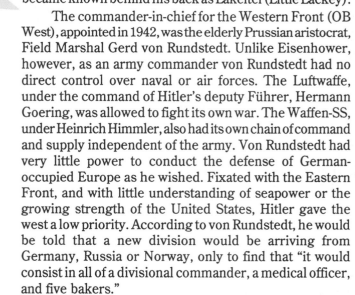

2 *Field Marshal Wilhelm Keitel, Chef des Oberkommando der Wehrmacht (Chief of the High Command of the Armed Forces; OKW), looks on as Hitler studies a map. The Führer increasingly took the conduct of the war into his own hands, ignoring the recommendations of his field commanders. Keitel, who in his memoirs called himself "a loyal shield-bearer for Adolf Hitler," did so little to restrain his leader's wilder schemes that other generals nicknamed him "Little Lackey" or "Nodding Ass."*
3 *Like Keitel, Colonel-General Alfred Jodl (nearest camera), chief of OKW Operations Staff, frequently allowed himself to be overruled by Hitler.*
(US National Archives)

4 *Arm band of the* Volkssturm *("People's Army"), the German home defense militia. This conscript force, consisting of all males between 16 and 60 previously considered too old, too young, or otherwise unfit for military service, was formed late in 1944.*

VON RUNDSTEDT

Karl Rudolf Gerd von Rundstedt was born on December 12, 1875 in Halberstadt, the eldest son of a hussar officer from an old Prussian family which traced its military traditions back to the 18th century. Inevitably he became a soldier, joining the 83rd Royal Prussian Infantry Regiment in June, 1893, and rising to train as part of the German military elite, the General Staff. He held several staff appointments during the First World War, finishing as chief of staff to XV Corps on the Western Front.

Von Rundstedt remained in the army after the war, rising steadily through command and staff appointments, including command of 2nd Cavalry Division in 1929. He reached the apparent pinnacle of his career in 1932 as the general commanding the Berlin Military District, and then First Army Group, the most important command in the small German Army. Raised in the traditions of army and family service, he had little time for the Nazis, with whom the army became increasingly involved, and he retired in 1938 as a colonel-general.

With the rise in tension which led to the Second World War, von Rundstedt was recalled to duty. He commanded Army Group South in the campaign against Poland in September, 1939, and Army Group A which led the decisive breakthrough and advance through France in June, 1940. As a result, he was promoted to field marshal in July, 1940, and made Commander-in-Chief West in October. Modestly, von Rundstedt took to wearing a colonel's uniform (representing the 18th Infantry Regiment of which he was colonel-in-chief) with his field marshal's insignia. In April, 1941, he was appointed to command Army Group South for the forthcoming Barbarossa offensive against the Soviet Union. In 1942, however, he was removed from command on the Eastern Front after disagreements on the conduct of the campaign, and reappointed as Commander-in-Chief West.

5

Von Rundstedt's second retirement in July, 1944, was even shorter than his first. On September 4 he reluctantly accepted the post of Commander-in-Chief West once more to defend against the Anglo-American onslaught, feeling compelled despite his personal pessimism and dislike of the Nazis to do so. Remarkably, he was one of the few senior commanders to escape the plots and accusations of the end of Hitler's Germany, and remained in his position almost until the end of the war. In March, 1945, he was captured by American troops while undergoing treatment for arthritis in a hospital. Indicted in 1948 for war crimes, he was considered too ill to stand trial, and died in Hanover on February 24, 1953.

5 *Gerd von Rundstedt, a career soldier and Prussian aristocrat, may have despised Hitler, whose military judgment he sometimes opposed, but served him well. Von Rundstedt was Commander-in-Chief West at the time of the D-Day landings, and although dismissed in July 1944 was soon reinstated.*
(The Bettmann Archive)
6 *Von Rundstedt (second from left) and Rommel (right) differed over how the Allied invasion should be met. Rommel favored a forward policy; von Rundstedt was more cautious.*
(Bundesarchiv)

ROMMEL

Erwin Johannes Eugen Rommel was born on November 15, 1891 in Swabia, southern Germany, the son of a schoolmaster. In 1910 he joined the 124th Infantry Regiment, and served with it on the Western and Italian Fronts in the First World War, winning promotion to captain and earning the *Pour Le Merite* or "Blue Max," the German Imperial Army's highest gallantry award. He stayed with the army after the war, but in 1935 he became military adviser to the Hitler Youth, and in 1938 commander of Hitler's bodyguard. Personally ambitious but politically naive, Rommel owed his rise to Hitler's patronage without ever becoming a convinced Nazi. In 1940 he was rewarded by Hitler for his service with command of 7th (Ghost) Panzer Division, and made a considerable reputation commanding it in France in 1940.

In January, 1941, Rommel was appointed to command the new Africa Corps in the Western Desert of North Africa. His campaigns in Africa made Rommel's reputation for daring, high-speed armored attacks, and in June, 1942, he was promoted as the youngest field marshal in the German Army, while his command grew to become Panzer Army Africa, and finally Army Group Africa. Defeated in his attempts to break through to Egypt, Rommel was finally driven back by Montgomery at the Second Battle of El Alamein in October, 1942. He was ordered back to Germany on sick leave in March, 1943, largely to prevent him being captured by the Allies with the last of Army Group Africa in Tunisia.

In July, 1943, Rommel was appointed to command Army Group B, at that time largely a paper formation, under Field Marshal Albert Kesselring in Italy. In November he was appointed Inspector-General of Fortifications, and in December Army Group B was made a reality, taking over the troops defending northern France and Belgium. Rommel worked to prepare the defenses with his usual energy, but despite his great reputation for winning battles he had never fought a successful campaign, and Normandy marked his third major defeat by Montgomery.

Rommel held no further command after being wounded on July 17, 1944. Recuperating from his wounds at his home at Ulm in Swabia on October 14, he was given the choice of taking poison rather than facing a public trial involving his family for his indirect involvement in the assassination of Hitler. He was pronounced dead on arrival at a hospital that day. A major monument to Rommel planned by the Nazi state was never built.

1 *The* Hoheitsabzeichen *("National Badge"), here in the silver-gray version for enlisted men of the Army and Luftwaffe, was worn on headgear and on the right breast of the uniform.*
2 *The* Allgemeines Sturmabzeichen *("General Assault Badge"), worn on the left breast of the uniform, was awarded to men after at least three combat assaults.*
3 *Rommel and Hitler greet each other with smiles and clasped hands – but in 1944 the field marshal would be forced to commit suicide at the Führer's order.*
(US National Archives)

4 *"Moscow's servants invade" says the Nazi newspaper* Volkischer Beobachter *("Racial Observer").* **5** *Did such propaganda inspire young Germans to resist the invasion more fiercely?* (Bundesarchiv)

might wish to reduce their own casualties, or the destruction involved, did not seem to occur to him, or to any other German commander. Hitler was also obsessed with the political importance of holding conquered territory, and repeatedly upset his subordinates' plans by issuing "no retreat" orders. When, in the Battle of Normandy, Hitler ordered that Atlantic Wall positions were to be defended "to the last drop of blood," all von Rundstedt could do before sending out the order was to change the wording to "defend to the last bullet."

In December, 1943, in typical fashion, Hitler appointed his favorite, Rommel, to command Army Group B, defending the northern coast of France and Belgium under von Rundstedt, but with a roving commission making him responsible for all coast defenses. Von Rundstedt regarded Rommel, nearly twenty years his junior and the son of a south German schoolmaster, as an upstart, and their relations were correct but cool. Von Rundstedt accepted that, while Rommel was prepared to obey his orders, he had direct access to Hitler and that his views would prevail.

THE DISPUTE OVER STRATEGY

In the months before D-Day, a major argument arose between Rommel and von Rundstedt over how best to defend against the Allied invasion that both were convinced would come somewhere in northern France. Von Rundstedt's view was that the Atlantic Wall could not be held for more than a day against a determined assault, and that its 120,000 garrison troops could be better employed elsewhere. While he agreed that the invasion should be destroyed on the beaches if possible, he was not convinced of where the Allied landings would come, or whether there would be more than one landing. OB West had a single armored reserve for Army Group B and Army Group G (covering the south of France), consisting of six armored divisions under General Leo Frieherr Geyr von Schweppenburg, and known as Panzer Group West. Von Rundstedt, with Geyr von Schweppenburg in agreement, wanted these divisions held back from the coast (at least thirty to forty miles inland), until the Allied intentions became clear. Then, as the Allies advanced, Panzer Group West would act as a counterattacking force to drive them back to the beaches. As a thorough professional soldier with a reputation for caution, von Rundstedt's plan for fighting the battle, giving up considerable ground in Normandy while trying to keep a reserve intact and his options open, was the way in which Montgomery also had expected the battle to be fought. The two enemies disagreed, however, on the probable result; von Rundstedt continued to believe, after the war, that he could have made the Allies pay heavily for victory if allowed to conduct the battle in his own way.

Montgomery had also judged Rommel's probable response to the D-Day landings correctly: "He will do his level best to 'Dunkirk' us – not to fight the armored battle on ground of his own choosing but to avoid it altogether by preventing our tanks landing by using his own tanks well forward." Rommel, unlike von Rundstedt, had prior experience of facing Allied airpower, and did not believe that it was possible to conduct large-scale armored counterattacks in the face of American and British bombers

7 *The* Deutsche Kreuz *("German Cross") in silver, seen here with a citation signed by Field Marshal Keitel, was given for outstanding leadership – a quality much needed by Germany in 1944. It was awarded in gold for gallantry in action.*

7

6 *Rommel inspects the crew of a self-propelled gun (note that it is based on the hull of a French Hotchkiss light tank, captured in 1940) on the Atlantic Wall in 1944. Rommel disagreed with von Rundstedt's decision to hold large armored forces in reserve, committing them in counterattack only when the main thrust of the invasion was identified. Believing that Allied air power would be able seriously to hinder the deployment of armored units, Rommel urged their concentration well forward at the likely landing areas. Hitler compromised, allowing Rommel to move some armored units forward – but keeping tight hold on the large reserves, which could only move with his sanction.* (Bundesarchiv)

1 *This young soldier, wearing a Luftwaffe camouflage smock over his Army tunic, appears confident of his ability to resist the invaders.* (Bundesarchiv)

1

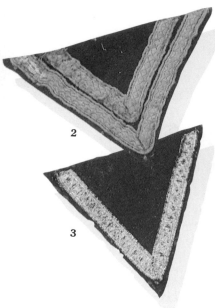

2

3

2 *Rank chevrons worn on the upper arm by an* Obergefreiter *(Corporal) with less than six years' service. After six years, the NCO wore a single chevron enclosing a star.*
3 *Rank chevron of a* Gefreiter *(Lance-Corporal; about equivalent to a Private First Class in the US Army).*
4 *As it was then: the view from a surviving German gun emplacement at Pointe de Hoc.*

and fighter-bombers. He wanted the armor of Panzer Group West well forward, as close to the coast of Normandy and the Pas de Calais as possible, to intervene against the Allied landings on D-Day itself. Rommel repeatedly stated his belief that if the Allies got firmly ashore then they could never be stopped.

The result of this dispute was one of many cases of Hitler's "divide and rule" tactics with his subordinates, and produced a compromise which followed neither plan of battle properly. Three of the armored divisions were placed under Army Group B, pushed up close to the coast by Rommel. Only 21st Panzer Division, however, was in Seventh Army area in Normandy, and it could not be moved without Army Group B authority. Rommel left the other two panzer divisions with Fifteenth Army in the Pas de Calais, from which they could not be transferred without Hitler's personal orders. The remaining divisions of Panzer Group West were held back by von Rundstedt away from the coast. But again, although these divisions came under OB West for training, they could not be moved into action without Hitler's personal permission.

This confused chain of command helped the Allies greatly on D-Day, slowing the intervention first of 21st Panzer and then the remaining divisions of Panzer Group West against the troops coming off the beaches. After D-Day, Panzer Group West became an operational headquarters under Geyr von Schweppenburg, taking over the defense of Caen from Seventh Army, both under Rommel's Army Group B. The resulting alignment of forces meant that in general terms US First Army faced the predominantly infantry force of German Seventh Army in the hedgerows near St Lô, while British Second Army confronted the armor of Panzer Group West (renamed Fifth Panzer Army in August) around Caen. Once more the old adversaries, Rommel and Montgomery, who had faced each other in October, 1942, at El Alamein, met again in battle.

THE GERMAN ARMY IN NORMANDY

The forces with which Army Group B defended Normandy were a characteristic German mixture. The armored troops were regarded by the Allies as very good, and the Waffen-SS divisions in particular developed a reputation for hard fighting. The new 12th SS Panzer Division (Hitler Jugend) displayed a fanaticism and toughness which surprised many Allied divisions also new to combat. But having been taught never even to consider surrender, the Waffen-SS soldiers made surprisingly cooperative prisoners. The remaining armored divisions also had soldiers of military age, but their equipment varied greatly, often including captured French, Czech, Polish or Yugoslav weapons. The 21st Panzer Division defending Caen had so many French tanks that it was the only German armored division ruled unfit to serve on the Eastern Front. Even the strongest of the German divisions were not as powerful, in terms of firepower and numbers, as most of the Allied divisions, which often had extra armored brigades attached.

The other German formations in Normandy regarded by both von Rundstedt and his Allied opponents as being of high quality were the paratroop divisions. Although by 1944 very few of the paratroopers had made a combat drop, their special selection and training made them formidable

fighters. In typical German fashion, however, paratroop and airlanding divisions were part of the Luftwaffe, not the Army. Late in the war, the Luftwaffe also created its own infantry divisions from airfield ground crews who were surplus to requirements. One of these, 16th Luftwaffe Field Division, took part in the defense of Caen, and was virtually destroyed by the Charnwood and Goodwood bombing. The 88mm anti-tank guns which formed such a menace to Allied tanks also came under the Luftwaffe as anti-aircraft guns (their original purpose) and German Army commanders found that their orders to the gunners were being countermanded or ignored. During Goodwood, Colonel Hans von Luck of 21st Panzer solved his immediate problem by threatening the Luftwaffe lieutenant in charge

4

of one battery with his pistol, telling him that "he could either die now on my responsibility or win a decoration on his own – he chose the decoration." This was hardly a long-term solution to the problem, which stemmed from Hitler's organization (or lack of it) of Germany for war.

Other than the armor and paratroop divisions, most of the German forces in Normandy were under-equipped, and contained soldiers who were over-age or suffered from disabilities, such as the "stomach battalions" formed of men who needed a special diet, and similar "ear battalions" and "foot battalions." Most of the German transport in Normandy was horse-drawn, and several of the coastal divisions had no transport provided at all. These static divisions were intended only for defensive fighting, and had to march into action. One of the most curious features of the Battle of Normandy was that although wearing German uniform, about one in ten of Rommel's troops was not German. Up to a quarter of the men in some divisions came from eastern Europe, including Poland, Hungary, Yugoslavia and the republics of the Soviet Union. These men were a mixture of true volunteers, who

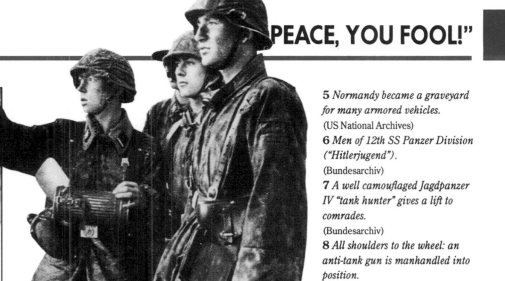

5 *Normandy became a graveyard for many armored vehicles.* (US National Archives)
6 *Men of 12th SS Panzer Division ("Hitlerjugend").* (Bundesarchiv)
7 *A well camouflaged Jagdpanzer IV "tank hunter" gives a lift to comrades.* (Bundesarchiv)
8 *All shoulders to the wheel: an anti-tank gun is manhandled into position.* (Bundesarchiv)

6

7

8

"MAKE PEACE, YOU FOOL!"

1, 2 *Uniform patches worn by East European volunteers in German service. As well as men from the Soviet republics of Georgia (1) and Azerbaijan (2), thousands more anti-Communist Soviet subjects, notably from the Ukraine, and from the Soviet-occupied Baltic republics of Latvia, Estonia, and Lithunia, fought for Germany.*

3 *One of Germany's "foreign legionnaires": a wounded Georgian (note sleeve patch).* (IWM: HU 3416)
4 *Captured* Hilfswilliger *("Hiwis") auxiliaries. Most were Soviet PoWs who, promised better* treatment, volunteered for non-combatant duty with German forces. Some were forced into combat.
5 *"As we fight, so you must work for victory," the heroic soldier tells German workers.*

had seen no future for themselves at home under German occupation (or in a few cases had genuinely welcomed the Germans as liberators from the Russians) and prisoners of war who found themselves just as much unwilling conscripts in the German Army as they had been in the Soviet Army. More than one prisoner taken by the Allies in Normandy had no idea of which country he was in.

hedgerows and villages, well camouflaged and dug-in, but unable to maneuver. Even if fighting troops and vehicles reached the front lines, their replacements, fuel and ammunition remained in short supply, cut off by Allied airpower. At the same time, the fighting in Normandy was taking an impossible toll of Army Group B. By the time that Caen and St Lô were finally captured, the German divisions were reduced to skeleton formations, some barely the strength of battalions.

Knowing their own weakness, the German commanders shared the surprise of the Allied airmen that 21st

7 Many Allied tactical air strikes targeted railroads and rolling stock. This locomotive will not deliver its armored freight ...
8 ... which will be missed in Normandy, where these German soldiers perhaps died because the tanks did not arrive.
(US National Archives)

6 *Keep the blackout – or risk destruction by RAF "terror fliers," the poster warns.*

Der Feind sieht Dein Licht!

Verdunkeln!

6

7

The absence of the Luftwaffe, and the effectiveness of the Allied air forces in sealing off the Normandy battlefield from the rest of France, meant that divisions arrived in Normandy days or even weeks later than they had expected, having already taken losses from air attack. The commander of Panzer Lehr Division (formed from the German armored training school), moving to the defense of Caen on June 7, described his division's route as a "fighter-bomber racecourse" which cost him five tanks, eighty-four other armored vehicles and 130 soft-skinned vehicles before even getting into action. German vehicles were forced to move only at night and hide by day. In Normandy itself, the sour joke spread that "if a plane shows up and it's painted white, it's American; if it's painted black, it's RAF; if it doesn't show up at all, it's Luftwaffe." As the battle wore on, tanks and assault guns were increasingly employed as armored pillboxes in the 8

1 *On the left breast of his camouflage jacket this veteran soldier wears the Iron Cross, First Class; above is the Army Close Combat Clasp (Nahkampfspange des Heeres), awarded after at least 30 continuous days in combat. He carries a 9mm MP-40 "Schmeisser" sub-machine gun; clipped to his belt are triple magazine pouches, each pocket containing a 32-round box magazine. Standard 6x30 binoculars hang from his neck; clipped to the jacket beneath is a signaling torch with a hooded beam.*
(Bundesarchiv)

4 *A 7.92mm Mauser 98k rifle, standard arm of the German infantryman throughout World War II, lies across a field service jacket and camouflage jacket. The former has on the right sleeve the specialist badge of a Funkmeister (radio operator). On it lies a Mauser Model 84/98 bayonet in a steel sheath, and a canvas-and-leather triple magazine pouch, seen also at (1). The latter has on the left breast a paratrooper's qualification badge. Headgear: (right) paratrooper's helmet, lacking the flared rim of the Model 1942 steel helmet at (1); (left) tropical field cap, with national eagle and cockade; .*

Army Group did not advance more quickly. An explanation very attractive to the Germans themselves was that they were simply better fighters than the Allies. In the front lines, German officers reported that they could win back positions lost to the enemy "by the platoon or section commanders leaping forward uttering a good old-fashioned 'hurrah!' which spurs on the inexperienced troops and carries them along." Some even reintroduced bugle calls for their troops to charge forward. This worked at the level of small fire-fights, but the refusal of higher commands to give ground, and the insistence on always launching counterattacks to retake lost positions, caused very heavy casualties. The hedgerow country of Normandy also worked to the advantage of the defender. On several occasions, the Allies failed to break through a thinly-held German line because they could not coordinate their forces in the maze of the farm country, or assumed that the few Germans firing at them were the outposts of a much stronger position further back. But the value of the bocage to the defense worked for both sides. Although the Germans managed to slow or limit the big British and American offensives to penetrations of a few miles only, those few miles could never be retaken. Slowly, the Allied advance ground the defenders in Normandy down, until by the end of July German divisional commanders were reporting that one more attack would break through.

2 *Arm band of a type worn by Werksschutzpolizei (Factory Protection Police), a force of guards and watchmen.*
3 *The War Merit Cross (here the Second Class with Swords) was awarded for general military virtue; unlike the Iron Cross, given only for acts of bravery.*

THE CRISIS IN COMMAND

The German failure to stop the invasion on D-Day and the next few days was accompanied only by Hitler's insistence that no ground should be given up, and that counterattacks should be launched to drive the Allies back into the sea. But after even a week of fighting, it was clear that this was impossible. "I am being bled white and getting nowhere," Colonel-General Josef (Sepp) Dietrich, I SS Corps commander and a former head of Hitler's bodyguard, complained to Rommel. "We need another eight or ten divisions in a day or two or we are finished." By June 18, Allied air and ground attacks had killed another corps

5 *Spit and polish: a young Sturmmann (lance-corporal) of the Waffen-SS shines up his boots. He looks hardly more than a child, foreshadowing the crumbling of the Reich in 1945, when Hitler Youth members in their earliest teens would be thrust into the firing line.* (Photo From Three Lions)

5

6

6 *Note the colored slide buttons on the signaling torch shown here: they allowed red, yellow, or green acetate strips to be pushed up over the lens.*

commander, together with four divisional commanders, and killed or wounded about 40,000 German soldiers. As Allied pressure on the battlefield and air control of the roads and railways of France ate away at the German strength in Normandy, Rommel and von Rundstedt found themselves increasingly in agreement that the one thing which might at least delay the Allied victory was to give up ground, and to allow their divisional commanders more control over their own troops. In response to repeated telephone and written requests from both field marshals, Hitler flew out on June 17 as far as Soissons to meet them. This was the closest to the Normandy battlefield that Hitler ever came. At Soissons, both Rommel and von Rundstedt argued that the Battle of Normandy was lost,

and that the correct strategy would be to retire behind the Seine to block further Allied advances. When Hitler rejected this, von Rundstedt argued instead for a major armored counterattack. Although this was approved, and would have coincided with the period of the "Great Storm," in which Allied air and ground forces were at their least effective, the required divisions did not reach Normandy in time or were sucked into the holding battle.

As with all his meetings with Hitler, Rommel came away still worried but reassured by the Führer's magnetic personality and confidence. Hitler placed great faith in the V-1 flying bombs which had begun their attacks on London and the Channel ports of Britain on June 16. Once away from Hitler, however, Rommel's doubts over the hopeless

"The Führer has ordered ... the long-range bombardment of England will begin in the middle of June." So began the "Führer Order" of Armed Forces High Command (OKW) on May 16, 1944. *"The bombardment,"* it decreed, *"will open like a thunderclap by night with Fzg.76 ...."* The cover name Fzg.76 (Flakzielgerät; *"anti-aircraft aiming device"*) denoted the Fieseler Fi.103 flying bomb, the first *"guided missile"* to play a significant part in warfare. It was Hitler's Vergeltungswaffen Eins (*"Vengeance Weapon One;" V-1*), a counter-terror to the Allied bombing offensive on Germany. It was followed by the V-2 (A-4) rocket, the world's first ballistic missile. The V-3, a multi-barreled launcher to fire finned missiles to a range of some 175 miles, was approaching completion when its installation near Calais was overrun during the Allied breakout from Normandy.

The Fieseler Fi.103 flying bomb, or V-1, which the Allies nicknamed the "Buzz-bomb" or "Doodlebug," was a pilotless aircraft with pulse jet propulsion that gave a maximum speed of about 400 mph. A pre-set magnetic compass and gyroscopic auto-pilot determined and maintained its course; a small air-log propeller in the nose (missing from the damaged specimen seen here) registered the distance covered; at the appropriate time the guidance system cut out the power and put the bomb into a steep dive. Its maximum range, carrying a 1,800-pound explosive warhead, was some 200 miles. (UPI/Bettmann)

2

1 *The V-1 was accurate only to within about a 10-mile radius. It was vulnerable to anti-aircraft fire (AAA massed along the British south coast destroyed more than half the V-1s brought down in flight) and fighter interception. Fighter pilots would sometimes fly alongside the V-1 and flip up a wing tip, disrupting its guidance system and sending it plunging into the Channel.*

1

2, 3, 4 *German propaganda promises devastation of London and the Channel ports by V-1s, backing its threats with spurious quotations. Most were aimed at London or the Allied supply centers of Antwerp and Liège. Of around 9,000 V-1s aimed at London, some 2,400 arrived (the first on June 13, 1944), killing 6,184 persons. The V-1's approach could be seen and heard (it sounded "like a motorcycle running underwater"), so its effect on civilian morale was not great. The V-2 rocket, arriving silently at a terminal 2,386 mph, was more terrifying. 518 V-2s hit London, killing 2,724 persons; Antwerp was hit by 1,341 V-2s, causing about 30,000 casualties.*
5 *US Army engineers explore a huge bunker in Normandy – possibly part of the unfinished installation for the V-3 long-range gun.*
(UPI/Bettmann)

Soldiers of the Invasion Army!

Do you know

that since 16th June, the new German weapon of retaliation which bears the name "V 1" is pounding on London day and night, and above all on the harbours of Southern England?

Do you know

that the number of victims already amounts to hundreds of thousands?

It is not to be wondered at that the utmost efforts are being made in England to draw a veil of silence over the appalling effects of "V 1"

But what is, inspite of strict censorship, the English press compelled to admit?

In the paper "DAILY MAIL", 24th June, the air-correspondent Collin Bednall writes:

"It is ridiculous to claim that the German attacks on Southern England by means of flying bombs are without military significance."

Another correspondent writes in the same issue:

"No air combat in history has ever been of so desperate a character as that of the British fighter planes against the new German weapon."

3

DAILY TELEGRAPH:
« An incredible stream of German pilotless bombers is dropping a rain of explosives over Southern England. There is widespread destruction in many places. »

EXCHANGE TELEGRAPH:
« Pauseless attacks with the new German weapon. The South coast has been shrouded for days in light and fire. »

EVENING STANDARD:
« English military experts are breaking their heads over the nature and construction of the new German weapon. The distinguished air expert, Oliver Stewart, writes: « This weapon may turn out to be the most important weapon in future air warfare. »

SVENSKA DAGBLADET:
« According to a London report, King George has left London for an unknown destination with a view to greater personal safety. »

STOCKHOLM TIDNINGEN:
« The London population is living in a ghastly nightmare. The thunder of explosions has been heard without interruption during five days. Eight story buildings are reduced to powder. No shelter affords protection against the terrific effects of the new German weapon. ...We are living in the very heart of terror. »

ARSHAM (ANKARA):
« To the man in the street, the most depressing feature is that there appear to be no means of alleviating the effects of the new weapon. Nothing is known about the nature of the weapon, its construction or its bases of departure. Both ground and air-anti-aircraft defences are quite ineffective. Experts are actively engaged in devising counter-measures. Meanwhile London and the towns of Southern England are burning. Attacks follow one another without intermission, striking new localities by day and night. The heart-rending anguish of Englishmen may be about intermittent. The heart-rending anguish of Englishmen may be readily understood. It is a bad look-out for them. »

4

5

6 *A V-1 in flight. The V-1 threat ended when its "ski-ramp" launching sites in the Pas de Calais were overrun in the Allied breakout.*
(UPI/Bettmann)

7 *V-weapons might have had more effect if fewer had been aimed at London and more, as the leaflet threatens, at Allied supply lines. Hitler might better have devoted the research and development effort expended on V-weapons to the jet aircraft program.*

CAUGHT LIKE FOXES IN A TRAP

English and American soldiers !

Why has Jerry waited ten days after the landings to use his so called secret weapon behind your back ? Doesn't that strike you as queer ?

It looks very much as though after waiting for you to cross the Channel, he had set a **TRAP** for you.

You're fighting at present on a very narrow strip of coast, the extent of which has been so far regulated by the Germans.

You are using up an enormous number of men and huge quantities of material.

Meanwhile the Robot-planes, flying low, scatter over London and Southern England explosives, the power and incendiary efficiency of which are without precedent. They spread death and destruction in the towns and harbours, which should be sending you much needed supplies.

They are cutting the bridge to your bases

In addition to the destruction and panic at home, trafic is disorganised, ships, even hospital ships, are held up.

How long can you keep up this foolish « invasion » in those circumstances ?

It's up to you to think of the best way to get out of the TRAP in wich you are CAUGHT.

Time is precious. To-morrow may be too late.

"MAKE PEACE, YOU FOOL!"

1 *Colonel-General Friedrich Dollmann was so shaken by the onset of the Epsom offensive that he committed suicide, taking poison at his HQ on or about June 28.*
(Bundesarchiv)

2 *The skill he showed in defensive operations in Russia won Field Marshal (Hans) Günther von Kluge (right), seen here with General Eberbach, the nickname "Clever Hans." He took over von Rundstedt's command on July 2.*
(Bundesarchiv)

3 *Rommel (in car) speaks to his adjutant Hellmuth Lang; Generals Meindl and Hausser (camouflage jacket) stand by.*
(Bundesarchiv)

1

2

3

4

4 *General der Panzertruppen Heinrich Eberbach relieved Geyr von Schweppenburg, fired for his "defeatist" attitude, as commander of Panzer Group West on July 6.*
(Bundesarchiv)

position of Army Group B once more asserted themselves. At the end of June both field marshals left France to meet Hitler in Germany once more, but without result. While they were away the Epsom offensive started, and the commander of Seventh Army, Colonel-General Friedrich Dollmann, committed suicide in the face of what seemed a certain Allied breakthrough. Rommel's other Army commander, Geyr von Schweppenburg of Panzer Group West, meanwhile submitted a report arguing that only by retreating from Caen could he save his forces from "melting away," and von Rundstedt forwarded this report to Armed Forces Headquarters with his personal endorsement. Hitler may have already decided to dismiss the old Prussian aristocrat, who never managed to hide his disdain for all Nazis, but von Rundstedt's next action put the matter beyond doubt. On July 1 he spelled out the situation in Normandy in a lengthy telephone conversation with Keitel. "What shall we do? What shall we do?" Keitel plaintively broke in. "What shall we do?" von Rundstedt replied, "Make peace, you fool!"

Next day, von Rundstedt was retired from his position, ostensibly on grounds of age and ill health, and replaced

5

6 Obergruppenführer-*SS
(Lieutenant-General) Josef "Sepp"
Dietrich was to the end one of
Hitler's most loyal supporters.
8 *Cuff title of 1st SS Panzer
Division Leibstandarte Adolf
Hitler; the "bodyguard" unit
Dietrich long commanded.*
9 *Death's-head (Totenkopf)
insignia of the Waffen-SS.*

5 *Although Rommel opposed the
appointment, Colonel-General
Paul Hausser became the first
Waffen-SS officer to take
command of an Army.*
7 *Hitler welcomes his old comrade
"Sepp" Dietrich to the "Wolf's
Lair" HQ at Rastenburg, East
Prussia.*
(US National Archives)

"MAKE PEACE, YOU FOOL!"

1 *Perhaps peace in mid-1944 would have been welcomed by this apprehensive soldier.*

2

3

5 *Crewman in sun-goggles scans the sky for "tank busting" aircraft from the hull of his Panther.* (Bundesarchiv)
6 *Printed ephemera.*

1

2 *The 7.92mm FG-42 (Fallschirmjägergewehr; "paratrooper's rifle") is shown with bayonet fixed and light bipod extended.*
3 *A Kfz.1/20 Schwimmwagen (amphibious car) is approached by a Tiger tank.* (Bundesarchiv)
4 *Identity book and ephemera.*

by Field Marshal Gunther von Kluge, regarded on the Eastern Front as the German Army's specialist in defending against armored breakthroughs. Geyr von Schweppenburg was also fired, and replaced on July 6 by General Heinrich Eberbach, known as a competent armored commander. As a sign of the times, Dollmann's replacement at Seventh Army was the first Waffen-SS officer to command an Army, Colonel-General Paul Hausser, appointed over Rommel's protests. This left Rommel as the only remaining member of the German high command that had begun the defense of Normandy on D-Day. Even Rommel, however, was in an increasingly weak position, and had lost whatever faith he ever had in stopping the Anglo-American advance. "The unequal struggle is drawing to a close," he reported to von Kluge on July 15. Two days later, just before the start of Operation Goodwood, his staff car was spotted on the road near Livarot by two Allied aircraft at about six PM and strafed heavily. Badly wounded and unconscious, Rommel was taken to the nearest village (which, by the kind of coincidence no writer of fiction would attempt, was called Ste Foy de Montgomery). Von Kluge took the opportunity to simplify the German command system by not replacing Rommel but taking over Army Group B directly. By July 20, however, there was very little action that von Kluge could take to affect the battle, and something much more important had occurred: officers of the German Army had tried to kill their Führer.

7 *German paratroopers, who are fighting as infantry in Normandy. One carries a slung FG-42: as its name – see (2) – suggests, this "assault rifle," combining the characteristics of rifle and light machine gun, was designed for paratroopers.* (Bundesarchiv)
8 *Nazi icons mark even the smallest artifacts.*

1 *Because July 20 was a hot, airless, day, Hitler chose to hold a conference in this wooden building, the Operations or Map Room, instead of in one of the concrete bunkers at the Wolf's Lair. Von Stauffenberg had expected to plant his bomb in the confinement of a bunker: its use in more spacious premises may have lessened its effect.*
(US National Archives)

THE PLOT TO KILL HITLER

Opposition to Hitler's rule in Germany had always existed, but had been both extremely risky and ineffective. The German armed forces, although many of its senior officers disliked both Hitler and his Nazis, were prepared to follow the orders of their commander-in-chief. For many soldiers, particularly the young who had grown up under the Nazi state, the Führer was "almost like a god," as one of them put it, "we had total faith in him." Although the German higher command went to war in 1939, it was always deeply pessimistic about Hitler's plans for conquest, and by 1943 several senior officers, including von Kluge, were to some extent involved in plans or plots to remove Hitler. In turn, Hitler himself had declared that if the German people could not conquer, it would be better for them all to be killed fighting than to live defeated.

2 *Propaganda Minister Josef Goebbels: on July 20 he was in Berlin, where he took decisive action against the conspirators' coup. A few days later, Hitler appointed him "Reich Plenipotentiary for Total War."*
(The Bettmann Archive)

The basis for the plot to assassinate Hitler was the belief, shared by most of the German high command, that the war on the Eastern Front was far more deadly for Germany than that against the British and the Americans. A large part of the German motive for fighting on after the war was clearly lost was the fear of what might happen to Germany in the face of Soviet conquest and occupation. To this was added the hope that the British and Americans, despite their proclamation of unconditional surrender, needed Germany as a counterweight to the Soviet Union after the war, and could not afford to let Germany be occupied. Plans developed by spring, 1944, for the assassination of Hitler, followed by an arrest of all other leading Nazis and the institution of a government under Colonel-General Ludwig Beck, former Army Chief of Staff. If the plot succeeded, the plotters hoped to be able to negotiate a peace with the Western Allies which would spare Germany from occupation.

The man selected to kill Hitler was Colonel Count Klaus Schenk von Stauffenberg, a young staff officer serving with Hitler's headquarters at the Wolf's Lair. The previous loss of an arm and all but two fingers of his remaining hand in battle made it impractical for von Stauffenberg to shoot Hitler. On July 20, after three

3 Reichsmarshall *Hermann Goering (in white uniform), Luftwaffe commander-in-chief, inspects the wrecked Operations Room. Goering, then the official nominee to succeed Hitler in the event of his death (but rapidly losing favor), rushed to Rastenburg immediately after the assassination attempt to assure the Führer of his unswerving loyalty.*
(Keystone)

4 *Seen soon after the explosion, Hitler shows no sign of injury. In fact, his right arm was partly paralyzed, his right leg burned, his hearing impaired, and his buttocks so bruised that he had, in his own words, "a backside like a baboon."*
(Keystone)

previous attempts which had been given up at the last moment, he placed his briefcase, containing a bomb, under the map table next to Hitler in one of the wooden huts at the Wolf's Lair during a lunchtime meeting, and then wandered outside. The bomb went off, killing four officers and seriously injuring others, but by the chance nature of explosions, Hitler escaped with partial deafness and a badly injured right arm.

Meanwhile, the conspirators in Berlin had sent out radio and teletype messages that Hitler was dead, and ordered the arrest of leading Nazis. Von Kluge, who had not been directly involved in the plot, hesitated over the messages until reports arrived confirming that Hitler was still alive. He remained in command in Normandy, but with suspicion hanging over him. Many others were arrested and executed in the months that followed for their part in the conspiracy, among them was Canaris as head of German Intelligence, and several of the lower-ranking commanders in France. Rommel's Chief of Staff at Army Group B, General Hans Spiedel, also fell under deep suspicion, but escaped arrest. When the Gestapo came for Rommel, who had only been slightly involved with the plotters, he was allowed to commit suicide in order to save his family. His death was announced as resulting from his wounds, and he was given a state funeral.

There was hardly a senior officer in the German Army who had not expressed dismay at Hitler's conduct of the war before July 20. While the Gestapo tracked down the conspirators, the defenders of Normandy fought on in an atmosphere of desperation, facing imminent defeat on the battlefield and the probability of arrest by their own side. On July 25, Hitler appointed his Propaganda Minister Josef Goebbels to the new position of "Reich Plenipotentiary for Total War" to mobilize national resources for a final struggle. But it was much too late. On the same day the Allied breakout from Normandy began.

5 Of 24 men present in the Operations Room when it was reduced to this shambles, four died: Generals Gunther Korten, Chief of Luftwaffe General Staff, and Rudolf Schmundt, Chief Adjutant to Hitler on OKW Operations Staff; Colonel Heinz Brandt (who, by moving aside the briefcase containing the bomb, may have unwittingly saved Hitler's life); and a stenographer called Berger.
(Keystone)
6 Seen here during his trial, Dr. Joseph Wirmer, a Berlin lawyer, was a key civilian member of the conspiracy. He was executed on September 8.
7 A bust of Hitler dominates the Volksgericht ("People's Court") during the trial of the conspirators; about 150-200 persons were executed as a direct result of the July plot. Some were hanged slowly with piano wire and their bodies afterwards displayed on meat hooks.
(Keystone)

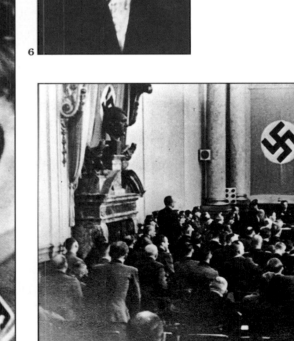

8 Count Ulrich-Wilhelm Schwerin von Schwanenfeld, adjutant to Field Marshal Erwin von Witzleben, served as the retired commander's liaison man with the plotters. Both von Witzleben and von Schwanenfeld, seen here during his trial, suffered death by hanging.
(Keystone)

THE LUFTWAFFE

The German High Command was certain that invasion was imminent, but uncertain of where it was to be launched. The Luftwaffe had approximately 600 aircraft in France which could be regarded as suitable strike aircraft to help oppose the invasion, but they were positioned to cover all the potential landing areas, so that less than half of them were actually in the vicinity of the Normandy beaches.

On D-Day, the response by the Luftwaffe to the landings was barely perceptible. The strength of the Allied air cover was such that there was no question of German long-range bombers and anti-shipping aircraft being used. The total German effort during daylight hours on D-Day was no more than 100 sorties, mostly by single-engined fighters. The bombers were thrown into the fray after dusk, but they suffered casualties not only from the Allied night fighters but also from their own flak, and little was achieved.

From D+1, reinforcements were made available from units based in Germany and Italy, and by the end of the week the number of effective aircraft had increased to around 1,000. However, their resources for reinforcement were soon exhausted and from then on, Luftwaffe strength on the Western Front steadily declined.

The Allied domination of the skies over the beachheads prevented the German long-range bombers from attacking at low level, while from high level they were unable to identify and engage specific targets. Their main effort was then shifted, concentrating instead on laying mines in the English Channel. Admittedly this caused significant disruption to

1 *Elusive enemy: the nose-gunner of a Heinkel He 111 medium bomber tries to bring sights to bear on a Spitfire.*
(Keystone)
2 *Goering in his glory: the be-medaled Luftwaffe chief greets Hitler in 1938.*
(Central Press Photos)
3 *RAF Mosquitos make a low-level strike on a German airstrip in Normandy; 1944.*

shipping engaged on the reinforcement and resupply of the invasion forces, but really only had nuisance value and was therefore unlikely to influence the eventual outcome.

Any plans which the Luftwaffe had made to provide close support for the defending ground forces were shattered from the first by the supremacy of the Allied air forces. Single-engined fighters were diverted to supplement the close support effort, but the aircrews' lack of training for this type of work meant that little was achieved, and by June 12 the units were ordered to return to their primary, air-to-air fighing role.

By the end of June, Allied bombing and the progress of the land forces had driven the Luftwaffe from its main bases in the operational area. Their units were forced back to bases as far away as Paris.

In their plans to resist the invasion, they had always believed that their predictably inferior numbers would be offset by the proximity of their bases. This advantage was already lost – they were now flying from bases no nearer to Normandy than the Allied aircraft operating from their airfields in southern England.

The Allied bombing offensive against strategic targets in Germany had continued in the weeks following D-Day. Prominent among those targets was the German oil industry, which had already been raided to such good effect that on August 11. A Luftwaffe general instruction was issued which imposed serious restrictions on flying activity of all kinds. Fighters operating in the defensive role against heavy bombers were allowed to continue without restraint, but any flight of any other kind had to be specifically authorized. This was the first time restrictions had been placed on operational flying; the Luftwaffe's teeth had been pulled. From now on, they would be in no position to have any significant effect on the progress of the liberating Allied forces.

4 *Gunners of a US AAA unit declare their intention further to thin the depleted ranks of the Luftwaffe.* (US National Archives)

5 *Luftwaffe issue: a leather map case and a steel "bin" for binoculars.*

6 *Luftwaffe forage cap: the strap could be unbuttoned and the sides of the cap turned down to protect the ears.*

7 *Waffenrock (uniform tunic) of a senior NCO, Luftwaffe.*

CHAPTER TEN
THE COBRA STRIKES

asualties in the fight for Caen and the hedgerows had been heavy. Since D-Day, 21st Army Group had lost over 80,000 men killed, wounded or taken prisoner, most of them infantrymen. Looking northward from the heights of Bourguébus ridge or Hill 112 in the misty sunlight, British and Canadian troops could still just see the D-Day beaches a few miles away, with the sun sparkling off the English Channel, the ships lying offshore and the barrage balloons floating overhead. To the northwest, the Mulberry harbor of Port Winston continued to unload the forces of 21st Army Group and its air support. Even to those who were responsible for Allied transport the figures were breathtaking: by the end of July over 1.5 million men, 300,000 vehicles and 1.8 million tons of stores had been landed in Normandy. Thereafter the Allies maintained a steady average of 16,000 men, 4,500 vehicles and 94,000 tons of stores moved each day up to the end of August.

If the view from the high ground of St Lô was obscured by the hedgerows, they could not disguise the fact that much of this force was American, including the headquarters of US Third Army under the redoubtable Patton, who had come to France in early July to help lead the breakout as Bradley's unofficial assistant. Just west of St Lô, three infantry divisions of "Lightning Joe" Collins' US VII Corps waited astride the St Lô-Perriers road to begin the attack. Behind them was Collins' powerful exploitation force of 2nd and 3rd Armored Divisions, and 1st Infantry Division, the "Big Red One," which had fought all the way from Omaha beach for this chance.

Previous page: GIs, one with a 2.36-inch "Bazooka" rocket launcher, follow a tank of US 2nd Armored Division along the road to Mortain.
(US National Archives)
1 *Youthful German PoWs show little distress at ending their fight against odds.*
(US National Archives)
2 *Generals George S. Patton (left) and Omar N. Bradley aboard a transport plane; September 1944.*
(Keystone)

On the other side of the line, Army Group B had been worn away almost to nothing, having lost nearly 100,000 men and receiving barely 5,000 in replacement. Panzer Lehr Division facing VII Corps had only forty tanks and 2,200 men left, barely the size of a brigade. The 12th SS Panzer Division was reduced to a single infantry battalion and a few tanks. Most of the German formations were in the same perilous condition, and the men on the ground had long since stopped looking upward for the Luftwaffe. Through Ultra, the Allies knew that the German forces facing the Americans were far too weak to stop the next onslaught. The overwhelming bulk of the German armored forces, 645 out of 835 tanks and seven out of nine panzer divisions, was still pinned-down south of Caen by the threat of a renewed British attack. As Rommel had always known, once they failed to stop the Allies on the beaches on D-Day the German defeat in Normandy was inevitable.

It was unsettling for many who fought in Normandy that at the front line itself these two great armies were

3 *Port Winston, the Mulberry harbor at Arromanches, where men and materiel continued to pour ashore in July-August.*
(IWM: BU 1021)
4 *Patch of US 2nd Armored Division ("Hell on Wheels"); part of General Collins' VII Corps in Operation Cobra.*
5 *A Hawker Typhoon fighter-bomber of the RAF raises the dust on a newly constructed Normandy airstrip.*
(IWM: CL 472)

5

6 Patch of US 1st Infantry Division ("The Big Red One"), dating from World War I, when the original "1" is said to have been cut from the cap of a German soldier.

6

7

almost invisible. Infantry dug themselves in along the hedgerows or in the houses. Tanks, jeeps and artillery pieces moved slowly for fear of raising tell-tale dust. Except for an occasional shellhole or ruined farmhouse, the landscape seemed empty. There was "a complete silence," remembered one visitor to the front line, "not even the sound of birds, a sense of being in an unreal world with no life." Only behind the front, out of sight of the enemy, did it seem that there was a war going on.

THE ALLIED PLAN

It is said that success has a thousand fathers, but failure is an orphan, and there was no shortage of generals to claim credit for the success of the American attack when it came, leading to many arguments and accusations after the war. The ordinary soldier's view of this was neatly summed up in the angry remark that "Now it starts – but

7 Beachhead in mid-July: the photograph conveys the enormous scale of the Allied undertaking. Close on 2 million tons of stores were landed by the end of July. (Keystone)

1 *Eisenhower, Bradley, and (right) "Lightning Joe" Collins. Collins' nickname was won in the Pacific, where he led US 25th Infantry Division ("Tropic Lightning") to victory on Guadalcanal.*
(US National Archives)
2 *An abandoned German 88mm Flak 18 anti-aircraft gun.*
(IWM: TC 15618)

anyone who wants to take a bow for himself is crazy!" Part of Montgomery's original plan for the battle, decided back in London before the invasion, was for US First Army to advance out of Normandy south and then westward, to capture the Britanny peninsula and with it the ports of Brest, Lorient and St Nazaire. The Allies believed that they needed these ports, together with Cherbourg, to sustain their armies for the next main effort, the drive across the River Seine and into northern France. Battles do not have precise schedules, but by any estimate this move into Brittany was long overdue. On July 10, Bradley offered to Montgomery his idea for an offensive to break through the hedgerow country and start the move toward Britanny. It was for this offensive, codenamed Operation

2

1

3 *Officers of the Highland Light Infantry of Canada gather for a briefing.*
(National Archives of Canada)
4 *Montgomery studies a map with his army commanders: Dempsey (back to camera), British Second Army, and Bradley, US First Army.*
(IWM: B 5322)

Cobra, that Operation Goodwood became the diversionary attack. It was later suggested by Montgomery's critics that he had expected Goodwood also to break out from Caen far to the south and south-east, something that Montgomery himself always denied. Bradley's plan, which he had worked out by July 13, was to use the heavy bombers once more to blast a way through the German lines, as the British had done for Operation Charnwood and were planning to do for Operation Goodwood. Later, Bradley would claim that the whole idea of using heavy bombers to support major offensives in this way had been

4

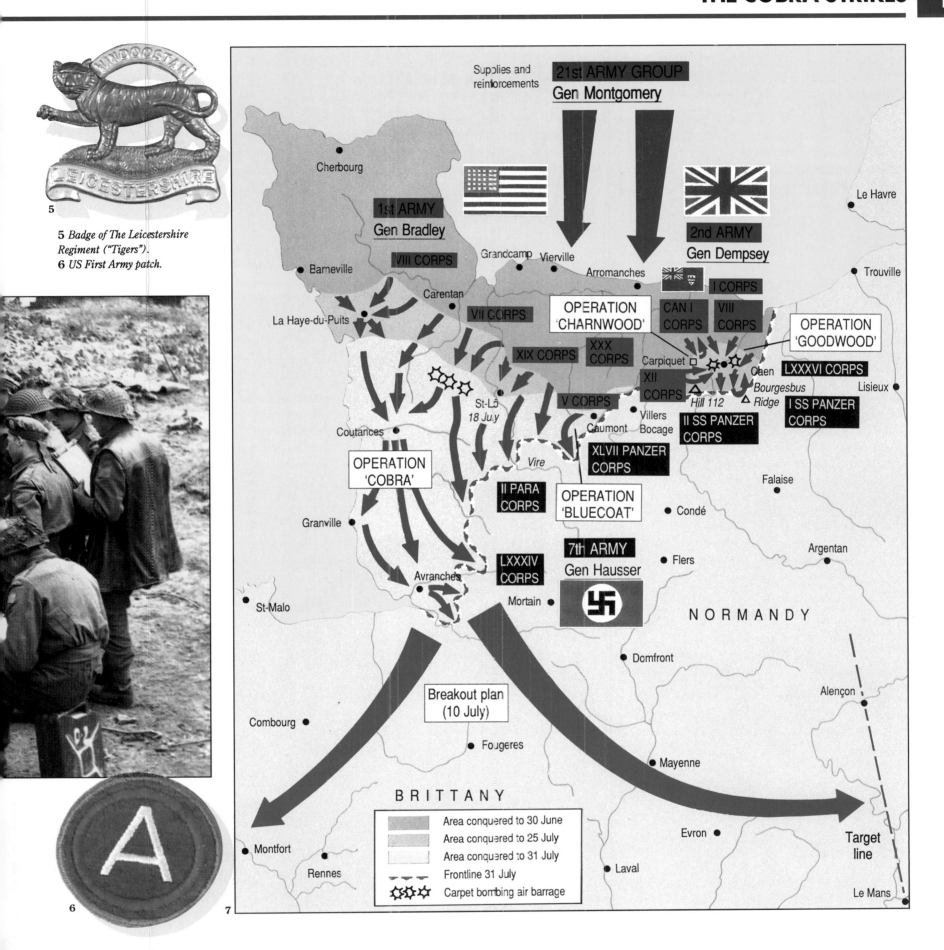

5 Badge of The Leicestershire Regiment ("Tigers").
6 US First Army patch.

Supplies and reinforcements

21st ARMY GROUP
Gen Montgomery

1st ARMY
Gen Bradley
VIII CORPS

2nd ARMY
Gen Dempsey

I CORPS

OPERATION 'CHARNWOOD'

VII CORPS

CAN I CORPS

VIII CORPS

OPERATION 'GOODWOOD'

XIX CORPS

XXX CORPS

XII CORPS

Carpiquet

Caen

LXXXVI CORPS

Bourgesbus Ridge

Lisieux

St-Lô 18 July

V CORPS

Hill 112

Villers Bocage

Caumont

II SS PANZER CORPS

I SS PANZER CORPS

OPERATION 'COBRA'

XLVII PANZER CORPS

Vire

II PARA CORPS

OPERATION 'BLUECOAT'

Falaise

Condé

Argentan

7th ARMY
Gen Hausser

LXXXIV CORPS

Avranches

Mortain

Flers

NORMANDY

Domfront

Alençon

Breakout plan (10 July)

Combourg

Fougeres

Mayenne

BRITTANY

Area conquered to 30 June
Area conquered to 25 July
Area conquered to 31 July
Frontline 31 July
Carpet bombing air barrage

Evron

Target line

Montfort

Rennes

Laval

Le Mans

Cherbourg
Le Havre
Barneville
Grandcamp
Vierville
Arromanches
Trouville
Carentan
La Haye-du-Puits
Coutances
Granville
St-Malo

his alone. For Cobra he planned a saturation attack against a single German division, Panzer Lehr, and then a drive-through by ground forces over the wreckage. Cobra was virtually an all-American show, with the bombers coming from USAAF Eighth and Ninth Air Forces. Bradley believed that the faults revealed by Charnwood, the heavy cratering and the long delay between the bombing and the ground attack, could be avoided by using smaller bombs and keeping the attacking troops well forward. Once more, at Montgomery's suggestion, he followed the British method of attack on a narrow front. The major

difference between the planning of Goodwood and Cobra was that Bradley had sufficient infantry to exploit the initial air bombardment, clearing the way in front of the armor. Even so, it was not expected that Cobra would achieve much more of an advance than Goodwood, for which so much had been hoped. Its objectives were set ten to fifteen miles away from the start lines, some distance from the west coast of the Cotentin at Granville, to envelop about six German divisions defending the line from St Lô to the coast. From this, it was hoped to unhinge the German line and strike out toward Brittany.

7 Map shows the course of US First Army's Operation Cobra, the breakout that would exceed all expectations. Part of its success was due to British Second Army's Operations Charnwood and Goodwood, which diverted powerful German forces.

ALLIED FIGHTER-BOMBERS

The Allied fighter-bombers engaged in Overlord were controlled by IX and XIX Tactical Air Commands of the USAAF Ninth Air Force, and by 83 and 84 Groups of the 2nd Tactical Air Force of the RAF. The Americans used the P-38 Lightning, the P-47 Thunderbolt and the P-51 Mustang, while the RAF also used the P-51, as well as Spitfires and Typhoons.

In order to obtain the maximum effect from the fighter-bomber squadrons, it would be essential to establish them on captured or specially constructed airfields in France as soon as possible after D-Day. In the meantime, during the Pointblank operations and the invasion itself, they were faced with transit flights from their bases in England.

During the prelude to Overlord they had been supreme in pin-point attacks against transport targets such as trains, convoys, bridges, and against airfield targets and radar stations. Targeting of the radar stations had been left until the last few days before the invasion to give the enemy the minimum of time to carry out repairs and get the stations back on the air.

On D-Day, most fighter-bomber operations were in close support of the landing forces. From H-Hour onward, squadrons were allocated to specific beaches, briefed to attack pre-arranged targets iden-

By noon on D-Day it was already becoming apparent that the unexpected deterioration in the weather would prevent the heavy bombers from successfully carrying out their attacks on towns in the rear, intended to block the roads and create chaos to impede the enemy's troop movements. The fighter-bombers were therefore ordered to seek out and engage any transport moving on the unblocked roads.

As the invasion and the breakout from the beaches progressed, the pattern of close air support continued. The work of the fighter-bombers has been described as "a fast-moving, far ranging aerial artillery which pounced on anything German which moved." As the Allied armor moved forward, each command tank wore its identifying fluorescent patch and carried an Air Support Control Officer who could call in the fighter-bombers as they were required.

By the end of June about forty fighter and fighter-bomber squadrons were operating from a dozen airfields in France. This was, unfortunately, well short of the eighty-one squadrons and twenty-seven airfields which had been anticipated in the Overall Air Plan. In some cases, airfields had been built by the engineering battalions but the forces on the ground had been unable to push the enemy back far enough to risk bringing in the aircraft.

1 *The Medal of Honor, America's highest military award, is seen here with its Air Force pendant: the head of "Lady Liberty."*

2

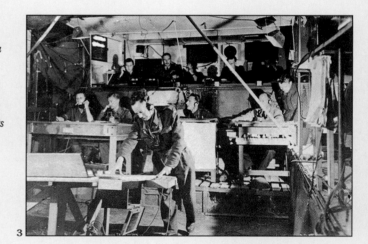

3

2 *With four 20mm cannon, as seen here, or carrying eight 60-pound rockets, the Typhoon was a potent "tank buster."*
(Fox Photos)
3 *Army-RAF liaison in ground attack operations: Group Control Centres sent Visual Control Points (one RAF, one Army officer) to the front to direct aircraft.*
4 *Pilots scramble on an order from a Group Control Center.*
(Keystone)

tified from the Pointblank reconnaissance missions. The squadrons were instructed to call up the Beach Headquarters Ship for their particular beach before commencing their attack, in case there were targets requiring more urgent attention. As the day progressed, the close support aircraft operated on a "cab-rank" system, flying standing patrols over the invasion area, from which they could be directed by liaison officers on the ground to attack specific targets as required. Other squadrons were dispatched further inland on armed reconnaissance patrols to search for targets of opportunity. As the day progressed the need for "cab-rank" aircraft decreased and they, too, were allocated to the armed reconnaissance role.

4

6 Like this shoulder sleeve patch, worn by personnel at USAAF HQ, Washington, D.C., USAAF insignia normally featured the colors blue, gold, white, and red.

5 USAAF Mustang pilots shoot the breeze after a mission. Although its most valuable role was that of long-range escort, the P-51 Mustang was also handy in ground attack.
(Keystone)

7 Groundcrew renew belts for ammunition needed by the eight 0.5in machine guns of the Republic P-47 Thunderbolt (nicknamed "Jug"; for

"Juggernaut"), the war's largest, heaviest fighter.
(US National Archives)

9 Developed from the Typhoon, the Hawker Tempest packed a powerful punch with bombs, cannon, or rockets. The Tempest V, seen here, was noted for success against V-1 flying bombs, claiming around 640 destroyed in flight.
(Aviation Bookshop)

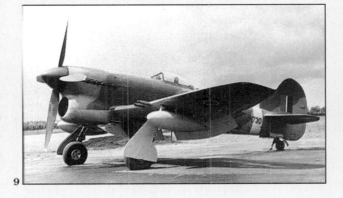

8 P-51 Mustangs over Britain in 1944; perhaps after escorting heavy bombers "there and back" to Berlin. With auxiliary fuel tanks, the Mustang had a range of around 600 miles. In the Pacific Theater it escorted B-29 Superfortresses in raids on Japan's home islands.
(US Army)

1 *Patch of US 30th Infantry Division ("Old Hickory"); raised in Tennessee and nicknamed for Andrew Jackson.*
2 *US tank crewman, in leather helmet with earphone flaps; holster for M1911 Colt .45 on pistol belt; M3A1 sub-machine gun slung.*

4 *Motorcyclists shepherd a convoy of British troops in jeeps, trucks, and Carden-Loyd Universal Carriers ("bren gun carriers").* (Keystone)

OPERATION COBRA

Bradley's original plan called for Cobra to start on July 19, something made impossible by the hard German resistance in defending St Lô. The following day, with St Lô in American hands, an unexpected heavy summer storm with driving all-day rain caused Cobra to be postponed once again (and also brought the fighting for the Bourguébus ridge to a virtual end on both sides). Mist and overcast skies caused similar anxieties to those which had dogged Eisenhower's original decision to launch the D-Day invasion back at the start of June. On July 23 it was agreed that there was a fifty percent chance of the weather being good enough for the bombers to see their target by one PM next day.

The first waves of heavy bombers were in the air on the morning of July 24 when the clouds closed in once more, and an extremely frustrated Bradley had to call off the operation. The message got through to those aircraft which had not taken off, and others flew home rather than bomb through the clouds. But about 300 aircraft released 685 tons of bombs over what they believed to be their target. On the ground, the soldiers watched in horror as the bombers flew in, not across the American positions from north to south, but down the Perriers-St Lô road along the line of the front, dropping bombs on German

3 *A flamethrower mounted on a German armored vehicle spreads destruction.*
5 *A change of livery for a Sherman tank that has fallen into German hands.*
(Bundesarchiv; both)

and American formations alike on either side of the road. Some 156 men of US 30th Infantry Division, waiting to attack, were killed or wounded. Alerted to the attack by the bombers, the Germans facing Cobra put down a heavy artillery bombardment, which they believed had stopped the attack and which cost more American casualties. In the face of this, the start of Cobra was reset for the following day, at eleven AM on July 25. Flying at between 12,000 and 15,000 feet, more than 1,880 American heavy and medium bombers released nearly 4,000 tons of bombs onto Panzer Lehr, backed up by fighter-bombers dropping smaller bombs, napalm (one of the first uses in war of that dreadful weapon), and white phosphorous.

6 *Heavy metal: a US 8-inch Howitzer M1 adds the weight of its 200-pound shell to an Allied bombardment.*
(IWM: EA 29632)
7 *Seen here during a night bombardment, the US 155mm gun M1 ("officially" nicknamed "Long Tom") threw a 96-pound projectile to a range of more than 14 miles.*
(Keystone)

1 *The badge of The Canadian Scottish Regiment features the cross of St. Andrew.*

2 *A morale-sapping message to German front-line troops is delivered by an officer of a Psychological Warfare Unit.* (IWM: B 6354)

3 *British armored troops advance through the Somme valley – the grave of many thousands of their forebears in the great World War I offensive 28 years earlier.*

4 *A GI of US 2nd Infantry Division approaches anti-tank gunners of British 3rd Infantry Division, as US and British forces link up near Vire in early August.* (IWM: B 8985)

5 *Badge of the 17th Duke of York's Royal Canadian Hussars (7th Reconnaissance Regiment; Canadian 3rd Division).*

Once more, some of the bombs landed on American troops, causing a further 601 killed and wounded. Among them was a senior American officer, Lieutenant-General Lesley McNair, who had been sent to Britain as Patton's supposed replacement commanding FUSAG after Patton's arrival in Normandy. The commander of US Army Ground Forces, McNair, more than anyone else, had built the magnificent armies waiting to begin Cobra, and had wanted to see them in action. He was buried with great secrecy.

The delays, and the double shock of being bombed by their own aircraft, "took the ginger," as First Army headquarters put it, out of the front-line troops of VII Corps. In 30th Division alone, 164 cases of shell shock were reported from the experience. Meanwhile, with no possibility of retreat, the defenders of Panzer Lehr fought in the bomb craters and the wreckage of their division almost literally to the last man. The result was even more disappointing than Goodwood had been for the British, as VII Corps advanced barely two miles into the German position. As American and German units became mingled together, a savage killing battle took a heavy toll on both sides. But, unlike the defenders of Caen, the Germans facing Cobra had neither armored reserves to call upon, nor any depth to their defensive positions. Collins added the leading troops of his armored divisions to the slow American heave on its second day, and more ground was gained. On the same day, July 26, US VIII Corps under Lieutenant-General Troy Middleton, holding the line west of VII Corps to the sea, joined in with an attack toward Perriers. Although the attack failed to advance more than a few hundred yards, it was enough to cause the German defenders in front of them to pull back next day. By July 27, VII Corps had fought its way through the German defenses. The leading columns of 2nd Armored Division, Patton's own old "Hell on Wheels" command, were twelve miles behind the old front line by the end of the day, out on the roads of France, moving south and west with almost nothing to stop them. To the west, the Germans facing VIII Corps were in danger of being trapped against the sea. What had for nearly two months been a static attrition battle in the hedgerows suddenly became a battle of movement, sudden ambushes, tanks surging down the little roads in a cloud of dust with fighter-bombers roaring overhead.

THE CANADIANS AND THE BRITISH

Canadian First Army had come officially into existence on July 23 under Lieutenant-General Henry (Harry) Crerar, consisting at first of Canadian II Corps and British I Corps. The new Canadian Army's first battle in Normandy, codenamed Operation Spring, was planned to start two days later, as an attack by II Corps due south from Caen, with the two Canadian infantry divisions leading once more, and two British armored divisions held in reserve behind them. The Canadians' objectives were set about three miles from their start line, through defenses that included 1st SS Panzer Division. The Canadians attacked at 3:30 AM on July 25, by coincidence on the same day as the rescheduled Operation Cobra, fuelling speculation that Montgomery planned a breakout on the eastern flank rather than the western. This was certainly believed by the Germans, who continued to treat the Canadian attack

as the main Allied offensive for two days, giving additional help to Cobra. Operation Spring, however, was stopped dead on its first day with heavy casualties. It was later suggested that it had always been planned as a diversionary attack. In 2nd Division, the Canadian Black Watch suffered 307 casualties trying to break through the German defenses, the worst losses for any Canadian battalion since Dieppe. In 3rd Division, the North Novia Scotia Highlanders lost 139 men in a fruitless attempt to take the village of Tilly la

3

4

CRERAR

Henry Duncan Graham Crerar was born on April 28, 1888 in Hamilton, Ontario. Although educated at the Royal Military College, Kingston, he decided to become an oil engineer rather than a soldier, keeping a reserve commission in the artillery. He was called for active service at the start of the First World War, and served throughout with the Canadian Corps on the Western Front, being decorated for bravery. Remaining in the Army after the war, he became Commandant of the Royal Military College in 1938 as a colonel. With the outbreak of the Second World War he was sent to London to organize Canadian troops in Britain. In 1941 he became Chief of Canadian Army Staff back in Ottawa, and in 1942 went back overseas as commander of Canadian 2nd Division and then as commander of the Canadian Corps in Italy, as a lieutenant-general. In January, 1944, he was appointed as commander of the Canadian Overseas Army in London, which later became Canadian First Army in Normandy. He commanded First Army, which at times also included British and Polish troops, to the end of the war in Europe. In 1946 he retired from the Army and from public life, and died quietly in Ottawa on April 1, 1965.

6 *Lieutenant-General Crerar took command of Canadian First Army on July 23, and on July 25 Canadians spearheaded Operation Spring, a southward push from Caen. It was halted by heavy losses among weary troops,* *but diverted strong German forces from Cobra.*
(National Archives of Canada)
7 *Going carefully: GIs probe for mines ahead of a Sherman.*
(Keystone)

1

2

Campagne. Another battalion sent to replace the high-landers described itself as "worn out." After the battle, the commanders of the brigade and both battalions were replaced. Many units among the British and Americans who had fought since D-Day and the first days of the Battle of Normandy were reaching the same state. A temporary expedient was to replace commanders, but the only practical solution was to rest the men or use another division.

With Operation Spring a failure, Montgomery moved his Guards Armored and 7th Armored Divisions from behind the Canadians over to the other end of the British line, next to the Americans, in order to support Operation Cobra. This in itself was a major achievement in the crowded lanes and roads of Normandy, showing remarkable traffic control as some units moved fifty miles between nightfall on July 28 and dawn two days later. The seemingly mundane skill of the military police of both US First Army and British Second Army in keeping vehicles moving and on schedule behind the front lines, assembling forces and their supplies, was one of the many underrated reasons for the Allied victory. At one British checkpoint, records showed that 18,836 vehicles passed in twenty-four hours, or one every four seconds throughout the period.

The British attack began on July 30, codenamed Operation Bluecoat and made once more by O'Connor's

VIII Corps, together with XXX Corps in support. The British drove from the high ground at Caumont down into the depths of the hedgerow country aiming for the town of Vire, another crucial road junction and the last line of resistance that the Germans could reasonably hold. By now the British troops, according to one of them, were "weary with the endless routine of marching and fighting, they were already punch-drunk with battle." There was little enthusiasm left in the infantry and armor, no pipers playing, only a determination to fight through. Few were aware that the enemy was in an even worse state, and to most of them it made little difference. Finally, like the Americans to the west, to take the ground away from the Germans they would have to get up and walk forward into the fire.

Once more the British blasted a path for their infantry with heavy bombers and artillery, although not as much of either as in previous operations due to the speed with which Bluecoat had been mounted. The troops of XXX Corps, attacking toward Mont Pincon, made almost no progress on the first two days, failing to get five miles despite light opposition, and Dempsey took the unusual step of replacing the corps commander, along with the commander of 7th Armored Division. As in their earlier battles, the British did not break out of Normandy but ground their way out against a German opposition that showed its usual tactical skill in leaving delaying parties or small fire-teams to slow down the advance. The front line was at last moving forward, but in the hedgerows it was anything but a dash.

3 *Trucks carrying Canadian infantry roll past a battery of 5.5-inch howitzers engaged in artillery support for the abortive Operation Spring.*
(National Archives of Canada)

4 *A Sherman "Crab" flail tank: one of the "funnies" developed by British 79th Armoured Division. Lashing chains on the rotating drum detonated mines to clear a 10-foot-wide track.*
(IWM: B 7495)

3

4

1 *Operation Bluecoat: British infantry with Carden-Loyd Universal Carriers (and note flail tank – see (4) – in background) move down from Caumont on July 30.*

2 *The British "Wasp," a flame projector fitted to a Universal Carrier, displays its sting.*

5

6

7

5 *Badge of The Royal Northumberland Fusiliers; in Normandy, 4th RNF were a machine gun and mortar unit.*

6 *Carriers loaded with British infantrymen prepare to advance south of Caumont on July 31. Air and artillery bombardment had attempted to clear the way for Bluecoat, but progress was slow.*
(IWM: B 8308)

7 *Shoulder flash of The Black Watch (Royal Highland Regiment) of Canada; severely mauled in Operation Spring.*

Multi-barreled "volley guns" appeared in the Middle Ages; the hand-cranked Gatling in the US Civil War; and the "modern" machine gun in the 1880s, when Hiram Maxim designed an "automatic" arm in which energy generated by the recoil of one cartridge was harnessed to chamber and fire another. The machine gun dominated trench warfare in World War I, when the light machine gun (LMG) emerged as a squad weapon. In World War II, such arms as the German MG-34 gave rise to the "general purpose machine gun" (GPMG), combining the portability of the LMG with firepower approaching that of the heavy/medium weapon.

1 *Of Czech-British origin (Br: Brno; En: Enfield): the British Bren LMG.*

1, 7 *The .303in Bren, seen also on a tripod mounting at (7), weighed 22.5lb (gun only) and fired up to 500 rpm from a 30-round box magazine.*

4 *Pre-loaded belts can be fed straight from the ammunition boxes into the machine gun.*
5 *German infantryman (right) advances on the double, shouldering an MG-34.*
(Bundesarchiv)

6 *The German Mauser MG-34 machine gun was (with the later MG-42) the first of the modern GPMGs. The example shown, on an integral bipod mount, is fitted with a 75-round saddle drum magazine; the air-cooled MG-42 fired also from a belt of up to 250 7.92mm rounds, to a rate of 800-900 rounds per minute.*

2 *A GI humps the 33lb (gun only) bulk of the water-cooled .30in Model 1917 Browning medium machine gun.*
(US National Archives)
3 *Water-cooled Vickers .303in machine gun: standard British MMG from c.1912 until 1966.*

5

8 *Bren gunner in action.*
(IWM: B 5382)

6

4

7

8

1 *A tracked personnel carrier leads jeeps and trucks of an American convoy through a shattered town.*
(US National Archives)

3 *As the pace of the Allied advance increases, the* New York Post *boasts on July 27 that US armies "sweep on in France".*

1

2 *Narrowly escaping "fallout" from a white phosphorus shell, GIs close in on a German sniper post at Brest, where fighting dragged on well into September.*
(IWM: KY 52460)

PATTON'S ARMY

Lieutenant-General George S. Patton Jr had experienced a very frustrating time since his failure to win preference over Bradley for command of US First Army in December, 1943. Used for the deception of FUSAG but denied much part in the planning of Overlord, Patton had little faith in Montgomery's plan for the battle. The two men, in many ways so similar despite their different nationalities and backgrounds, had fought as Army commanders in Sicily, and at best, their relationship could be described as friendly rivalry. Both were convinced of their own military genius, and both hated to lose. While Montgomery was criticized for excessive caution, Patton had landed himself in trouble more than once with his love of taking flamboyant risks. But Patton's readiness to take chances with the lives of his men had produced results, and he had not failed yet. Of all the Allied commanders in Normandy, his approach to war was the most similar to that of the German commanders, and he was the Allied general whom they most feared.

Now was Patton's chance to redeem himself and restore his career. On July 28, as the Germans fell back and the way opened up in front of Cobra, Bradley at once put VIII Corps under Patton's US Third Army command. The formality of bringing Third Army into operational existence took another four days, by which time Patton's forces were already moving out of Normandy and into Britanny, with orders from Bradley to "maintain unrelenting pressure" on the Germans. While this was happening, with Patton looking after his western flank, Bradley reverted to his broad front methods, spreading the offensive across US First Army into a general advance, linked to the British Bluecoat offensive.

With the Germans withdrawing in front of him, one of the more unkind remarks made by hostile First Army soldiers about Patton's advance was that "he didn't break

out – he walked out." It was nevertheless a very impressive walk, at a speed which gave the enemy no time to recover and seal up the front. Middleton's VIII Corps was already pushing south as fast as its engineers could clear the German minefields. On July 27 Patton ordered 4th and 6th Armored Divisions through the infantry to spearhead VIII Corps advance down the roads. This armored drive took place in the middle of an infantry battle, itself in the middle of a minefield. By the evening of July 28 the leading armor held the town of Coutances, with the two divisions strung out behind their spearheads, but air reconnaissance showed that there was no fixed German defense in front of the advancing divisions. In the next three days, VIII Corps captured over 7,000 prisoners, and dealing with German troops who wanted to surrender became the single biggest factor slowing down the American advance. At one point, without knowing it, the leading column of 4th Armored Division almost overran the forward headquarters of German Seventh Army. By the morning of August 1, 4th Armored had secured three crossings over the River See, two of them in the crucial seaside town of Avranches, with the famous Mont St Michel island monastery just offshore.

5¢ **New York Post**
COMPLETE NEWS-MAGAZINE SECTION-COMIC FEATURES
TWO SECTIONS   NEW YORK, THURSDAY, JULY 27, 1944   40 PAGES

Americans:
SWEEP ON IN FRANCE
—Story on Page 2

Russians:
STORM OVER VISTULA
Story on Page 3

3

4

2

4 *Black American soldiers keep their weapons at the ready. The enlisted man (right) holds a .30in Model 1903 Springfield rifle.*
(US National Archives)

7 *US Army Engineers engaged in reconstruction of river bridges near Coutances, partially destroyed by the retreating Germans.*
(US National Archives)

8 *The smoke of battle still hangs over the devastated town of Coutances on the evening of July 28, just after its capture by armored units of US Third Army.*

5 *Patch of US 3rd Armored Division; "Spearhead."*
6 *Flamboyant, hard-driving Lieutenant-General George S. Patton, Jr., nicknamed "Old Blood and Guts."*
(US National Archives)

PATTON

George Smith Patton, Jr. was born to a wealthy California family on November 11, 1885. He attended the Virginia Military Institute and West Point, graduating in 1909, and joined the 15th Cavalry Regiment. A keen sportsman, he became the first American to represent his country in the modern pentathlon at the Olympic Games in Stockholm in 1912. In 1916 he obtained a place as an aide to Brigadier-General John J. ("Black Jack') Pershing for the Mexican War. In 1917, with American entry into the First World War, Pershing was selected to command the American Expeditionary Force to France, and took Patton with him. Patton was appointed second-in-command of the new US Army Tank Corps, and finished the war as a colonel, having been wounded in action.

Seeing no future in tanks, Patton returned to the cavalry, and by 1938 had worked his way up to colonel again. With his independent wealth he had no need to remain in the Army, but he believed in himself as a soldier. In 1940, with the expansion of the army, he was given 2nd Armored Brigade to command, a year later 2nd Armored Division, and in 1942, command of I Armored Corps in the United States. In November, 1942 he commanded part of the Torch landings on the north coast of Africa, landing virtually unopposed in Morocco. Patton developed a reputation for hard driving, and in March, 1943, he was given II Armored Corps in Tunisia after its defeat at Kassarine Pass, being promoted to lieutenant-general. For the invasion of Sicily in July, 1943, Patton was given command of US Seventh Army. Although successful, Patton was a controversial commander. He was dismissed from Seventh Army after two incidents in which he slapped American soldiers suffering from battle fatigue, claiming that they were cowards.

With the appointment of Bradley, who had been his deputy at II Armored Corps, to command First Army in Normandy, Patton's career appeared to be over. He was too good a commander to lose, however, and was brought back to command Third Army in Normandy in July, 1944, leading it successfully up to the end of the war in Europe and being promoted to full general. Never at home with politics, he was dismissed from Third Army in Germany in September, 1945 for his leniency toward former Nazis, and given command of Fifteenth Army, a paper formation. On December 9, 1945, Patton broke his neck in a car crash. He was taken to an American military hospital in Heidelberg, where he died on December 21.

1 *Caught by a German photographer as battle smoke rolls above her home, a French housewife's look of weary resignation embodies what must often have been the mood of civilians caught up in the Normandy battles.*
(Bundesarchiv)

2 *Tanks, scout cars, halftracked troop carriers, and (right) a Willys MB Jeep with .30 caliber Browning MG, churn up a village lane.*
(US National Archives)

3 *A Tiger tank, apparently in trouble, is passed by an SdKfz.166* Brummbär *("Grizzly Bear") tank destroyer.*
(Bundesarchiv)

Events now moved very swiftly. Generals and soldiers who for weeks had thought of the Battle of Normandy in terms of advances of a few hundred yards were now planning in terms of miles. Patton, new to the front and with his relaxed command style encouraging subordinates to press hard, was the perfect commander for the job. In twenty-four hours he pushed his two armored divisions and two following infantry divisions through Avranches over a single bridge. In the next twelve days, averaging advances of ten miles a day, 4th and 6th Armored Divisions overran Britanny, with the rest of VIII Corps following. As at Cherbourg, however, the German garrisons kept firm

hold on the main ports. "We're winning this war the wrong way," complained Major-General John Wood commanding 4th Armored, "we ought to be going to Paris!" It took until August 15 for Bradley to recognize that the Germans holding the Brittany ports were not going to be bluffed into surrender, and to turn VIII Corps' forces eastward.

With the offical activation of Third Army, Bradley's headquarters was also changed to become 12th Army Group, making him equal with Montgomery under Eisenhower. But with the situation of the battle so fluid, Eisenhower left Montgomery in charge. While the original Cobra plan had been intended as a modest advance with the securing of the Britanny ports the first priority, Bradley now ordered Patton, with Montgomery's approval, to send the rest of Third Army eastward into the French countryside and to drive for the River Seine. With the German front breaking open before US First Army and British Second Army, von Kluge described his position as "a madhouse." The Germans had known for some time that they had lost the Battle of Normandy. Now the Allies knew it too.

4 *Clearing a newly-captured town of snipers was a task calling for extreme caution and, as the GI with the M3A1 "grease gun" demonstrates, no little agility. His buddy crouches with his M1 carbine at the ready as they seek to discover whether there are enemy hold-outs taking cover in a house at Coutances.*
(UPI/Bettmann)

5 *Chow among the ruins: men of a US Army engineering unit take a break while they eat cold rations.*
(US National Archives)

HITLER'S LAST THROW

The one person on the German side not ready to concede defeat was Adolf Hitler. Despite von Kluge's repeated requests to be allowed to pull his forces back, Hitler, relying on his maps at the Wolf's Lair, planned instead to counterattack. It was a plan made without reference to what had happened to the German Army in Normandy, moving pins on a map as if the divisions that they represented were at full strength, properly supplied with fuel and ammunition, and could maneuver at will without having to face Allied airpower, to which the power of artillery and tanks in increasing numbers was being added as the Allied armies found space to spread out. On August 2, as Patton's forces were driving eastward deep into France, Hitler issued his own orders for an attack by five armored divisions at the little town of Mortain, just north of the hinge between US First and Third Armies. It was here, Hitler decreed, that the Germans would break through all the way back to the coast at Avranches, cutting Patton off

from the rest of the Allied forces and bottling up the Normandy beachhead once again. In the atmosphere of suspicion generated by the recent assassination attempt, few of Hitler's generals were prepared to argue with him, but none showed any faith in the idea.

Mortain, a dot on the map for Hitler, was in the heart of the worst of the hedgerow country, the Suisse Normande, and hardly ideal for armored sweeps of the sort that had characterized the Eastern Front. Fuel shortages and Allied airstrikes meant that it took three days to assemble the

6 *Arms raised in surrender, a long line of newly-captured Germans moves towards the rear, passed by one of Patton's speeding Shermans fresh from the conquest of Avranches; August 1.*
(UPI/Bettmann)

1 Feldgendarmerie *(Military Field Police) patrol of a Fallschirmjäger (paratroop) unit. Note the* Ringkraken *(metal gorget) – seen in more detail at* **(2)** *– around the neck of the NCO seated on the bonnet of the utility truck.*
(Bundesarchiv)

2 Feldgendarmerie Ringkraken: *the gorget worn as a distinguishing mark when on duty by Military Field Police personnel of the German Army. On the matt silver shield, the bosses, national eagle, and legend are picked out in gold luminous paint, for high visibility. In all armies military policemen are traditionally unpopular among the lower ranks and are usually given nicknames that reflect this: in the German Army, the* Ringkraken *gained the* Feldgendarmerie *the sobriquet of "Chained Dogs."*

4, 5 *The* Feldgendarmerie Ringkraken *marks the figure at* **(4)** *as that of a Military Field Policeman; he holds a traffic direction baton (bearing the message: "Stop: Police") much like those seen at* **(5)**. *He wears a* rubberized waterproof coat and carries an MP-40 "Schmeisser" sub-machine gun, with triple magazine pouches (along with a waterproof map/document case) on his belt.

3 *German infantrymen grab a lift on a tank. In combat zones, a major task of* Feldgendarmerie *was to ensure that any stragglers quickly returned to the front line.*
(Bundesarchiv)

6 Feldgendarmerie *missed these stragglers, who had holed up in a convent at Avranches. Nuns negotiated their surrender to the incoming Americans.*
(UPI/Bettmann)

remnants of four panzer divisions, with about 140 tanks, to make the attack. To add to the Germans' problems, Ultra gave the Allies a few hours' warning that the attack was about to happen. When the Germans came forward through the hedgerows just after midnight on August 7 they found the troops of 30th Division in a hasty defense, having reached the town four hours earlier. Mortain itself fell to an attack by 2nd SS Panzer Division, but the rocky hill to the east, Hill 317, was already held by 2/120th Infantry Regiment. As dawn came up, Allied fighter-bombers and rocket-firing aircraft joined in the destruction of the German armor. A promised maximum effort of air support from the Luftwaffe was intercepted by Allied fighters and never materialized over the battlefield.

Within 24 hours of the first German attack, US VII Corps had seven divisions under command, quite enough to stop the Germans if they made any further progress, and although the 30th Division lost 300 men in the day's fighting, it held its ground. The battalion headquarters of

2/120th Infantry was overrun by the Germans, but 700 men of the battalion under Captain Reynold Erickson remained on the hill. Despite losing half their number, the men of 2/120th Infantry held Hill 317 against the Germans for five days. The battalion was given a Presidential citation, while Erickson and each of his four company commanders received the Distinguished Service Cross.

Long before relief reached the men on Hill 317 the German attack was finished. By nightfall on August 7 the Americans had taken 350 German prisoners, and estimated the number of remaining enemy tanks at Mortain as thirty or less. Hitler's gamble had not only failed, it had doomed the German troops in Normandy by preventing them from withdrawing, and by using up their armor. By August 8, Patton's leading tanks were at Le Mans, over fifty miles south and east of Mortain. "This is an opportunity that comes to a commander not more than once a century," Bradley observed, "We are about to destroy an entire German army."

7 Prisoners of war taken by US VIII Corps at Coutances.
(UPI/Bettmann)
8 An American military policeman in a forward area is distinguished by his white-banded, lettered helmet and, unseen in this photograph, an "MP" brassard on his left arm.
(US National Archives)
9 Equipment of a US MP includes web leggings, brassard, pistol belt, and night stick. The all-white helmet which gained US MPs their least insulting nickname, "Snowdrops," was worn only in rear areas.

6

7

8

9

Early in 1945 the number of prisoners of war (PoWs) held by all combatants was about 4 million (including estimates of PoWs held by the USSR, Soviet PoWs held by Germany, and Chinese PoWs held by Japan). Germany held c.765,000 French, c.550,000 Italian, c.200,000 British and Commonwealth, c.125,000 Yugoslavian, and c.90,000 American PoWs. Japan held c.108,000 British and Commonwealth, 22,000 Dutch, and 15,000 American PoWs. The Allies (excluding the USSR) held c.630,000 German, c.430,000 Italian, and c.11,600 Japanese PoWs. (Italy, having changed allegiance, had men held by both sides.) Allied PoWs (other than East Europeans) held by Germany, and Axis PoWs held by the Allies (other than the USSR), were generally treated in accordance with the Geneva Convention of 1929, which enjoined humane treatment monitored by representatives of neutral countries.

2

1

3

1 Allied psychological warfare publications assure Germans that if they surrender they will be given safe conduct and fair treatment. The German language leaflet promises that PoWs held in the USA and Canada will be allowed to earn 80 cents per day for camp duties, with which they may purchase cigarettes, soft drinks, and candy.

2 A German teenager surrenders at Coutances. By August 1944 the difficulty of handling an increasingly large number of captured Germans threatened to slow the Allied advance.
(UPI/Bettmann)
3 Men of the German garrison at

Boulogne march into captivity after their surrender to Canadian troops late in September 1944.
(Associated Press)
4 Newly captured PoWs bring in one of their wounded.
(US National Archives)

4

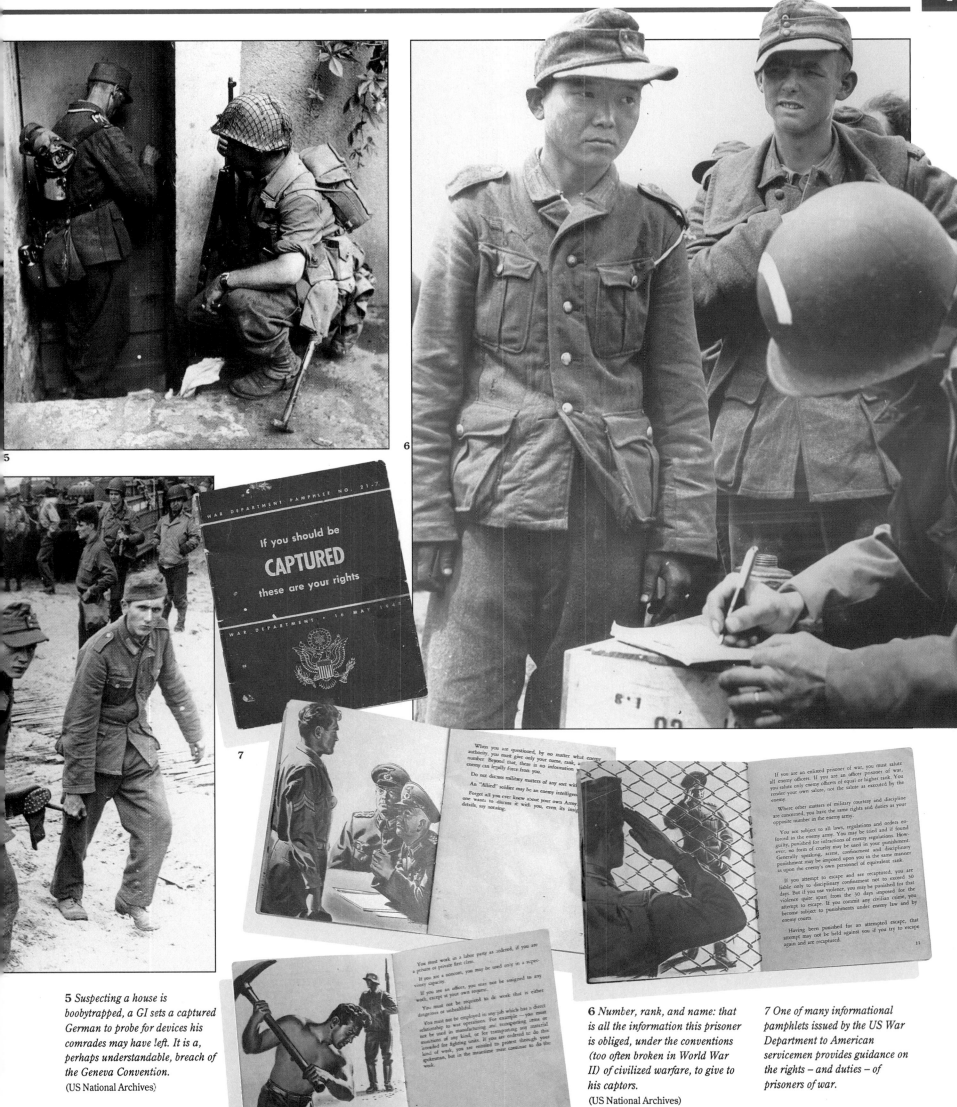

5 Suspecting a house is boobytrapped, a GI sets a captured German to probe for devices his comrades may have left. It is a, perhaps understandable, breach of the Geneva Convention.
(US National Archives)

6 Number, rank, and name: that is all the information this prisoner is obliged, under the conventions (too often broken in World War II) of civilized warfare, to give to his captors.
(US National Archives)

7 One of many informational pamphlets issued by the US War Department to American servicemen provides guidance on the rights – and duties – of prisoners of war.

CHAPTER ELEVEN

DEATH OF AN ARMY

The failure of the German counterattack at Mortain left the whole of Hausser's Seventh Army sitting inside a rapidly forming pocket of Allied troops, bounded to the west by US First Army, to the south by US Third Army, and to the north by British Second Army. British XXX Corps, under the newly-arrived Lieutenant-General Brian Horrocks, finally secured Mount Pincon on August 6. O'Connor's VIII Corps was also within reach of Vire, but a small change in the Army boundaries led to the task of taking the town falling to the Americans. Like all advances through the Suisse Normande, this was a hard fight against determined opposition, in marked contrast to the open driving of Patton's Third Army. In a night attack starting on August 6, US 29th Infantry Division cleared the rubble and ruins of Vire of the last of its German defenders. The attack was led once more by the 116th Infantry, the Stonewall Brigade, who had fought through Normandy from Omaha beach to the edge of the hedgerow country. In an advance of twenty miles from St Lô to Vire, the 29th Division had lost nearly a thousand men.

In order to complete the pocket on the northeastern side, Montgomery ordered Canadian First Army to attack south once more, with its II Corps aimed at Falaise. With this little historic town in Allied hands, Fifth Panzer Army would join Seventh Army inside the Allied trap. Apparently joining in the spirit of British racing terminology, Crerar on August 7, launched Operation Totalize down the Falaise road. For this, Canadian II Corps was more than five divisions strong, including the newly- arrived Canadian 4th Armored and Polish 1st Armored Divisions. Lieutenant-General Guy Simmonds, commanding II Corps, had some claim to have invented the armored personnel carrier for the attack by ordering turretless Sherman tanks known as "Kangaroos" and tracked gun platforms called "Unfrocked Priests" (a Priest was a type of self-propelled gun) to be used to carry some of his infantry.

Previous page: Mourners for the dying Third Reich. (Bundesarchiv)
1 *Lieutenant-General Brian Horrocks took command of British XXX Corps in August.* (IWM: B 9302)

The Canadians knew that two Waffen-SS divisions had been pulled out of the line in front of them only four days before Totalize to take part in Hitler's planned counterattack, leaving the front held by one weak infantry division. Crerar hoped for the Poles to reach Falaise, about eighteen miles from the start line, in a single sustained drive. RAF Bomber Command laid on the support, by now expected, from over 1,000 bombers, followed by the ground attack just before midnight, aided by "artificial moonlight" from powerful searchlights reflecting off the clouds. By mid-morning the first phase of the operation, an advance of five miles, had been achieved. But the second phase, passing the two armored divisions through the infantry, was marred by Canadian inexperience and small pockets of German resistance, as reinforcements arrived from part of 12th SS Panzer Division and a weak battalion of Tiger tanks. The Canadian difficulties were increased when the heavy bomber support from US Eighth Air Force, which appeared after midday, again managed to hit its own troops, causing over 300 Canadian and Polish casualties. At least one Canadian unit vented its feelings by opening fire on the American bombers.

Whereas in the Cotentin peninsula the Germans were prepared to give up ground to the Americans rather than be trapped, between Caen and Falaise they knew that to retreat would doom the whole of Army Group B. The formidable Michael Wittmann, now a captain, led his Tiger into action with his customary aggression, being finally killed while taking on five Canadian Shermans single-handed at close range. "Panzer" Meyer of the Hitler Jugend stopped one German retreat by standing in the path of the fleeing men, a cigar clenched between his teeth, and demanding if the troops would leave him to face

2 Canadian armor moves up, accompanied by infantry in trucks, carriers, and (in foreground) an M3 halftrack armored personnel carrier.
3 Railroad installations at Vire after its capture by US 29th Infantry Division on August 6-7. (US National Archives)

5

7

4 Cloth insignia of XV Corps; US Third Army.

5 A Tricolor in the hands of a World War I veteran welcomes Canadians of the South Saskatchewan Regiment to a French town.
(National Archives of Canada)

6 Colonel-General Paul Hausser, whose German Seventh Army was threatened by encirclement after the failure of the Mortain counteroffensive. The veteran tanker had spent 33 years in the German Army before joining the Waffen-SS in the 1930s. He was wounded in action at Falaise.
(Bundesarchiv)

7 Kurt "Panzer" Meyer, the ruthless commander of 12th SS Panzer Division (Hitler Jugend), whose tanks temporarily stalled the Canadian advance down the Falaise road.
(Bundesarchiv)

6

THE POLES

Poland collapsed in the face of the German onslaught in September, 1939, with Soviet forces joining in to occupy eastern Poland in October. Members of the Polish Army, and many other Poles determined to fight, escaped from the German occupation of their country. Some went by the northern route through Scandanavia to Scotland. Others went into internment in nearby neutral countries and made their way abroad. Many survived the first German occupation, to leave by the southern route down through central Europe to the Balkans. Other Poles, or people of Polish ancestry, came from around the world to fight. The Free Poles established a reputation as among the best and most ruthless fighters on the Allied side.

Through a long historical connection, the majority of the Free Poles, perhaps 100,000 soldiers and airmen, volunteered for French service, supplying three infantry divisions, a cavalry division and a mountain brigade to the French Army. With the collapse of France in 1940, no more than 18,000 escaped to Britain, joined by more Poles from overseas. The soldiers were re-equipped and reorganized by the British to form Polish 1st Armored Division, inheritor of the old cavalry titles of regiments which had fought against the Germans in 1939, and Polish 1st Parachute Brigade, which fought with distinction as part of British I Airborne Corps at Arnhem in September, 1944. In 1942, the Polish government-in-exile in London, under General Wladislaw Sikorski, negotiated with the Soviet Union the release of Poles taken by the Soviet forces in 1939. Leaving the Soviet Union through Iran, they also were re-equipped by the British, and fought as Polish II Corps in Italy, earning the distinction of capturing Monte Cassino monastery.

General Sikorki died in an air crash in July, 1943. Unable to return to a Poland occupied by the Soviet Union after the war, the Free Poles established themselves throughout the world, many going to Canada after their experiences fighting alongside the Canadians. The government-in-exile continued in existence in Britain until the collapse of communist authority and the establishment of the new Polish constitution in 1990.

5

2 *The Polish Eagle – seen on the berets of officers at (1) – was the badge of Free Polish forces.*

1 *With Montgomery are Major-General Stanislaw Maczek and officers of Polish 1st Armored Division. Note the "Jerusalem Cross," worn by Poles who had fought in the Middle East, on battledress of officer nearest camera.*
(IWM: B 8762)
3 *Admiral Swirski, Commander in Chief of the Polish Navy.*
4 *Tanks of Polish 1st Armored Division ready to roll.*
(IWM: B 8826)

3

4

7

5 *In a night attack immediately before the Canadian advance, more than 1,000 RAF heavy bombers broke the ground for Operation Totalize. Men of Canadian II Corps watch the bombardment from their start line.*
(National Archives of Canada)
6 *GIs examine a six-barreled* Nebelwerfer *("smoke thrower;" the weapon was originally*

designed as a chemical mortar) rocket launcher, abandoned – and perhaps, as a warning notice suggests, boobytrapped – by the retreating Germans.
(US National Archives)
7 *Smoke rolls over the Falaise road following the Totalize air bombardment.*
(IWM: HU 52367)

the enemy alone. By these and similar desperate actions a handful of German tanks and infantry defending the villages of the open Falaise plain stopped the Canadian offensive by the end of the second day, in a repetition of the British experience in Operation Goodwood. Trying to maintain the momentum, Lieutenant-General Simmonds ordered his armored forces to to press on through the night. This was an extremely dangerous action for Second World War tanks, which had virtually no night-fighting capability, and most of the armored troops quietly ignored the order. The British Columbia Regiment (28th Armored), with two companies of the Algonquin Regiment, attempted to advance but lost its way in the dark, and misreported its position as it came under Tiger attack the next morning. Attempts to reach the regimental group or give it fire support were directed to the wrong location. The Canadian force was destroyed with the loss of forty-seven tanks – virtually the whole armored regiment – and 240 men. By August 10 the advance was clearly at an end, having reached only half the distance to Falaise.

PATTON AT ARGENTAN

Montgomery's original plan had been for Canadian First Army, after securing Falaise, to drive southward to Argentan, so closing Army Group B in a giant encirclement. On August 8 Bradley proposed a new plan, turning Patton's XV Corps northward to Argentan, well outside its existing

8 *A Canadian infantryman lies dead on the road between Caen and Falaise. After creeping forward for three days against savage German resistance – and tragically losing men also to "friendly" air attack – the Totalize advance finally stalled on August 10, only about half way to Falaise.*
(National Archives of Canada)

1 *An aerial reconnaissance picture taken in mid-August shows Allied armor moving in a well-ordered column into a village in the Falaise area. A P-51 Mustang in RAF livery (note "invasion stripes") patrols overhead. Tactical air forces continually harassed the retreating Germans and guarded the Allies against any attempts the Luftwaffe might make to disrupt the advance.*
(Keystone)

boundaries, in order to trap the German Seventh Army. Eisenhower was enthusiastic, if still reluctant to interfere in what was becoming a complex (if not actually chaotic) battle, and Montgomery was grateful for the proposal. By the time that Totalize came to a halt, XV Corps had already reached a line north of Le Mans, about sixty miles almost due south of the Canadians. Serving with the Americans was French 2nd Armored Division, coming into action against the Germans on French soil for the first time. The use of the French division underlined the problems of coalition warfare when, either in their enthusiasm to get into action or entering into Third Army's freewheeling spirit, the French disregarded the boundaries allocated for their advance and drove onto US 5th Armored Division's roads. The resulting traffic jam delayed the advance to Argentan by half a day, allowing the Germans to reinforce their position north of the town, and for a handful more of their soldiers to escape eastward from the Allied trap.

2 *Wrecked locomotives and rolling stock litter the railroad depot at Argentan, vital objective in the battle to close the Falaise Gap. Patton bitterly resented Bradley's order that brought his XV Corps to a halt south of the town.*
(US National Archives)

3 *A GI advances through the ruins of Argentan on August 20. Next day the town was secured by US First Army.*
(US National Archives)

Ignoring Bradley's fears that his force would be too weak to close the trap for the Germans, Patton ordered his commanders to disregard the stop line set for them just south of Argentan. Late on August 12, he reported the leading units of 5th Armored as being inside the town, which in fact remained in German hands, although some troops of 5th Armored, having negotiated their way past the French, were just north of it. Never one to hesitate, Patton demanded permission to carry on northward "and drive the British into the sea for another Dunkirk." When Bradley refused to let his men go further north than Argentan, Patton characteristically – and wrongly – blamed Montgomery for trying to steal his thunder.

pocket not hitting their own ground troops was also a factor. After the war, the decision to halt Patton at Argentan would become an endless source of needless argument and controversy. For a few days, between the success of the Cobra breakout and the capture of Argentan, the Allied generals had actually had full control of the battle, almost independent of their enemy's ability to interfere. Now, in the woods, the bocage and the Falaise plain, and in the skies above, the battle was back in the hands of the fighting soldiers once again.

OPERATION TRACTABLE

After the disappointments of Spring and Totalize, the Canadians decided that nothing less than another full set-piece attack would be enough to break the German line. Rather than aiming directly for Falaise, Montgomery

4 *This Panther tank of 116th Panzer Division was knocked out in the shadow of St. Germain Cathedral, Argentan.* (IWM: B 9537)

5 *A British sniper finds cover near the wreckage of a Tiger tank of a Waffen-SS Panzer division. In the foreground a Waffen-SS trooper has literally died with his boots on; just beyond the corpse is a German 50mm light mortar.* (IWM: B 6154)

5

ordered Crerar to swing east of the town, and then south towards Argentan to link up with US Third Army and close the pocket for good. Organized in two days, the attack was essentially a renewal of Totalize for which Simmonds dispensed with written orders, reflecting a growing experience within his II Corps. The original codename of Operation Tallulah (which was neither easy to say nor to spell) was replaced on August 13 by that of Operation Tractable. At noon the next day, using smokescreens to provide cover, Canadian 3rd Infantry and 4th Armored Divisions attacked, with help from the Funnies of 79th Armored Division. "Hit him first, hit him hard, and keep hitting him," Lieutenant-General Crerar ordered his men. Once more heavy bomber support was laid on for the attack, with nearly 1,000 aircraft of RAF Bomber Command striking at German targets on the flanks of the Canadian drive. An error in identification led to seventy-seven aircraft, most of them, ironically, from 6 (Royal Canadian Air Force) Group, bombing short onto their own troops, for which Bomber Command firmly blamed itself. As on previous occasions, troops being bombed by their own side were hardly at their most

The problem for the Allies of what was now being called the Falaise pocket turned out to be greater than the generals trying to solve it. All the Allied problems of coordination, coalition warfare, the need for caution and for limiting their own casualties, together with the difficulties of finishing off German troops who were fighting for their lives, combined to make the closing of the Falaise gap a difficult and dangerous encounter. Eisenhower was genuinely concerned that the meeting between Canadians and Americans might result in unintentioned shooting, a "calamitous battle between friends." The accuracy and reliability of the Allied air forces that were busy destroying the Germans inside the

6

6 *Infantrymen of US First Army move into battle-scarred Argentan. Its fall on August 21 marked the closing of the Falaise Gap.* (US National Archives)

Mortars are short-barreled bomb-throwing weapons firing at angles greater than 45 degrees, and used mainly by the infantry for bombardment. When the bomb strikes the ground it is almost vertical and subsequently the lethal fragmentation spreads in all directions over a wide area. "Bazookas" are one-piece rocket-launchers – light steel tubes which electrically ignite hollow-charge anti-tank rockets. Both the Americans and the Germans claim the credit for the invention of the weapon. The "Bazooka" first appeared in North Africa in 1942, while the German equivalent, the Panzerschreck ("Tank terror"), was first used on the Russian front in 1943. The "Bazooka" was named after the trombone played by a popular American radio comedian of the day .

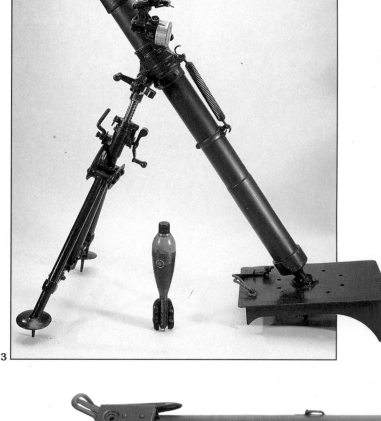

3 *A British 3-inch (76mm) medium mortar. Used mainly as an infantry company support weapon, these fired a bomb of about 7lbs in weigh to a range of approximately 2,000 yards.*

1 *A U.S. Infantryman poses with a Geman RP54 Panzerschreck.*
2 *German 81mm mortar bombs in their carrying case.*

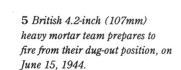

5 *British 4.2-inch (107mm) heavy mortar team prepares to fire from their dug-out position, on June 15, 1944.*

4 *The standard German light mortar was the 50mm L.gr.W.36. This weapon had a maximum range of about 570 yards and broke into two parts (baseplate and barrel) for carrying. Weight was 31lbs.*

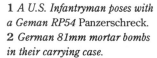

6, 7 *Canadian troops examine a captured German RP54 Panzerschreck. Weighing 20lbs and measuring 5'4", these were clumsy weapons to handle. The bomb weighed around 7.25lbs and the two-man team (loader and firer) would carry four rounds.*
7 *The earlier RP43 version, essentially the same as the RP54, but without the integral face shield. With this version, it was safer to wear a helmet and goggles when firing – not always possible in the heat of battle.*

8 *The U.S. 2.36-inch M1 rocket-launcher or "Bazooka." Their effective range was approximately 100 yards, much the same as the Panzerschreck, and the rocket could penetrate up to 3 inches* (75mm) *of armor. The launcher was loaded from the back and the rocket was fired by a burst of electric current from a circuit completed by the trigger.*

(9) *The German 81mm mortar Gr.W.34 and* **(10)** *the U.S. 81mm M1 mortar. These were the standard medium infantry mortars of their respective armies and were virtually identical in both design and performance. Maximum effective range was 2,500 yards, weight was 125lbs, and the weapons broke down into three parts for transportation.*

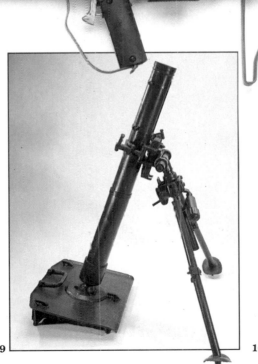

1 *A Canadian supply truck on the way to Falaise. Farther along the highway another truck burns – perhaps a victim of the tanks of 12th SS Panzer Division (Hitler Jugend), whose desperate fight against odds kept open the gap in the Allied encirclement between Falaise and Argentan long enough for part of German Seventh Army to make its escape.* (UPI/Bettmann)

troops entered the bombed and ruined town that afternoon, but trapped parties of the Hitler Jugend refused to surrender, including sixty men occupying the local high school buildings who fought literally to the death until the early hours of August 18. Canadian bulldozer operators trying to clear routes through the town for traffic after the battle could hardly find where the streets had once been.

COMMAND DECISIONS

For the generals on both sides in Normandy, trying to control a battle involving armies that numbered more than a million men each was no easy task at the best of times. Controlling the rout and slaughter of the Falaise

2 *Tanks of Canadian 4th Armored Division in Operation Tractable, the successful thrust to Falaise on August 14-16. Note that the tank in the foreground, and another in the distance, are fitted with mine-clearing "flails."* (National Archives of Canada)

enthusiastic, and the Canadians on the ground once more demonstrated their feelings by shooting at their own planes. Nevertheless, swathed in dust and smoke clouds, the Canadian attack covered the seven miles toward Falaise in two days, breaking through the thin German defensive line. By nightfall on August 15, Polish 1st Armored Division had swung across the River Dives at the little village of Jort, eight miles northeast of Falaise, cutting the main road out of the pocket. At Point 159, a mile north of Falaise, troops of 12th SS Panzer Division held on until noon on August 16 before being forced back. Canadian

pocket was impossible. In the heat of battle, careful judgements commited to paper and argued over for days or weeks were replaced by improvisations made with a glance at the map and a hasty telephone call. It was not surprising, when the arguments started after the war, that the generals' versions of events did not always agree with each other. The main outlines of what happened are, however, reasonably clear. On the Allied side, with the closing of the Falaise pocket left to the Canadians, the Americans continued their drive toward the River Seine. After Bradley's decision not to allow him north of Argentan,

3 *Radio operator on a Tiger. Most of these formidable tanks went to Waffen-SS units.* (Bundesarchiv)

4 *Tiger Mark I knocked out in the Falaise-Argentan battles. The German heavies took severe toll of* Allied tanks, but themselves suffered heavy loss from rocket-firing Typhoon fighter-bombers. (US National Archives)

5 *Major David Currie (left, with pistol), South Alberta Regiment, is seen immediately after his* heroic defense of St. Lambert-sur-Dives, thwarting the final German breakout attempt, for which he won the Victoria Cross. (National Archives of Canada)

Patton started part of XV Corps eastward to join the rest of Third Army on August 14, and gave up his remaining divisions at Argentan to First Army on August 16. While this was happening, Bradley decided to continue his attack north from Argentan, believing that the Germans were already escaping from the pocket in large numbers. The handover of command resulted in the American attack not starting until August 18, intended to link up with the Canadians near Chambois and Trun, east of Falaise. The American advance, against bitter German opposition, took them halfway to Chambois, effectively

closing the pocket to all but the most desperate Germans by bringing the last of their escape routes within artillery range. Meanwhile, British Second Army and the rest of US First Army, attacking through the broken, wooded country, gradually wore the last German resistance down.

For the German generals, there was no question of controlling events short of trying to avert a full-scale disaster. Back at the Wolf's Lair, however, Hitler was still planning to "hurl the Allies into the sea." On August 9, after the failure of his first attempt at Mortain, he ordered the creation of an even stronger armored force to repeat

6 *Canadian infantrymen cooling their feet after the Falaise advance appear to be threatened with a shower bath as dispatch riders ford a flooded farmyard. A nearby river had been dammed to permit armor to cross.* (UPI/Bettmann)

249

the operation. This military fantasy produced some benefit for the Germans fighting in the pocket, as "Panzer Group Eberbach," containing most of the remaining German armor, was used north of Argentan to block the American advance. On August 15 von Kluge almost suffered the same fate as Rommel when his staff car was caught in a slow-moving traffic jam of trucks, tanks and carts inside the pocket. Von Kluge's car and radio truck were attacked by Allied aircraft and his radio destroyed, leaving him out of touch with his headquarters for the rest of the day. After another day arguing on the telephone and the teleprinter, Hitler at last agreed on the afternoon of August 16 to von Kluge's repeated demands that Army Group B should withdraw, authorizing a redeployment east of the River Dives. But suspicions ran high in Hitler's headquarters about von Kluge's involvement in the bomb plot of July 20, and his mysterious disappearance coupled with his demands for a retreat led finally to his dismissal. On August 17 Field Marshal Walther Model arrived to take command of OB West and Army Group B next day. After explaining the hopeless situation to Model, and writing a frank letter to Hitler, von Kluge drove away eastward. On the road he committed suicide by taking poison. "You

2 *Field Marshal Walther Model took command of OB West and Army Group B on August 18.* (Bundesarchiv)

1 *Left: M1944 blouse of a German infantryman, with Infantry Assault Badge; above, pennant and M1943 field cap. Center: leather jacket of Untersturmführer (Second Lieutenant) of Waffen-SS Panzer unit; above, field cap. Right: field* *jacket of an Unteroffizier (Lance-Sergeant), Panzer regiment; above, side cap.*
3 *Left to right: Tank Battle Badge; Iron Cross, First Class; Wound Badge in gold (for five or more wounds).*

have fought an honorable and great fight," his letter to Hitler concluded, "Show yourself now also great enough to put an end to a hopeless struggle when necessary."

SAINT LAMBERT AND THE MACE

The final act of closing the Falaise pocket was left to Polish 1st Armored Division and Canadian 4th Armored Division, ordered on the afternoon of August 17 to drive southeast from the River Dives and secure Chambois, only ten miles away, placing a stopper in the pocket now being compressed by the Americans and British. In the confusion of the fighting at close quarters, even the Allied fighter-bombers could not guarantee identifying targets accurately. The Poles reported that, although within reach of Chambois, they could not advance because of Allied bombing, and fuel and other supplies needed for the Canadian tanks was also lost to Allied air attacks. Both divisions pressed on, backed by the rest of Canadian II Corps.

4 The swastika is an ancient good luck sign: Nazi doctrine declared it a symbol of "Aryan supremacy."
5 Tunic of a General, Army of the Third Reich. Beneath the medal ribbons are the Iron Cross, First Class, and Tank Battle Badge. Above, left to right: Feldmütze (side cap); Schirmmütze (uniform cap), with gold cords for General's rank; Einheitsfeldmütze (field cap).
6 Tunic of a Lieutenant, Panzer Lehr Division. On the right breast is the Deutsches Kreis (German Cross) in gold, awarded for gallantry in action. The ribbon of the Iron Cross, Second Class, is worn in a buttonhole.

1 *Burning out resistance: a Churchill "Crocodile" tank turns its flame projector on buildings that may harbor German snipers.* (IWM: B 9691)

2 *Mopping up in Falaise: Canadian infantrymen check out the railroad depot.* (UPI/Bettmann)

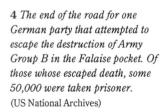

3 *This trooper was one of some 10,000 Germans who died in the Falaise pocket.* (Keystone)

4 *The end of the road for one German party that attempted to escape the destruction of Army Group B in the Falaise pocket. Of those whose escaped death, some 50,000 were taken prisoner.* (US National Archives)

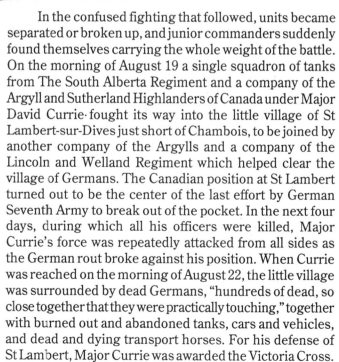

In the confused fighting that followed, units became separated or broken up, and junior commanders suddenly found themselves carrying the whole weight of the battle. On the morning of August 19 a single squadron of tanks from The South Alberta Regiment and a company of the Argyll and Sutherland Highlanders of Canada under Major David Currie· fought its way into the little village of St Lambert-sur-Dives just short of Chambois, to be joined by another company of the Argylls and a company of the Lincoln and Welland Regiment which helped clear the village of Germans. The Canadian position at St Lambert turned out to be the center of the last effort by German Seventh Army to break out of the pocket. In the next four days, during which all his officers were killed, Major Currie's force was repeatedly attacked from all sides as the German rout broke against his position. When Currie was reached on the morning of August 22, the little village was surrounded by dead Germans, "hundreds of dead, so close together that they were practically touching," together with burned out and abandoned tanks, cars and vehicles, and dead and dying transport horses. For his defense of St Lambert, Major Currie was awarded the Victoria Cross.

By the most bitter of ironies, the attack by Polish 1st Armored Division coincided with the final destruction by the Germans of the uprising in their home capital of Warsaw, which had begun at the end of July. The order to strike back at the Germans given by the divisional commander, Major-General Stanislaw Maczek, was greeted with enthusiasm, and little mercy was shown on either side. By August 19 the Poles were across the exit road from Chambois, holding the high ground north of the village which Major-General Maczek christened the "Mace" (*Maczuga* in Polish) from the appearance of its contours on the map. In the early evening Poles of 10th

as they could hold the Mace the Germans were trapped. "Our brigade is cut off." Koszutski told his officers, "No question of surrender. I speak as a Pole." Not until the following day did the Canadians break through once more to the Polish position on the Mace, to find the whole area strewn with burned out vehicles and dead soldiers of both sides. "The picture was the grimmest the regiment has so far come up against," reported the relief force, "the Poles cried with joy when we arrived." By breaking the German counterattack the Poles had firmly closed the Falaise pocket, and guaranteed the destruction of the Germans in Normandy.

5 *A British 5.5 inch gun: Allied artillery relentlessly hammered the retreating German columns.*
(IWM: B 7414)
6 *Anything with wheels, including horse-drawn farm carts, was seized on by the fleeing Germans.*
(US National Archives)

5

Cavalry Brigade arrived in Chambois, more or less simultaneously with Americans of 359th Infantry Regiment coming from the south. Both sides later claimed to have actually captured the village.

The Falaise pocket was closed, but not yet secure. Unknown to the Poles, II SS Panzer Corps was planning to attack the next day from the northeast, to link up with the attempts by Seventh Army to escape from the pocket. On August 20, under attack by Germans from both sides, the Polish division was cut off from the rest of Canadian II Corps and broken into three main groups, of which the strongest, about eighty tanks and 1,500 soldiers under Lieutenant-Colonel Stanislaw Koszutski, continued to hold the Mace. With increasing numbers of wounded, the defenders were already short of food, fuel and ammunition when the German attacks started, but realized that as long

6

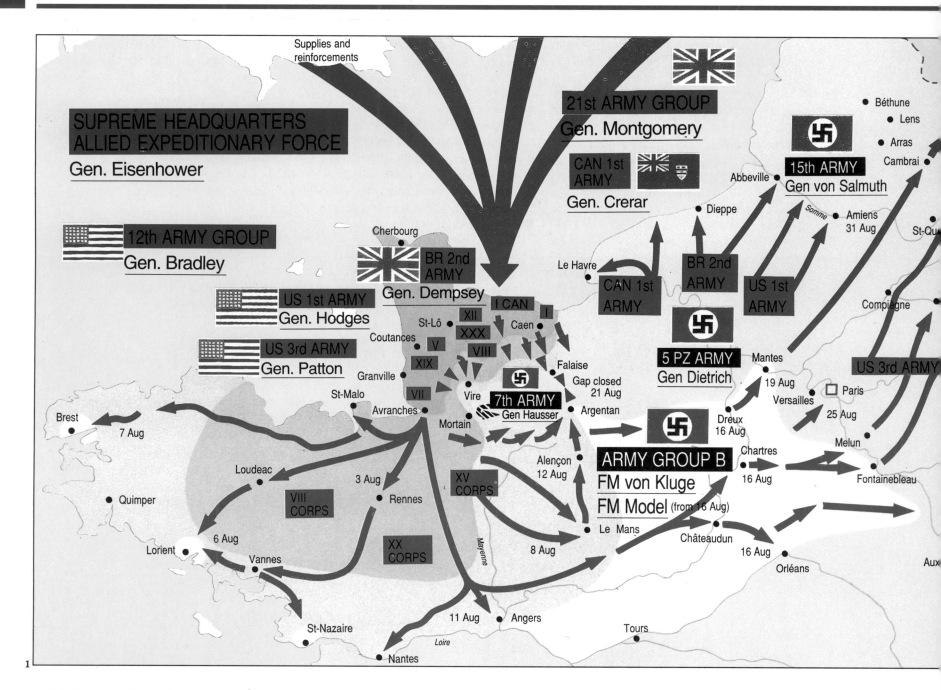

Supplies and reinforcements

SUPREME HEADQUARTERS ALLIED EXPEDITIONARY FORCE
Gen. Eisenhower

12th ARMY GROUP
Gen. Bradley

US 1st ARMY
Gen. Hodges

US 3rd ARMY
Gen. Patton

21st ARMY GROUP
Gen. Montgomery

CAN 1st ARMY
Gen. Crerar

15th ARMY
Gen von Salmuth

BR 2nd ARMY
Gen. Dempsey

CAN 1st ARMY

BR 2nd ARMY

US 1st ARMY

5 PZ ARMY
Gen Dietrich

US 3rd ARMY

7th ARMY
Gen Hausser

ARMY GROUP B
FM von Kluge
FM Model (from 16 Aug)

I CAN — XII — XXX — VIII — I
V — XIX — VII

XV CORPS

VIII CORPS

XX CORPS

Cherbourg · St-Lô · Coutances · Granville · St-Malo · Avranches · Mortain · Vire · Caen · Falaise · Gap closed 21 Aug · Argentan · Alençon 12 Aug · Le Mans · Mantes · Dreux 16 Aug · Versailles · Chartres · Châteaudun · Orléans · Angers · Tours · Nantes · St-Nazaire · Rennes · Loudeac · Quimper · Lorient · Vannes · Brest

Béthune · Lens · Arras · Cambrai · Abbeville · Dieppe · Amiens 31 Aug · St-Qu · Compiègne · Paris · Melun · Fontainebleau · Aux

Le Havre

7 Aug · 6 Aug · 3 Aug · 8 Aug · 11 Aug · 19 Aug · 25 Aug · 16 Aug

Mayenne · Loire · Somme

2 *Thankful, no doubt, that the slaughter in the pocket is at an end, German soldiers file into captivity under the eyes of British infantry and armored units.*

INSIDE THE POCKET

For those who survived the Falaise pocket, the memory of individual horrors remained, but the actual experience of the last few days merged together into a shapeless nightmare. "I had never known such tiredness,"·recalled

one German survivor, "it caused hallucinations and a complete sense of non-being." As ammunition and fuel ran out, the artillery and drivers replaced the infantry in the front line so that they could sleep. "We could have slept for days. Next morning it was worse." In the crush of the narrow country roads breakdowns and slow-moving vehicles created traffic jams and stoppages, with no room to overtake or turn around if discovered by the roving fighter-bombers. Even more feared were the spotter aircraft used by the Allies to direct artillery fire into the pocket. "We cursed the little dark-green, high-wing airplanes," confessed one German, "they were the angels of death to us." As the German forces inside the pocket disintegrated, it was almost impossible for gunners and aircraft not to find targets. Men on foot, cyclists, horse-drawn carts, tanks and trucks became mixed together in a rush to escape.

The Germans still found that the threat of a Tiger, a Panther or an 88mm gun could be enough to bring an Allied advance to a halt, giving them time to retreat. A two-man "tank-busting" team with a panzerfaust could be enough to stop a major attack in the hedgerows, and the Germans were confident that they could hold their ground against most Allied troops. Some did not actually realize that they were trapped inside the pocket until after it had been formed, and fought on regardless. "It is

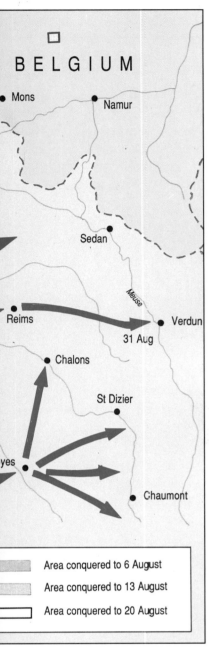

BELGIUM

Mons

Namur

Sedan

Reims

Meuse

Verdun

31 Aug

Chalons

St Dizier

oyes

Chaumont

Area conquered to 6 August

Area conquered to 13 August

Area conquered to 20 August

1 *Map shows the Allied breakout in northwest France in August 1944. Following the virtual annihilation of Army Group B in the Falaise-Argentan pocket, Allied armies moved eastward on a broad front. By the end of the month, Paris had been retaken and the Allies were advancing across the Meuse and Somme rivers.*

4

5

surrendered Polish volunteer told his captors, "If you didn't you got a bullet in the back." Very few of these eastern volunteers showed any enthusiasm for the German cause in the final stages of the battle. An interesting exception was "Panzer" Meyer's Cossack orderly, who fought with him to break out across the Dives with the remains of his division. Meyer, himself wounded and with his head swathed in bandages, reported that only one in five of his infantry and tanks escaped the pocket. The final German losses inside the Falaise pocket and beyond, as the retreating columns of Army Group B were harried by pursuing Allied aircraft and tanks, cannot be accurately given. About 80,000 men were caught in the pocket, of which perhaps 10,000 died there, with another 50,000 being taken prisoner. Eisenhower described the dead lying so close together in the pocket that it would have been possible to walk for hundreds of yards on nothing but their bodies. Allied estimates of the number of German tanks and other vehicles destroyed range between 5,000 and 9,000, not counting the horse-drawn vehicles.

But, even after such a great victory, Allied pessimism and caution persisted. Some commanders, Bradley among them, continued to believe that more Germans had escaped the pocket than was in reality the case. Once more, it took the Allies time to realize what they had done to the Germans. Army Group B had been destroyed as a fighting force. No more than 30,000 men and 120 tanks in any condition escaped to reach the Seine, and those divisions which were not completely destroyed were reduced to the size of battalions. Hausser of Seventh Army was among those who got out, but was badly wounded with his lower

3 *Grim graffiti: a Canadian soldier inspects a Hakenkreuz ("hooked cross" or swastika) and Third Reich eagle carved by a German hand on an ancient fortification at Falaise. This might easily be erased, but the scars left on Europe by Nazi aggression would be longer lasting.*
(UPI/Bettmann)

7

4 *Insignia of Canadian II Corps; mauled in the Totalize offensive on Falaise.*
5 *Insignia of V Corps, US First Army.*
6 *GI with a Browning machine gun guards a packed PoW cage. The German commander in the final days at Falaise, Field Marshal Model, would commit suicide when trapped in the Ruhr pocket in April 1945.*
7 *In Falaise an ancient warlord looks down on his modern counterparts: Canadian soldiers relax in the shadow of William the Conqueror, Norman invader of England in the 11th century.*
(UPI/Bettman)

3

6

rumored that our division is encircled by the enemy," the commander of 3rd Parachute Division told his men on August 14, "The army, British or American, which can encircle or capture our division does not exist." Others were kept fighting by Waffen-SS squads patrolling the rear areas of the pocket, threatening to shoot or hang anyone who retreated. "You had to shoot straight," a

jaw shot away. On August 25 Eberbach, who had taken over command of Hausser's troops along with his own, reported his effective strength as just under 18,000 infantry, 314 artillery pieces and forty-two tanks, about the strength of one Allied division. The Battle of Normandy was a worse disaster for the Germans than Stalingrad. Nothing could stop the Allies now.

OPERATION DRAGOON

On August 15, which Hitler later described as "the worst day of my life," as Field Marshal von Kluge was reported missing in the depths of the Falaise pocket, a major Allied amphibious landing involving 30,000 troops took place in the south of France, near Toulon. Originally codenamed Operation Anvil, this secondary landing began as an American proposal in August, 1943, to create a major diversion from Normandy by taking place simultaneously with D-Day (or, in one variant, a month earlier), using troops from Italy and the Mediterranean. The British were unenthusiastic, believing that the forces could be better employed in Italy itself. Nevertheless, the Western Allies promised the Soviet Union, at the Tehran conference in November, 1943, to undertake Anvil in some form as well as Overlord.

Shortage of shipping and landing craft made it impossible to launch the invasion of southern France at the same time as the D-Day landings, or for some weeks afterward. At the start of July the landing was set for August 15, too late to influence the outcome of the Battle of Normandy. Churchill, who made a last unsuccessful attempt to get Roosevelt to cancel or divert the operation, made his feelings clear by ordering a late change of the codename to Dragoon.

Protected by a force of seven British and two American aircraft carriers, the assault force comprised 880 ships and 1,370 landing craft. The main assault was preceded by a landing on the night of August 14 by French and British Commandos and a combined American-Canadian special service force. An airborne drop by American and British paratroop brigades followed. At eight AM on August 15 the main landing was made by three American divisions and a French armored group. The German Army Group G, covering the south of France, had already been stripped of many of its divisions for the Normandy battle, and with the collapse of Army Group B it began to retreat northward. Marseilles fell on August 23, and the advancing Allies moved up the Rhône valley to link up with the Allied troops from Normandy. The Dragoon forces grew by September, 1944, to become Sixth Army Group under Lieutenant-General Jacob Devers, consisting of US Seventh Army and French First Army. Overshadowed by Montgomery and Bradley, Devers remained the third of Eisenhower's Army Group commanders for the rest of the war.

2 *Invasion obstacles near Cavalaire, one of US VI Corps' Dragoon landing sites. (US National Archives)*
3 *Lieutenant-General Jacob Devers; Sixth Army Group.* (IWM: IA 13766)

1 *Before the Dragoon landings, Allied tactical air forces made precision strikes on German communication routes. Here, B-26 Marauders hit the railroad bridge over the Rhône River at Arles.* (UPI/Bettmann)

4 *Operation Dragoon: commando and airborne assaults preceded the main landings by US and French forces, between Cannes and Hyères, August 15.*

Lyons
Rhône
Grenoble
Valence
ITALY
Montélimar
Gap
19th ARMY
Gen Wiese
Digne
Avignon
Durance
Nice
Aix
Cannes
Fréjus
Marseilles 28 Aug
Hyères
1st AIRBN TASK FORCE
Toulon 28 Aug
US VI CORPS
Gen Truscott
US 7th ARMY
Gen Patch
FRENCH ARMY B
Gen de Lattre de Tassigny

5 *American and British paratroopers drop in support of the Dragoon landings.* (US National Archives)

6 *American LCTs (Landing Craft, Tank) line the beach at St Raphael, near Fréjus. Some 94,000 men and 11,900 vehicles were put ashore on August 15; there was little opposition, and only about 200 men were lost.* (US National Archives)

7

8

9

7 *US Army engineers lay a steel mesh road along a beach. Immediately after the landings, US forces struck eastward to Cannes and Nice; French armor headed for Toulon and Marseilles.*

8 *Some 15,000 men of German Nineteenth Army were taken prisoner by late August.*
9 *A German turret gun emplacement.*
(US National Archives; all)

After survival, the subjects that most interest the fighting man probably are sex, liquor (and, in World War II, cigarettes), mail, furloughs – and food. Until the later 19th century, servicemen generally had to cook their own rations: British soldiers in the Crimea were issued raw meat, flour, and coffee beans – and starved for lack of firewood. Armies often "lived off the land": in the US Civil War, Sherman's "bummers" (foragers) stripped the Southland like a plague of locusts. The US Army had no centralized logistic service until the creation of its Quartermaster Department in 1912. By World War I mobile field kitchens provided hot meals just behind the front lines, while advances in food preservation made available a variety of portable rations to men in the firing line. However often they cursed service cooks or condemned their cold rations – GIs called the ETO campaign award "the Spam Medal," after a much issued brand of canned meat – Allied servicemen of World War II were generally well fed, if not always well contented, warriors.

1 *Selection of items from the emergency rations (C-, K-, and 10-in-1 Rations) issued to US troops in the field. Note tiny*

Emergency Field Cooker, used to heat up food in the mess kit ("meat can").

3 *Leaflet issued with British emergency rations includes instructions for "brewing up" tea in the field.*

2, 4 *The Nazi emblem appears even on the handle of a can opener; shown also at (4) with flatware issued to a German serviceman.*

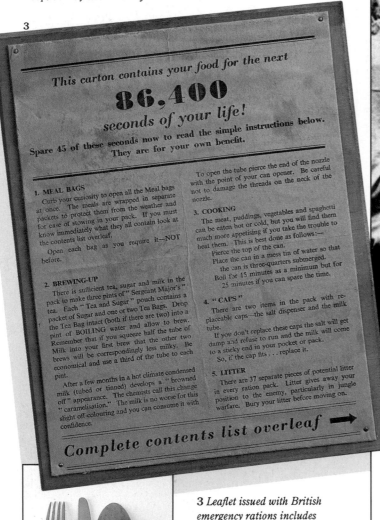

5 *Canadian soldier with a midget field cooker scrambles eggs 'liberated' from a Normandy farmyard.*
(UPI/Bettmann)
7 *British mess tins, "eating irons," field cooker, and emergency ration packs – including cigarettes, matches, and "bumf" (toilet paper).*

6 *German field cookery utensils include a water can and a "hay box" – an insulated container to keep food hot as it is carried from field kitchen to foxhole.*
8 *Galvanized ashcans make sinks for US servicemen to wash up their tableware.*
(US National Archives)

9 *Living off the land: some German paratroopers patronize a mobile dairy …*
10 *… while comrades manning a light AA weapon chow down.*
(Bundesarchiv)

CHAPTER TWELVE

"PARIS MUST NOT FALL"

With the closing of the Falaise pocket, the Battle of Normandy was over. Army Group B, the largest and strongest Army Group in the German order of battle, had been crushed and virtually wiped out. Only three divisions anchoring the northern flank of the German position still existed as fighting formations. Of thirty-eight German divisions committed to the battle, twenty-five had been destroyed and were never reformed. Two German panzer divisions had to be rebuilt from scratch, and the remaining nine were reduced to skeletons.

Every battle which ends in a major victory is also followed by a pursuit, in which the destruction caused to the defeated side is often greater than in the battle itself. But in the pursuit from Normandy, as in the battle, the Allies showed their customary caution and lack of drive compared to the German skill in conducting a rearguard action. The first problem came in disentangling the American, British and Canadian forces after the Falaise pocket had been eliminated. While the battle was still going on, Patton's Third Army was plunging eastward on a broad front, trying to stake out as much territory as possible and prevent the Germans re-establishing a secure defensive line. On August 19, while the Poles and Canadians were fighting east of Falaise, a task force from US 79th Infantry Division reached the River Seine about twenty miles north of Paris, at Mantes-Gassicourt, and crossed unopposed that night, as the first Allied troops across the river. On the same day, more of Patton's forces reached Melun, about the same distance south of Paris. US First Army, now under Bradley's former deputy, Lieutenant-General Courtney Hodges, crossed north of Paris together with the British and Canadians, advancing almost without opposition.

Previous page: *Men of the French Resistance (note Cross of Lorraine armband) lie in ambush, armed with a .30 caliber Browning machine gun and British Sten guns.*
(US National Archives)
1 An M29C Weasel tracked amphibian carries British soldiers through floodwater.
(Keystone)

At the same time, the Germans found that they could rely on the Allies halting every evening to regroup, rather than pressing on, and this gave the forces of Army Group B some chance of escape. Every bridge over the Seine west of Paris had been destroyed long before by Allied bombing. But bad weather for three nights from August 20, including fog in Britain which grounded Allied night fighter and bomber aircraft, allowed the Germans to build a pontoon bridge, floated out into the river at nightfall, and to run twenty-three ferries across the Seine. If only a handful of tanks escaped from the Allies, about 2,500 other vehicles eluded them. Allied airpower, however, continued to take a heavy toll of the German formations as they fled eastward.

5

THE GERMAN OCCUPATION OF PARIS

With the collapse of France in 1940 Paris was declared an open city. It was occupied peacefully and by agreement between the Germans and the surrendering French on June 14. On June 22 France signed an armistice. The population of Greater Paris, normally about 3 million, had shrunk below 700,000 as people fled from the approaching Germans, but gradually returned to normal as people came back to the city. As part of the armistice agreement, Paris and the northern part of France remained under German military control. The Paris police continued to function under the Prefect of Police, but this difficult position changed hands four times in four years.

German military administrative services and officers took over most of the hotels in central Paris, where the Gestapo also established their headquarters. Newspapers and theaters reopened under German control, and restaurants and night clubs also stayed open to entertain Germans and French collaborators. The first attacks on Jewish families in Paris by French fascists, inspired by the Germans, came as early as August, 1940. By May, 1941, 5,000 Parisian Jews had been rounded up by the Germans. In June, 1942, all Jews were ordered to display the yellow Star of David badge, and in July, 1942, some 30,000 Parisian Jews were rounded up and shipped to concentration camps.

Resistance to the Germans in Paris was extremely difficult, although the Left Bank, the Paris student quarter, became a center of opposition to the occupation. The first Resistance newspapers appeared in December, 1940, along with the first cases of Parisians being shot for Resistance activities. In August, 1941, came the first shooting of a German soldier by the Paris Resistance, for which hostages were rounded up and shot in response, and the Germans announced that all Parisians were considered hostages. The highest-ranking German killed by the Paris Resistance was the senior Nazi functionary Julius Ritter in September, 1943.

In 1944 all Frenchmen were, in theory, conscripted for the German war effort as laborers, and a two-mile stretch of the Paris metro was closed off and turned into an underground factory for aircraft parts. Statues had been taken down and melted for their metal content, and monuments destroyed, including one to the great actress Sarah Bernhardt (the Divine Sarah), who was Jewish. Shortages in Paris, and resistance to the Germans, increased greatly with the D-Day landings, and reached a peak with the uprising just before liberation.

6, 7 On June 23, 1940, within a few days of German forces raising the Nazi flag in Paris, Hitler made a flying visit to the city, touring its cultural landmarks in the company of Nazi "intellectuals" such as the architect Albert Speer (on Hitler's right in photograph). In spite of savage repression – shamefully abetted by some French collaborators with Germany – the Resistance was active in Paris.
(Keystone)

7

6

2 Eisenhower with General Jean-Marie de Lattre de Tassigny; French First Army.
(Keystone)
3 GIs paddle flat-bottomed boats across the Seine River near Nantes; August 20.
(US National Archives)
4 How to behave in France: do not dwell on the nation's collapse in 1940!
5 Montgomery with the FFI's General Marie-Pierre Koenig.
(IWM: B 6930)

1 *Visiting the French theater of operations, General George C. Marshall (left), US Army Chief of Staff throughout World War II (and, from December 1944, a five-star General of the Army), is seen with Lieutenant-General Jacob L. Devers, USA (right), and General de Lattre de Tassigny, commander of French First Army in Devers's Sixth Army Group.* (Keystone)

2 *A French woman and children (the patched pants of one of the latter illustrating the wartime necessity to "make do and mend") meet friendly GIs in a newly-liberated village.* (US National Archives)

3 *For four years it has been chalked on walls to infuriate German occupation troops – and now the "V for Victory" sign is openly made by French civilians cheering Allied troops on the way to Paris.* (UPI/Bettmann)

the failure of the Mortain counterattack, it would have been militarily possible for American troops to have reached the city. But the Allies had no desire to repeat the experience of Caen over again on a much greater scale, destroying the capital of France street by street in order to free it from German occupation. Moreover, although Paris itself had remained almost untouched by Allied bombing, the destruction of the transport and railway system supplying the capital meant that any Allied force accepting responsibility for the city would also be committed to feeding it and supplying it with fuel. Allied planners calculated that Paris would need at least 4,000 tons of supplies at once if liberated, enough to keep eight divisions running. By another calculation, the transport and supplies needed to feed Paris would also be enough to keep the SHAEF forces driving toward Germany for another three days. This was the reason for the decision to bypass Paris from the north and south, leaving the city as a problem for the German garrison.

The fate of Paris was also bound up in the attitude taken by the Germans as the Allies crossed the Seine. Rome, which had fallen to the Allies on June 4, had been declared an open city and had changed hands without fighting. But Warsaw, which had risen in an unsuccessful revolt, was being systematically destroyed by the Germans while the Battle of Normandy was being fought. Whatever action the Allies took, Paris might also be destroyed, or turned into a German fortress like the Channel ports, most of which continued to resist Allied attempts to storm or bluff them into surrender. With de Gaulle recognized as head of the French government in exile, and his troops fighting alongside the Americans only a few miles from Paris, the situation was politically difficult for Eisenhower. It was not simply a matter of cold calculation. The people of Paris had endured four years of German occupation, and now salvation was within reach.

In the later stages of the Battle of Normandy the growing strength of the American forces meant that Bradley had been able to exercise increasing freedom from Montgomery's command. With the creation of 12th Army Group, and the development of the Falaise pocket, Montgomery's authority over the Americans declined to the point that Bradley would later almost deny his contribution to the victory. Eisenhower set September 1 as the date on which he would formally assume command of all SHAEF land forces from Montgomery, who would revert to commanding 21st Army Group alone, and in the last two weeks of August Eisenhower become more heavily involved in the battle than at any time previously. Politics and alliance warfare were Eisenhower's great strengths, and there was one major political decision remaining before the battle was over: the liberation of Paris.

As the German occupation of France crumbled with their defeat in Normandy, the fate of Paris remained very uncertain. As a military objective, Paris had little attraction to the Allies. At any time from the middle of August, after

On July 14, in defiance of the Germans, Paris had celebrated Bastille Day openly for the first time in four years, with French national flags hung from the buildings. The recovery of the French capital – preferably not in ruins – would be one of the most important political acts of the war.

Finally, there was the issue of French 2nd Armored Division, equipped and organized by the Americans, and placed by de Gaulle under Eisenhower's authority as part of the SHAEF forces. In the original planning, the main purpose of putting the French armored division with the forces in Normandy, instead of making it part of French First Army for the Dragoon landings, was so that an important French formation should be present at the liberation of Paris. The men of the French division were aware of this, and as early as August 14 its commander began to press the American to release the division and send it to Paris. Instead, by August 21 the whole of US V Corps under Lieutenant-General Leonard (Gee) Gerow, to which French 2nd Armored belonged, was out of contact with the enemy, having been squeezed out by the British advance. By that time, changing events in Paris itself had made the French determined to sit idly by no longer.

THE PARIS UPRISING

The luckless German corps commander responsible for the part of the front on which Operation Cobra had fallen on July 25 was Lieutenant-General Dietrich von Choltitz, sacked by von Kluge three days later for failing to stop the American juggernaut. Instead of being recalled to Berlin, however, von Choltitz found himself appointed military commandant of the fortress of Greater Paris, with orders to prepare the city for defense. Von Choltitz's predecessor as governor of Paris, the aristocratic Lieutenant-General Hans Freiherr von Boineburg-Lengsfeld, was under suspicion and in danger for his life, having obeyed the first orders from Berlin sent by the bomb-plotters on July 20 to arrest all Gestapo members within the city. He was busy trying to convince the Nazi authorities that his action had been an innocent mistake, with some help from Speidel, still Chief of Staff at Army Group B who was under deep suspicion himself.

As the result of these events, von Choltitz of all the senior officers of the German Army was the best placed to know the power of the Allied armies and recognize that the war was lost. But he was also under no illusions as to what might happen to himself and his family in Germany if he refused to obey orders. As he would later point out, he also had no desire to become known as the man who destroyed Paris. Von Kluge visited von Choltitz in Paris just before August 15, and the two generals agreed that the bridges over the Seine at Paris should be preserved for German troops rather than destroyed. Von Choltitz then steered a careful middle course, improving his defenses while taking no action to destroy parts of the city for military reasons.

As the hub of German security and police organization, Paris had deliberately not been made a major center for the French Resistance, which was itself a mixture of different factions. All knew that control of Paris and the seat of French government would be crucial in establishing political power in France after the war. Although Koenig remained de Gaulle's Chief of Staff, his appointment as commander of the FFI came under

Eisenhower as part of SHAEF, and was only accepted with reluctance by some of the Resistance factions. On August 16, weighing all the complex factors together, de Gaulle through Koenig ordered the FFI in Paris not to rise in revolt, but to sit quietly and leave the liberation of Paris to the approaching Allied troops.

This was too much to ask of the people of Paris, who had a long tradition of uprising and throwing off oppression. On August 16 the Germans executed thirty-five young Frenchmen for acts of defiance against the occupation forces. On August 18, apparently without direct orders and contrary to de Gaulle's instructions, the rail networks of Paris ground to a halt in a strike, and the Paris police quietly vanished from the streets, many to reappear, armed, at the heads of gathering mobs. By the following day the disorder had spread to become a full-scale revolt against the Germans. FFI members captured the Hotel de Ville (the City Hall), police stations and municipal buildings. As on many other occasions in the city's history, the cobblestones of Paris were dug up to make improvised barricades or missiles. Dressed in any kind of uniform or none at all, members of the FFI took to the streets in an open battle with the Germans. The supposed leaders of the various FFI factions had little choice but to join in.

4 De Gaulle rallied the Free French, but his relationships with other Allied leaders were sometimes stormy.
(IWM: B 5490)
5 "Aux armes, citoyens!" Members of the FFI man a Parisian barricade.
(Central Press)
6 As well as Germans, at least 1,000 French people died in streetfighting during the Paris uprising.
(US National Archives)

THE LIBERATION

Normandy was a quiet farming community which had been peaceful and self-contained for generations. The German occupation was unopposed, and it was in the interests of neither side to create trouble for the other. Norman farmers grew rich by smuggling eggs, vegetables and meat to Paris to sell on the black market, while German troops found themselves in a quiet area to rest and retrain. An entire German division occupied the Channel Islands off the Normandy coast (the only part of Britain occupied by the Germans during the war) and remained there until the war's end.

Over 1.8 million French soldiers were left in German prisoner of war camps as a result of the defeat of 1940. A German attempt in 1942 to organize a scheme of "guest workers," whereby one French prisoner of war would be released for every three Frenchmen volunteering to work in Germany, was a failure, with only 7,000 volunteering. In 1943 the Germans created the Milice, to help them hunt down Resistance fighters, which was joined by about 30,000 Frenchmen. Generally, the majority of people concerned themselves neither with the Resistance nor the Milice. Inevitably, some close friendships and even marriages with German soldiers did occur. On D-Day near Ouistreham the British killed a sniper who turned out to be a young French girl whose German soldier fiancé had been killed in action that morning, and she had sworn to kill every Allied soldier in revenge.

Allied troops were surprised and disappointed by the wariness and even hostility with which they were greeted by the population of Normandy at first. After the experience of Dieppe, the French were not at all sure how long the Allies would be staying. Many blamed the British for deserting France in 1940, while considerable damage was done to their homes by Allied bombing and shelling. American officers reported that the people of St Lô seemed "pathetically anxious" to understand why Allied bombers had destroyed their town.

It was only with the breakout from Normandy that many French people became convinced that the liberation was really happening. Some took the opportunity to inflict reprisals on collaborators, including the practice of shaving the heads of girls felt to have been too friendly with the Germans. Most celebrated, and the Allies experienced the true joy of liberated people for the first time. Ironically, crowds pressing flowers, food and drink on the advancing armies became a serious problem during the pursuit.

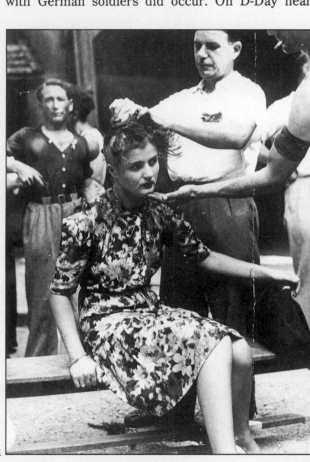

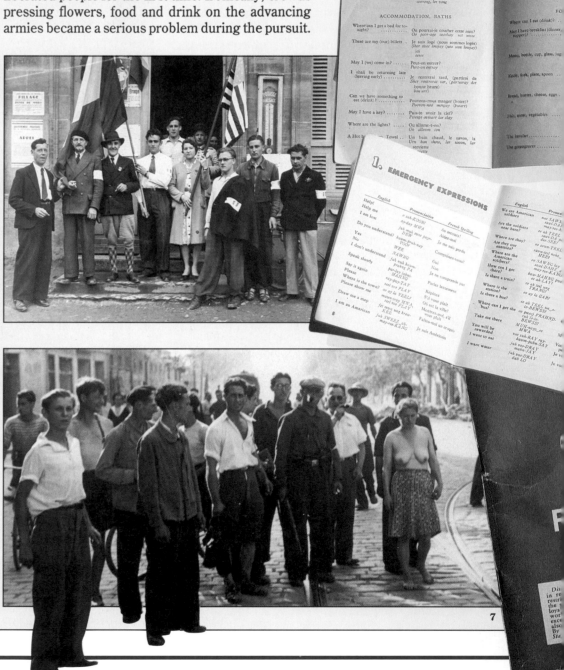

1, 3 *For some unlucky French people liberation was followed by retribution. "Kangaroo courts" tried and often executed men accused of collaboration, while many women accused of sexual relations with German servicemen were publicly humiliated. Here, one has her hair cut off; another is paraded half naked through the streets at gunpoint.* (US National Archives)

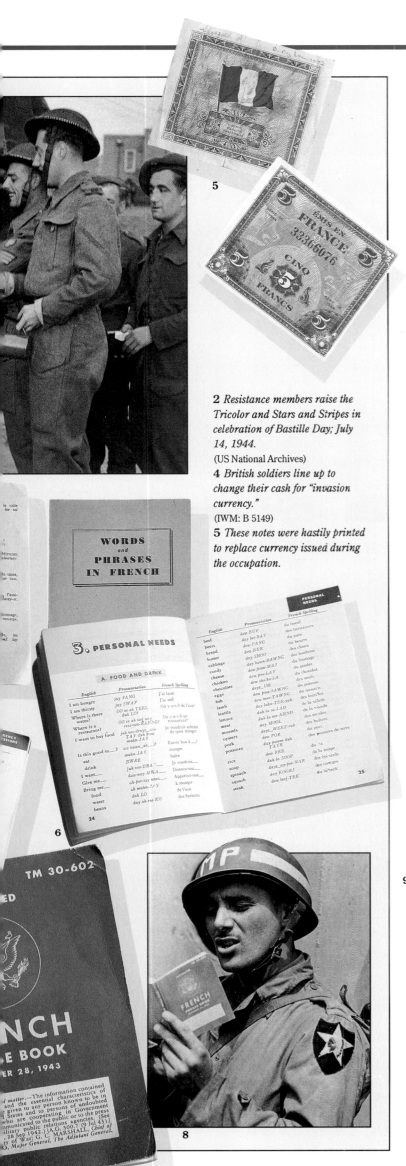

2 *Resistance members raise the Tricolor and Stars and Stripes in celebration of Bastille Day; July 14, 1944.*
(US National Archives)
4 *British soldiers line up to change their cash for "invasion currency."*
(IWM: B 5149)
5 *These notes were hastily printed to replace currency issued during the occupation.*

WORDS *and* PHRASES IN FRENCH

3. PERSONAL NEEDS

A. FOOD AND DRINK

PERSONAL NEEDS

TM 30-602

To keep control of Paris and defend it against the approaching Allies, von Choltitz had about 5,000 effective troops (although twice that number were taken prisoner by the Allies before the city was secured). The number of FFI involved in the uprising was probably no more than 3,000 at first, although the numbers grew with the telling in later years, and after the war 23,000 Parisians applied for recognition of their part in the fighting. The FFI had virtually no weapons except for those it could capture from the Germans, and the fighting in the streets cost the French at least 1,000 dead and 1,500 wounded. All the time, the situation threatened to get out of control completely into an all-out war involving the destruction of the city and massive loss of life.

At the end of the first full day of the uprising, von Choltitz received a visit from the Swedish Consul-General in Paris, Raoul Nordling, who had an unusual proposition. With Nordling as intermediary, von Choltitz arranged what he called "an understanding" (or *entente*) with the

6, 7 *American and British authorities were anxious that their servicemen should behave well in liberated Europe, and made sure that all received booklets on etiquette and, as seen here, phrase books. From the pages shown, the authorities apparently believed that "Personal Needs" were mainly concerned with food, and "Emergency Expressions" with finding the way back to billets. Many men no doubt had different views.*

leaders of the FFI. In return for an end to the fighting, von Choltitz recognized the FFI, even without uniforms, as serving Allied soldiers entitled to proper treatment under the Geneva Convention, and accepted that parts of the city were under FFI control. By August 20, combined FFI and German patrols were out on the streets policing the ceasefire. But the agreement was an extremely vague one. No actual boundaries were established, and no time limit was set for the truce to end. Like all other attempts by either side to control the people, the ceasefire was never really effective, and sporadic fighting continued in various parts of the city for the next few days.

From Paris, von Choltitz presented his decision to von Kluge as necessary to stop what he saw as largely communist-inspired rioting, and as enabling him to keep

8 *An MP of US 2nd Infantry Division appears to have some difficulty in getting his tongue round the phrases in the booklet also seen at (7).*
(US National Archives)
9 *But this gesture means the same in any language: a German straggler surrenders to the Resistance in Paris.*

1 *Shoulder title worn by men of Fighting France serving with Allied armies.*

2 *Men of French 2nd Armored Division take cover in the shadow of the Arc de Triomphe as they fight their way into Paris. Bodies litter the Étoile square (much later renamed in honor of General Charles de Gaulle).*
(IWM: EA 37079)

his troops would be out of food within two days. Both von Choltitz and Speidel were aware that others might be listening to their conversation, and that they or their families would be held accountable for their actions. Speaking almost in a private code, von Choltitz told Speidel that while he did not have the resources to destroy the more than seventy bridges of Paris, he had placed explosives in the key buildings including Notre Dame cathedral, and was ready to level the Arc de Triomphe to improve the field of fire, and to block the Seine using the Eiffel Tower as a barricade – none of which was true.

THE LIBERATION OF PARIS

While this had been happening, French 2nd Armored Division had been sitting within reach of Paris, with its commander, Major-General Viscomte Jacques-Philippe de Hautecloque, a nobleman whose family was still in France and who had taken the name Leclerc (the Priest)

4 *Wrecked vehicles, including a German light tank (a French Renault FT-17, captured in 1940), litter the courtyard of a public building after the Parisian uprising.*
(US National Archives)

3 *FFI fighters on the hunt for Germans in newly liberated Paris. The danger of such irregular warfare getting out of hand caused de Gaulle to order dissolution of the Parisian FFI.*
(Associated Press)

the bridges of Paris open and to strengthen the outer defenses of the city against the Allies. When Hitler heard of the truce, he issued unambiguous orders that Paris must be held against the Allied advance, and any anti-German actions within the city suppressed by the utmost force. "The Seine bridges will be prepared for demolition," Hitler ordered, "Paris must not fall into the hands of the enemy except as a field of ruins." Von Choltitz' response to this order was to telephone Speidel and to argue against it. The FFI were in charge of key administrative buildings, the city was close to chaos and could not be defended, and

to protect them, growing increasingly frustrated. On August 20 de Gaulle himself arrived in France. The following day, in a symbolic act, Leclerc ordered a small reconnaissance patrol of 150 men in light tanks and armored cars toward Paris. Trying to establish that Leclerc was still under his orders, "Gee" Gerow, commanding V Corps, canceled the move, forcing Leclerc to recall his men, and protested to Hodges at First Army. In response, de Gaulle in turn protested to Eisenhower that if orders for Leclerc to go to Paris were not forthcoming, he would issue them on his own authority. In the midst of this political tangle, on August 22 a delegation from the Paris FFI led by its Chief of Staff Roger Gallois arrived at Patton's headquarters with claims, passed on to Bradley, that although the Resistance now controlled the city the truce would end the next day, and that a bloodbath would result, but that von Choltitz would withdraw if facing Allied troops. It was essential, the delegates argued, for the Allies to reach Paris by noon on August 23. None of this was strictly true, but if Paris was in the hands of the FFI, recognized as part of the SHAEF command, then Eisenhower could reinforce them with French 2nd Armored Division as a purely military action. On this rather twisted reasoning Eisenhower came to the decision that solved everybody's problems. On the afternoon of August 22 Leclerc was ordered to drive for Paris.

Eisenhower was intent, however, on making this an Allied military operation, under Gerow at V Corps. The US 4th Infantry Division was sent along with Leclerc's troops, and the British were also asked to provide a token force to take part in the liberation, which for reasons

that the Americans could not establish afterward never appeared. More practically, the Americans and British started to organize an airlift of thousands of tons of supplies to feed and provide fuel for the city. Inevitably, the drive of French 2nd Armored to enter Paris turned into a triumphal march of liberation as they drew closer to the city. Once more, in their enthusiasm or lack of concern for their Allies, the French drove onto the American division's roads, causing another traffic jam. But the German defenders refused to withdraw without a fight, and Leclerc was anxious to cause as little destruction as possible to the historic buildings of Versailles on his approach from the southwest. By nightfall on August 24, his division had taken over 300 casualties and was still only on the outskirts of the city. "To hell with prestige," Bradley instructed Gerow, "tell the 4th to slam on in and take the liberation."

This decision was pre-empted by another small, symbolic act. As dusk fell on August 24 Leclerc ordered forward once more a small light armored patrol. Three

5 *Lieutenant-General Dietrich von Choltitz, German military commandant of Greater Paris, signs articles of surrender to the Provisional Government of the French Republic on August 25. Lacking means adequately to defend the city, von Choltitz acted with sensible moderation: he agreed to a "truce" with the FFI and, when Hitler ordered Paris reduced to a "field of ruins," prevaricated until it was too late to put the order into effect.*
(Central Press)

6 *Reporting the jubilation in liberated Paris, a British newspaper notes de Gaulle's return to the city "in triumph" on August 25. The French leader's insistence on a victory parade next day led to considerable friction with other Allied commanders.*
7 *Major-General Jacques-Philippe Leclerc, commander of French 2nd Armored Division, wears a tanker's helmet and carries his characteristic walking stick.*
(US National Archives)

1 *General de Gaulle acknowledges the cheers of his countrymen.* (US National Archives)
2 *The monument to Napoleon's victories looks down on the symbol of a new French triumph: the Sherman tank "Auvergne" of French 2nd Armored Division.* (Planet News)
3 *Although a black market in food flourished during the occupation, many ordinary citizens went hungry. Now they cheer the arrival of British supply trucks.*

1

3

light tanks and a platoon of infantry under Captain Raymond Dronne of the Route Regiment de Tchad, leading in the tank "Romilly," reached FFI headquarters at the Hotel de Ville in the center of the city late that night. Von Choltitz' headquarters were only a few hundred yards away. He telephoned Speidel, let him listen to the cheering crowds, and asked if there were any more orders before putting the telephone down. Von Choltitz' last act was to order a general retirement behind the line of the Seine. The next morning, August 25, French 2nd Armored Division and US 12th Infantry Regiment led by 102nd Cavalry Group, entered Paris. Appropriately, the forces met at about noon between the Hotel de Ville and the Place de la Concorde, the great triumphal square in the city center. Von Choltitz allowed himself to be taken without resistance, and Leclerc caused a minor storm by accepting his surrender of Paris in the name of the Provisional Government of the French Republic rather than as Eisenhower's representative. Hitler's reaction to the news that Allied troops had entered the city was to demand "Is Paris burning?" When told that no destruction had taken place, he demanded the bombardment of the city by aircraft, V-1 flying bombs and long-range artillery, which did not take place. American troops secured eastern Paris and the French the western half, but fighting continued on after the ceasefire and surrender as French and American soldiers, French civilians and German soldiers continued to die in the streets until August 29. Of the three great myths of the liberation of Paris – that it was

4

August 18 were not supporters of de Gaulle, and there was a real danger of uncontrolled fighting continuing against the Germans, or even breaking out between the factions of the FFI. On August 28 de Gaulle announced that effective the following day, the FFI in Paris was dissolved and its duties passed on to the uniformed military forces. In case there should be any hesitation, a show of force and solidarity was arranged, as de Gaulle asked Eisenhower for an American division to repeat the liberation parade from which American forces had been excluded a few days before. The British, once more invited to take part, once more mysteriously failed to appear. So it was that on August 29 an American division marched down the Champs Elysees from the Arc de Triomphe to the Place de la Concorde, past de Gaulle, Leclerc, Bradley and Gerow on a saluting rostrum. With the pursuit across the Seine in full flow, Bradley had been able to provide a division only by diverting through the city center a formation which had to pass over the Seine bridges on its way to the

4 *The nearer the Allies approached Paris, the greater grew the welcome given them by civilians who had, at first, feared the liberators might be driven back.*
5 *In June 1940 the victorious Germans underlined France's subjugation by staging a ceremonial parade through the Arc de Triomphe. Here, some four years later, Allied troops proclaim France's liberation in the same way.*
(US National Archives)

5

6

saved by the Germans, liberated from within by a popular uprising, or liberated by French troops alone – none is actually true.

De Gaulle arrived in Paris late on August 25 to cheering crowds, but made an official entry into the city the next day with a parade along the Champs Elysees lined by troops of Leclerc's division. Gerow was invited to take part with one officer, twenty men and an equal number of British. Instead, with fighting still going on, Gerow ordered Leclerc to cancel the parade. When his order was ignored, Gerow appealed to Hodges and Bradley. "Who the devil is the boss in Paris?" he wanted to know. The result was a compromise: Gerow was confirmed as Allied commander in Paris, but de Gaulle was allowed to keep Leclerc's division, not returning it to Eisenhower until September 4. The parade went ahead with shooting and sniping clearly audible nearby, and de Gaulle in some danger. The last large contingent of Germans, some 2,600 men in the Bois de Boulogne, finally surrendered that afternoon.

There was one more, rather fitting, act to the liberation of Paris. Many who had risen in revolt in Paris since

7

battle front. Eisenhower later hazarded that this was the only time in history that troops had marched in review through a major city and then on to a pitched battle on the same day. The troops chosen were from the US 28th Infantry Division, led by their new commander, Brigadier-General "Dutch" Cota, who had come ashore with the men of 29th Division on Omaha beach on D-Day.

6 *Only French troops took part in the first victory parade on August 26, but on August 29, US 28th Infantry Division marched from the Arc de Triomphe, down the Champs Élysées, to the Place de la Concorde – before boarding trucks that took them straight into battle.*
(US National Archives)
7 *General de Gaulle in the Champs Élysées during the parade of August 26. He was in some danger from German snipers nearby. Nor did all Frenchmen welcome him: Communist Resistance members saw him as a representative of a corrupt "old order."*
(Central Press)

World War I saw the first extensive military use of the internal combustion engine and other recent advances in personal transport. In 1914 Britain's Army Service Corps had 100 mechanically driven vehicles; in 1919, around 120,000. Motor vehicles were used up to the fighting line. Not all were designed for military use: in 1914 a French division was rushed to the Battle of the Marne in Parisian taxi cabs; London buses sometimes carried British troops "up the line." Both sides formed (not very effective) "bicycle battalions"; messages were carried by dispatch riders on motorcycles. Although animal transport remained vital to some World War II operations – the German blitzkriegs of 1939-41 made extensive use of draft horses – infantrymen now often rode to battle in trucks or tracked carriers. Compact vehicles, from folding bicycles to utility trucks, were developed for airborne troops and other special forces.

1 *Men of The Royal Warwickshire Regiment in Normandy, July 1944, appear to be deriving little benefit from their bikes!*
(IWM: B 6333)
2 *Folding bicycles were sometimes dropped with airborne troops.*
3 *Abandoned German draft horses allow GIs to become temporary cavalry; 1944.*
(UPI/Bettmann)
4 *Captured Germans improvise transport for a comrade unable to walk.*
(US National Archives)

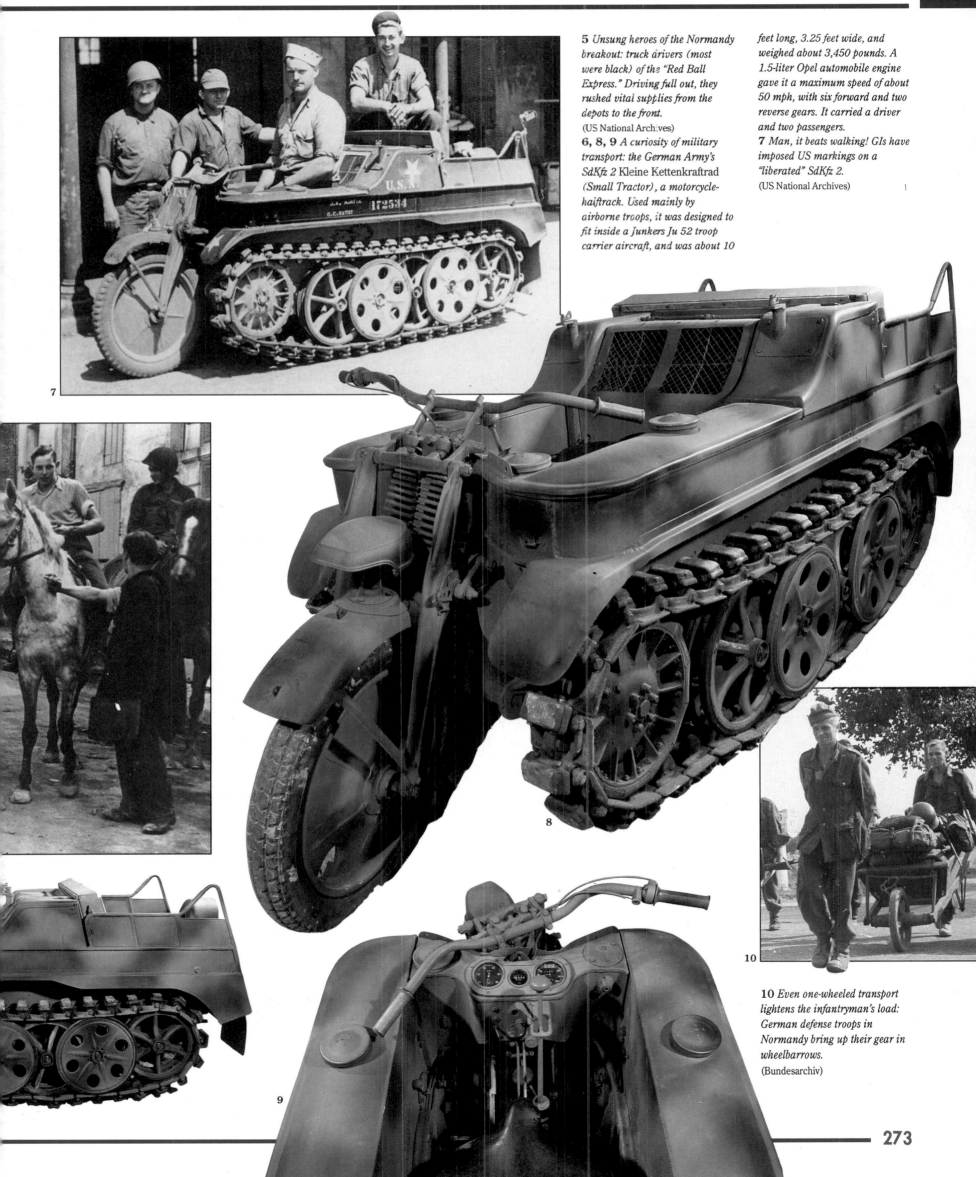

5 *Unsung heroes of the Normandy breakout: truck drivers (most were black) of the "Red Ball Express." Driving full out, they rushed vital supplies from the depots to the front.*
(US National Archives)

6, 8, 9 *A curiosity of military transport: the German Army's SdKfz 2 Kleine Kettenkraftrad (Small Tractor), a motorcycle-halftrack. Used mainly by airborne troops, it was designed to fit inside a Junkers Ju 52 troop carrier aircraft, and was about 10 feet long, 3.25 feet wide, and weighed about 3,450 pounds. A 1.5-liter Opel automobile engine gave it a maximum speed of about 50 mph, with six forward and two reverse gears. It carried a driver and two passengers.*

7 *Man, it beats walking! GIs have imposed US markings on a "liberated" SdKfz 2.*
(US National Archives)

10 *Even one-wheeled transport lightens the infantryman's load: German defense troops in Normandy bring up their gear in wheelbarrows.*
(Bundesarchiv)

1 *A price in English currency adds verisimilitude to a German propaganda pamphlet. Survive, it says, by surrendering – or by becoming hospitalized with a self-inflicted wound.*
2 *US regulations said "dog tags" must be worn (around the neck) always. They bore name, service number, date of latest anti-tetanus shot, blood type, name and address of next-of-kin (until 1944), and religion.*

GENERALS AND SOLDIERS

A parade is a good way to end a battle. Cota had been lucky enough to survive the Battle of Normandy from start to finish. Many, even on the winning side, were less lucky, although the dry calculations and statistics do little to convey the scale of the Battle of Normandy, or of the suffering that it caused. By August 30, the Allies had landed over 2 million men (and women, including military nurses) in Normandy, of which 209,672 had become casualties and 36,976 were dead. To this last figure a further 16,714 Allied aircrew lost over Normandy or on flights supporting the battle must be added. For those who had fought through Normandy unscathed, there was still another eight months of hard fighting before the end of the war in Europe. Often forgotten are the French

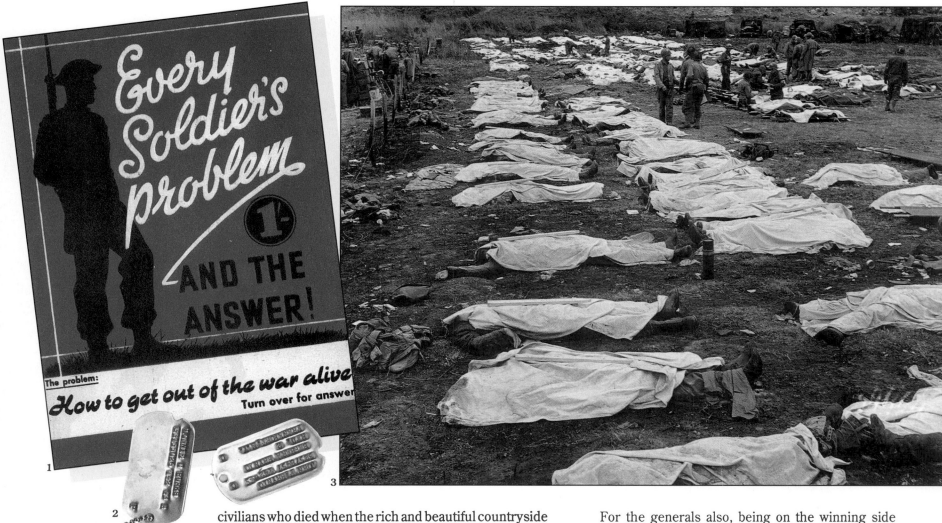

civilians who died when the rich and beautiful countryside of Normandy, peaceful for centuries, had become a battleground. Their numbers cannot be calculated, but it is today a sobering experience to stand in the center of a little bocage village and realize that none of the buildings are more than forty years old. If winning the battle had this price, then losing it was worse. The exact numbers and losses in the German armed forces that defended Normandy from the D-Day beaches to the Seine cannot be established. About 1 million German troops (or men in German uniforms) were involved, of which at least 240,000 were either killed or wounded, and a further 200,000 taken prisoner. The proportions of losses to troops involved for Normandy were about the same as for any other hard-fought battle leading to a rout, going back to ancient times. What was horrifying was the scale of the destruction, and the number of dead.

For the generals also, being on the winning side helped guarantee survival and more. Montgomery was promoted to field marshal, in partial compensation for losing command of the Allied land forces. Eisenhower, Bradley, and their army commanders were also promoted before the end of the war, which they all survived with honor. For most of the British, Normandy confirmed Montgomery's claim to military genius as another major victory. For most of the Americans, the failure to make progress at Caen and the apparent stalemate marked the end of his reputation, and he was seen as a suspect figure for the rest of the war. Perhaps only Eisenhower could have resolved the strains in the SHAEF forces that followed Normandy. After the war, attitudes became hardened to the point that the story of Allied command decisions in Normandy cannot now be disentangled from the claims and counter-claims. To the generals, military glory mattered.

5 Captured German helmets bear the "battle honors" of GIs who fought their way from the Normandy beaches to the heart of the Third Reich.
6 Last favor for a buddy: a GI letters a body bag for a dead comrade.
(US National Archives)
7 An obelisk on Omaha beach commemorates the men of US 1st Infantry Division.
8 The Normandy American National Cemetery overlooks Omaha beach. Of 9,286 men buried here, the graves of 307 are marked: "Here rests in honored glory a comrade in arms known but to God."
9 The 2,049 graves in the Canadian War Cemetery at Bény-sur-Mer include those of 335 men of 3rd Canadian Division killed on D-Day.

6

3 There is no discrimination in death. The sheeted bodies of GIs and Germans killed in one of the Normandy beachhead battles lie side by side awaiting burial details.
(UPI/Bettmann)
4 American casualties are brought in to a field hospital in Normandy, where 209,672 Allied personnel were wounded between June 6 and August 30, 1944.
(US National Archives)

8

9

1

1 *"Once I had a comrade ... ."*
begins a German soldiers' lament
dating back to a time before the
Third Reich. Here, a German
soldier searches for a lost friend
among the graves of the unnamed
dead.
(US National Archives)
2 *The armies have passed – and*
now civilians must try to rebuild
their lives among the ruins.
Villagers in Normandy salvage
household goods.
(IWM: B 6593)

4

5

6

To most others, including many of the soldiers who fought in Normandy, the argument over exactly which general gave what order seemed unreal. From D-Day onward, Normandy was a hard fight in which it was enough each evening to have survived the day. Even when resting, the combat troops were aware that "you are simply being fattened up, like pheasants in pre-war Septembers, for a particularly important occasion." The most that the Allied soldiers asked of their leaders was that their lives should not be thrown away without a reason, and that the result should be victory. From Eisenhower downward, the Allied commanders provided that victory at the lowest cost in human life to their own side that they could achieve.

The same cannot be said of the German forces. Starting with Rommel and von Rundstedt, every general holding a senior command appointment for the Battle of Normandy was killed, wounded or replaced by Hitler before the battle was over. Few survived the war, and many who did served sentences for war crimes, including the massacre of prisoners, the torture or murder of civilians, and the use of slave labor. In Normandy they had thrown away the lives of their troops in operations which they knew to be hopeless. In most cases, their defence was that they were obeying orders.

The strength of the German defense in Normandy in the face of Allied firepower, and the fact that German troops continued to fight in hopeless circumstances, have caused many to ask the reasons. One, certainly, was the strength of the Normandy hedgerow country in providing a natural defensive barrier. A few of the German troops fought because they believed, even in 1944, in the Nazi state. "You will hear a lot against Adolf Hitler in this camp, but you will never hear it from me," "Panzer" Meyer told his captors after Germany's surrender, "As far as I am concerned he was and still is the greatest thing that ever happened to Germany." Meyer seriously offered to raise a new "SS Division Europa" from surrendered Germans to fight for the Allies against the Japanese. Most Germans fought because, like their generals, they felt they had no choice, and because the Allied demand for unconditional surrender left them with nothing to do but defend their country, themselves, and their friends. "Our future looks hopeless," one German soldier trapped in the Falaise pocket wrote home on August 18, "and I think it is only right that I write to you that most likely we will be taken prisoner." He was lucky enough to surrender in safety.

There is little doubt that the Allied success on D-Day made their victory in Normandy a virtual certainty. Normandy itself was the largest battle fought by the Western Allies against Hitler's Germany during the Second World War, and although small compared to the fighting on the Eastern Front, it was also the largest amphibious military undertaking in history. By breaking the back of the German Army and the Nazi state at a time when both were badly overstretched, it ranks among the decisive battles of the Second World War, as the battle which put the Allied victory and the defeat of Nazi Germany beyond doubt or dispute. More important than victory, from the liberation of France the hope became real for the liberation of Europe, and for eventual peace.

3 As the elderly French woman scavenging for food knows only too well, hunger marches in the wake of war.
(US National Archives)
4 The lovingly tended grave of a British paratrooper in the cemetery at Bréville, where there also stands a memorial to men of British 6th Airborne Division.

7

5 A woman and child stand among the rubble of Mortain, Brittany, scene of a savage German counterattack during the August breakout battles.
(UPI/Bettmann)
6 The grave marker of an Obergefreiter (Corporal) killed one week after D-Day, in the German Cemetery at La Cambe. Here, in one of six German war cemeteries in Normandy, 21,160 service personnel are buried.
7 A wreath at the Merville Battery in remembrance of the men of 9th Battalion, The Parachute Regiment, who fell there early on June 6.

BIBLIOGRAPHY

Omaha Beachhead (U.S. Department of the Army, Washington D.C., 1984).

Utah Beach to Cherbourg (U.S. Department of the Army, Washington D.C., 1984).

Stephen E. Ambrose, *Pegasus Bridge* (Allen & Unwin, London, 1984).

Stephen Badsey, *Normandy 1944* (Osprey, London 1990).

Correlli Barnett, *The Audit of War* (Macmillan, London, 1986).

Eversley Bellfield and H R Essame, *The Battle for Normandy* (Batsford, London, 1965).

Ralph Bennett, *Ultra in the West* (Hutchinson, London, 1979).

L.F. Ellis, *Victory in the West* (HMSO, London, 1982).

John A. English, *The Canadian Army and the Normandy Campaign* (Praeger, New York and London, 1991).

Carlo d'Este, *Decision in Normandy* (William Collins, New York and London, 1983).

Edwin R.W. Hale and John Frayn Turner, *The Yanks Are Coming* (Midas, New York, 1983).

Shelford Bidwell and Dominick Graham, *Fire-Power* (Allen & Unwin, London, 1982).

Martin Blumenson, *Breakout and Pursuit* (U.S. Department of the Army, Washington D.C., 1961).

Angus Calder, *The People's War* (Jonathan Cape, London, 1969).

Peter Calvocoressi, Guy Wint, John Pritchard, *Total War* (Allen Lane, London, 1972).

David Chandler, *World War II – Battle on Land* (Mallard, London and New York, 1990).

Larry Collins and Dominique Lapierre, *Is Paris Burning?* (Gollancz, New York and London, 1965).

Martin van Creveld, *Fighting Power* (Arms & Armour, London, 1983).

Martin van Creveld, *Supplying War* (Cambridge UP, London, 1977).

Napier Crookenden, *Drop Zone Normandy* (Ian Allen, London, 1976).

Gerard M. Devlin, *Paratrooper* (Robson, London, 1979).

Dwight D. Eisenhower, *Crusade in Europe* (Heinemann, New York and London, 1948).

John Ellis, *Brute Force* (Andre Deutche, London, 1990).

John Ellis, *The Sharp End of War* (David & Charles, London, 1977).

J.P. Harris and F.H. Toase, *Armoured Warfare* (Batsford, London, 1990).

G.A. Harrison, *Cross-Channel Attack* (U.S. Department of the Ary, Washington D.C., 1961).

Max Hastings, *Bomber Command* (Michael Joseph, London, 1979).

Max Hastings, *Overlord* (Michael Joseph, London and New York, 1984).

Jock Haswell, *The Intelligence and Deception of the D-Day Landings* (Batsford, London, 1979).

J.J. How, *Normandy – The British Breakout* (Kimber, London, 1981).

David Irving, *The War Between the Generals* (Alan Lane, London and New York, 1981).

Sidney Jary, *18 Platoon* (Jary, Carshalton Beeches, 1987).

John Keegan, *Six Armies in Normandy* (Jonathan Cape, London and New York, 1982).

George E. Koskimaki, *D-Day With The Screaming Eagles* (Vantage, New York, 1970).

B.H. Liddell Hart, *The Other Side of the Hill* (Cassell, London, 1948).

James Lucas and James Barker, *The Killing Ground* (Batsford, London, 1978).

Alexander McKee, *Caen – Anvil of Victory* (Souvenir, London, 1964).

Kenneth Macksey, *Commando Strike* (Leo Cooper, London, 1985).

1 *The Rifle Number 4, Mark I caliber .303 (T), fitted with a Number 32 Type Telescope, was the standard British snipers' weapon from early 1942 until the war's end.*

2

S.L.A. Marshall, *Night Drop* (Methuen, New York and London, 1962).

Samuel W. Mitcham, *Hitler's Legions* (Leo Cooper, London, 1985).

Field Marshal Viscount Montgomery of Alamein, *From Normandy to the Baltic* (Hutchinson, London, 1947).

Norman Polmar and Peter B. Mersky, *Amphibious Warfare* (Blandford, London, 1985).

Richard Rohmer, *Patton's Gap* (Arms & Armour, London, 1981).

Cornelius Ryan, *The Longest Day* (Gollancz, New York and London, 1960).

E.K.G. Sixsmith, *Eisenhower as Military Commander* (Batsford, London, 1973).

Milton Shulman, *Defeat in the West* (Secker & Warburg, London, 1947).

C.P. Stacey, *The Canadian Army 1939-1945* (King's Publisher, Ottawa, 1948).

C.P. Stacey, *The Victory Campaign* (Queen's Publisher, Ottawa, 1960).

Willis Thornton, *The Liberation of Paris* (Rupert Hart-Davis, London, 1963).

Warren Tute, John Costello, Terry Hughes, *D-Day* (Sidgwick & Jackson, London, 1974).

Russell F. Weighley, *Eisenhower's Lieutenants* (Sidgwick & Jackson, London, 1981).

Chester Wilmot, *The Struggle for Europe* (Collins, London, 1952).

Peter Young, *D-Day* (Bison, London, 1981).

2 *German Model 1924 Stielhandgranaten (stick hand grenades). The wooden handle, it was thought, made it possible to throw the grenade farther than the oval German Model 1939 "egg" grenade, or the oval grenades used by Allied troops.*
3 *The American air-cooled Browning Model 1919A4 .30 caliber light machine gun, shown here on the standard M2 tripod, was a sturdy, reliable weapon.*
4 *A man of a Luftwaffe Field Division with an MG-42 general purpose machine gun.*
(Bundesarchiv)
5 *One dead man serves as a reminder of some 246,000 Allied troops and 240,000 Germans who became casualties somewhere between the Normandy beaches and the Seine River.*
(US National Archives)

INDEX

INDEX